Thoughtful
Cooking

Thoughtful Cooking

Recipes Rooted
IN THE New South

WILLIAM STARK DISSEN

PHOTOGRAPHY BY Johnny AND Charlotte Autry

Countryman Press

An Imprint of W. W. Norton & Company
Independent Publishers Since 1923

For information about permission to reproduce selections from this book, write to
Permissions, Countryman Press, 500 Fifth Avenue, New York, NY 10110

For information about special discounts for bulk purchases, please contact
W. W. Norton Special Sales at specialsales@wwnorton.com or 800-233-4830

Manufacturing by Toppan Leefung Pte. Ltd.
Book design by Allison Chi
Production manager: Devon Zahn

Countryman Press
www.countrymanpress.com

An imprint of W. W. Norton & Company, Inc.
500 Fifth Avenue, New York, NY 10110
www.wwnorton.com

978-1-68268-808-3

10 9 8 7 6 5 4 3 2 1

Dedicated to my children, Kira and Cole.
You are my most precious recipe!
You both make me so proud to be your father.
Thank you for lifting me up, and for always
dreaming big. Shoot for the stars!

Contents

132 Fall

199 Winter

Introduction

WHAT IS "THOUGHTFUL COOKING"?

True people-to-people or people-to-land connections are hard to rekindle in this digital age. Sometimes it's downright scary: asking people to put down their phones and look up at the trees, to go to markets and use all their senses to smell, taste, touch, see, hear, to talk to each other face to face rather than text, to be outside and feel the shift in the air right when it's about to rain for the first time in spring, to wash dirt off radishes and other root vegetables and appreciate that dirt, to literally smell the peppery difference between store-bought arugula and arugula harvested that morning. *Thoughtful Cooking* isn't designed to be convenient and quick, it's inconvenient in all the right ways: it asks the home cook to be in the moment, to take a breath, and to connect.

We are living in a time when people feel more disconnected than ever, from each other, from the land, from experiencing life and using their senses. Ironically, we're having more conversations in mainstream media about the foods we eat, and yet, with the current overflow of online information, it seems harder than ever to know where to start as a home cook, let alone where to start your day. *Thoughtful Cooking* is meant to be a door to a lifestyle shift, a vibe shift, to learning a new way of how to approach cooking and the world around us. It's more than just feeling good about the ingredients you source: it's about true connection, which is both challenging and deeply rewarding in this life.

While many of today's cookbooks are fast and easy, keeping everything closed up and neat and tidy in 30 minutes or less, *Thoughtful Cooking* is about shifting your mindset and unfolding from within, allowing yourself to explore and be curious. It's a form of self-care. After being conditioned for so long to stay on the surface of themselves, it's hard for folks to go deeper, to slow down, to stop the rush from obligation to obligation. I've been there myself. The real work and pleasure of sourcing, cooking, eating, and nourishing ourselves and others starts when we decide we want more out of life. Because we can't wait to live any longer. We can't wait for good food to come to us when we can go outside and see what's all around us, right now, waiting to be plucked and handled and sustainably harvested and turned into an amazing, life-is-worth-living experience. Even a simple summer tomato sandwich has the ability to transform, especially when we aren't trying to balance our phone on our other hand, waiting for the perfect Instagrammable moment.

The concept of *Thoughtful Cooking* came about over years of writing menus as a chef at my restaurants. I've always prioritized telling a story through my menus and with the food I prepare for our guests. I've spent years with my hands in the dirt pulling "weeds" that I forage to create exciting menu items. I've spent countless hours at farmers' markets learning about how the farmers grow their vegetables and when the prime time is to harvest them, and I've spent just as much time at the docks talking to our fishermen who follow the science to know what fish are the most sustainable to take from our waters. These experiences have helped me to tell my story through our food, so our guests can create a connection to not only my restaurants, but to a life experience they have had along their own way. Food can articulate a thought, spark creativity, and bring back memories and emotions through one single bite. Eating seasonally and sustainably is an act of self-care and at the same time an act of embracing our community. This is a book about spontaneity while also planning ahead, about taking risks and experiencing the world through all your senses. Finding a new ingredient, observing a ritual, and seeing the bigger picture are all part of the journey to becoming a more *thoughtful* cook.

Appalachian Roots

Along my path to becoming a chef and while being one, I have always been in touch with nature and have been curious about our connection to the land and the seasonal world around us. This con-

nection started while growing up in the heart of Appalachia, playing in the forests and streams of the West Virginia mountains. As a kid I yearned to be outside and to get away to explore as much as possible. I was definitely the annoying child who asked "why" all the time. Fortunately for my parents, nature was able to answer many of my questions and fulfill my inquisitive personality with the wild mushrooms, petrified wood, Native American arrowheads, and plants and animals that I found during my daily adventures beneath the forest canopy.

My mother's family were farmers who truly lived off the land. They had a garden and pollinated it with their own honeybees, they raised livestock and poultry, and tended a large, bountiful garden irrigated by a mountain creek. As a child living on the outskirts of suburbia, this was a magical place to visit and see family. My grandmother, Jane, cooked meals straight from the garden that were so inspirational I can remember everything about them: the delicious stick-to-your-ribs country cooking, my family sitting around the table sharing laughter and enjoying a meal, the hot sweaty summer weather up in the holler, and the Westerns playing on their TV. Food so good it made memories, yet so simple because it came from the garden right out the back door. Have you ever had the chance to "sit a spell" on a front porch, and shuck beans and corn to "put up" for the year in the canning cellar? To tell stories and tall tales while talking to relatives and neighbors?

Appalachian people are the salt of the earth and love their home and their community immensely. I know I take this wonderful place with me wherever I go, and I will be forever grateful for my childhood in these hills and valleys.

Food is meant to be shared across the table with people we love and as a way to forge new relationships. The people who embrace our local and sustainable food culture, and the way they take care of the land and water to protect their investment in the future, have taught me that growth happens when we can learn from the past and embrace today, all while looking ahead toward the future. Community has been one of the most important parts of my connection to food. Recognizing the changing of the seasons, and creating relationships with those who are growing, harvesting, fishing, and foraging for the ingredients I crave, has enabled me to tell the story of the world around me through food.

My Culinary Journey

I've always been hungry. My path as a chef started young. I was a voracious kid fortunate to have a family that indulged my interests in food. While I was young, I was constantly moving: playing sports, hiking in the woods, and on the go. Dreaming about my future, I thought I would go to college and eventually work a professional job, buy the house with the white picket fence, have the 2.5 kids, drive the Volvo, and all that.

But then the kitchen started to call me. One of my first jobs was washing dishes at a local country club in my hometown. One day, the garde-manger cook called out from work and the chef asked me if I could make salads and sandwiches. And as they say, the rest is history. I became hooked on cooking and the energy of a professional kitchen, and I haven't looked back since.

From college to culinary school to grad school, I was able to free my mind and also learn more about the culinary arts and business management. This journey led me to the Old North State (North Carolina) where I was drawn to the mountain town of Asheville. I became the chef and owner of The Market Place Restaurant, which is now more than 45 years old (15 of those years with me at the helm), and is considered one of the preeminent farm-to-table restaurants in the country. I have since gone on to open another equally successful restaurant in Charlotte—Haymaker Restaurant, which I founded as the executive chef and owner—as well as two casual brands, Billy D's Fried Chicken and Little Gem Restaurant. Each with its own unique identity, but all anchored in local and seasonal food.

Cooking has taken me around the world many times over, and each adventure has helped to make our world a smaller place for me. The people that I meet, and cultures I learn about, become less foreign and more familiar. When we break bread together and shed our fears about others, we truly build longer tables and tear down walls.

Food is an adventure worth traveling for, and I am inspired by the travels I have taken and those yet to come.

Cooking in Season

While this book is naturally an extension of my professional restaurant kitchens, it's also a vibe shift from the day-to-day grind. We'll meditate on the seasons and how they inform not only our ingredients and cooking styles, but how our choices affect the world around us. As the seasons unfold and the weather changes, so do the flavors we crave, so we'll take this journey of *Thoughtful Cooking* through the four seasons of the year. Each chapter, or "season," has been organized in this book by what's fresh, ripe, and inspiring from our local farms and markets. We will take the time to ponder on how these cycles teach us about our ingredients and the way we cook, and also about the time we take to spend with our friends and loved ones around the table.

I can always hear my French culinary instructor preaching mise en place every day in class back in

culinary school. *Mise en place* literally translates to "everything in its place." While in the kitchen, we need to be neat, clean, and organized so that we can free up our mindspace to cook and connect with the food. In *Thoughtful Cooking,* we will take the time to think through our recipes, get everything in order, and get our ingredients (and our mind) prepped for success. Preservation is also important in the seasonal kitchen, and we will take the time to look ahead and plan for different types of preservation of foods such as pickles and jams that we can "put up" in our pantry for menus later in the year.

Sustainability

Eating seasonally is naturally an act of sustainable living. When we think about what's fresh and what the earth is providing, we're taking a step toward treating Mother Earth a little more kindly. I didn't start out thinking I would be a chef who would advocate for "green peace," but my work led me to ask questions about our food system. It's not as simple as buying from the organic section in our grocery store. This is a chance to think a little more deeply when we're cooking and to navigate the seasons together through these recipes on the pages ahead. Along the way, I'll provide insight about how to put those principles into practice, such as picking the ripest strawberry or choosing the most sustainable salmon from your fishmonger. We'll conclude each season's chapter with the section Deep Thoughts, about how we can be better cooks by being better stewards of our planet, and why it's important to think about how our choices can change the world by voting with our forks. In the Spring chapter, we dive head first into Ocean Stewardship and protecting our oceans. The Summer chapter brings an abundance, and we discuss the importance of the preservation of the harvest and also preserving culture and commu-

nity. The Fall is a time of harvest when our gardens and markets are most bountiful, and so we slow down and take time to showcase why eating local helps to support a framework of sustainable agriculture. Because "we are what we eat," the Winter chapter finishes with thoughts on being a thoughtful eater. The power of "good food" goes beyond the flavors on the table and shows us that we all have the ability to make positive changes whenever we break bread together.

My Cooking Style

Let's not forget about the food! *Thoughtful Cooking* does not need to be complicated or fussy. My cooking style is wrought in simple dishes made with the freshest ingredients, and of understanding the seasons and slowing down to understand the moment in time. I love food that is bright and fresh. No matter what I am cooking, I always look for ways to make explosive flavors on the plate while still creating an approachable dish. It can feel daunting to create delicious, tantalizing food for your friends and family. I'm here to help. I have spent years behind the stove at many of the nation's best restaurants, learning everything from modernist cuisine and "tweezer food" to Grandma's Sunday gravy and Southern shrimp and grits. Over the years I have learned a number of easy tricks to make delicious food that also feeds the soul. What I've learned reflects the heart of *Thoughtful Cooking,* and my own cooking philosophy. With a little mise en place and planning, we can all cook beautiful food with seasonal ingredients that will not only delight the palate but also feed the mind, body, and soul.

Many recipes in this book are accompanied by a Thoughtful Tip, where I might give my secrets for how to source the ripest ingredients, or provide an efficient trick on making a recipe easier to execute. Look to these tips for things such as advice on how to "can" the freshest ingredients to preserve for the winter months, how to best roast a steak to delicious perfection on the grill, and how to make a savory tomato pie with the ripest summer tomatoes. Some of these approaches I've learned from collaborating with amazing chefs during my world travels, and others I've picked up on my own through years of repetition in professional kitchens.

Teaching others has always been my mission as a chef: to learn about life, live with passion, and pursue the quest for knowledge. I hope you join me on this adventure as we find new ways to think about food and the world around us. Cheers!

Tools of the Trade

Here is a list of my favorite cooking tools and equipment to help in your everyday cooking. Kitchen tools serve a distinct purpose and they also help make your daily tasks easier. These are tools I work with every day.

KORIN KNIVES: I work with a set of Glestain chef knives as my everyday workhorses, and I also work with a carbon steel Masamoto gyuto (chef's knife) and petty knife. I use these in my restaurants because I can get blades that are sharpened specifically for left-handed folks like myself.

SHARPENING STONES: A chef is only as sharp as their knife! Keep your blades tuned up on a good Japanese whetstone. I use coarse grit, medium grit, and fine grit stones to keep my knives razor-sharp.

SHARPENING STEEL: F. Dick Sapphire Cut Round Steel is what I use to hone my knives between sharpenings and to keep blade edges on point.

KITCHEN SHEARS: From cutting herbs to cutting the backbone out of a whole chicken, kitchen shears are always in my collection. Like choosing a good knife, choose a set of shears that fit well in your hand and stay sharp.

JAPANESE MANDOLINE: These are ultra-sharp slicers that you can find at your local Asian market. They aid in slicing root vegetables like radishes, and they can make slices that are paper thin.

VITA-PREP BLENDER: This is *the* blender to buy. It will help to make amazing purees and soups. This blender also comes through in a pinch for grinding spices and making smoothies.

MICROPLANE: This is my go-to for zesting citrus fruits, grating garlic, or finely grating Parmesan cheese.

ALL-CLAD STAINLESS STEEL POTS AND PANS: I put together a set of All-Clad Copper Core pots and pans over the course of the last decade. They have heavy induction bottoms, so they work on a gas range or an induction electric burner. They are easy to clean.

LODGE CAST IRON PANS: Cast iron conducts heat like no other and holds heat for a longer period of time than steel pans. Take good care of your cast-iron cookware, and plan to pass it down from generation to generation as a family heirloom.

LE CREUSET ENAMELED CAST-IRON POTS: This French brand is not only a workhorse but adds bold colors to your kitchen decor. But don't think it's all about looks: We use these pots and pans in our commercial restaurant kitchens, and they can take a beating. For soups, braises, and more, we reach for Le Creuset pots and pans.

THERMOMETER: From learning the temperature of hot oil to cooking a steak to perfection, a good instant-read thermometer that takes accurate temperature readings is imperative. My go-to is the Thermapen One.

CUTTING BOARD: I love a good, solid wood cutting board, and Boos Block is where the buck stops with their butcher's block-style boards. For boards that are dishwasher safe, I like the San Jamar Tuff-Cut cutting boards.

SCALE: Having a good digital scale will help you to refine your craft as a cook and ensure your recipes are precise. Oxo makes an 11-pound stainless steel scale that weighs in grams and ounces for precise measurements.

KITCHEN SPOONS AND SPATULAS: I always keep a few Rubbermaid high-temp spatulas around for scraping down pots and pans, as well as a good wooden spoon for making sauces and using in my enameled cast iron. My favorite kitchen spoon is my Gray Kunz sauce spoon, and I use a Gray Kunz perforated spoon for cooking, plating, and more.

WHISK: A good balloon whisk and a French whisk are wonderful tools for mixing and fluffing up ingredients like egg whites.

Y-SHAPED PEELER: These horizontal peelers are far superior to their vertical cousins. From peeling carrots to extracting orange peel for an old-fashioned cocktail, this style of peeler is the best.

OFFSET SPATULA: From a large offset spatula for cake work to a small offset spatula for plating to a small and wide spatula for flipping ingredients in the pan, these tools help give our hands the dexterity that a spoon cannot provide.

FISH SPATULA: When cooking delicate seafood, a good fish spatula will aid in gently turning over a fillet of fish to keep it intact. Lamson products are my go-to.

FISH TWEEZERS: When butchering whole fish, you need this specific tool to pull out those tiny fish pin bones. Messermeister makes my favorite set of fish tweezers.

CAKE TESTER: For checking the doneness of a cake or testing a piece of fish, I always have one in my apron pocket.

CONICAL FINE MESH SIEVE: These tools are wonderful for straining the larger sediment from stocks and soups so that your sauces and soups are velvety smooth.

Larder

When I was in culinary school, I met a friend from Hawaii who taught me about being able to speak to all the taste buds when cooking. He said that if we can incorporate sweet, sour, salty, bitter, and umami into our cooking, then people are bound to love our food. He was right! Here are some of the ingredients I can't live without when I'm in the kitchen.

DIAMOND CRYSTAL KOSHER SALT: This is my favorite salt to season with, and it's what I use for every recipe in this book. It's like an old friend and is trusted for every recipe I write.

J.Q. DICKINSON HEIRLOOM FINISHING SALT: This sea salt hails from West Virginia, but wait: There aren't any oceans there! Siblings Nancy Bruns and Lewis Payne extract ancient seawater from the Iapetus Ocean trapped underneath the mountains of Appalachia. The result is pure, delicious heirloom finishing salt.

DUKE'S MAYONNAISE: Although I love to make homemade aioli, Duke's is the creamiest and most flavorful mayonnaise around. I use it as a base for an endless amount of recipes.

CITRUS: A good punch of acidity takes a flat dish to the next level. Brighten up soups, sauces, vegetables, meat, and seafood with a zip of fresh citrus juice and zest.

VINEGAR: Sour power! Vinegars are my go-to base for vinaigrettes and dressings. I love champagne vinegar, apple cider vinegar, and aged sherry vinegar to start the base of a good dressing, but they're equally good for finishing a dish to level out the flavor.

PICKLES: Just like citrus and vinegar, a good pop of tang goes a long way. Packed with salt and acid, different varieties of pickles help to elevate a dish. One of my go-tos is pickled red onions. I like to add them to a fresh herbal sauce such as a gremolata or sprinkle them over my lox bagel in the morning.

HOT SAUCE: Some like it hot! Then again, a little heat goes a long way. I use hot sauce to provide depth and balance to a dish. Even when I'm not looking to create a spicy dish, a little heat from a good hot sauce provides the right amount of depth. And if you like it spicy, stir in a little more!

GOOD EVOO (EXTRA VIRGIN OLIVE OIL): While olive oil has a lower smoking point than its counterparts like canola or peanut oil, it is a great and healthy option for cooking. I usually keep a milder grade of olive oil for cooking and look for a brighter, spicier, and fruitier style such as Arbequina for finishing.

WILDFLOWER HONEY: With real honey you can taste the plants and flowers that the honey bees have been pollinating. My preference is for wildflower honey, because it provides a soft and floral sweetness to a recipe to help balance out a sauce or to add a note of sweetness without overpowering a dish.

MISO PASTE: Miso's greatest strength is providing a deep umami flavor to vegetarian dishes. I like to use it on meat, too—try it in a marinade on grilled chicken or pork to add an extra layer of savory goodness.

STONE-GROUND GRITS AND CORNMEAL: Here in the South, we love some grits and corn bread. Finding a resource for freshly stone-milled corn can be tough, but it's worth the effort—you can taste the difference. I use dried corn for dredging fried catfish as much as I do in a velvety polenta.

FRESH HERBS: A hint of thyme or a sprig of rosemary help elevate a sauce to higher ground. Parsley and chives add the right amount of herbal excitement to finish a salad, or they can be chopped into a sauce like a gremolata. Find the flavors you love and use a handful in your next recipe.

NUTS AND SEEDS: They provide crunch, earthiness, and texture to your recipes. Pistachios, pecans, walnuts, cashews, and almonds are among my favorites. Slowly roast them, and then puree them into a sauce for added depth and nutrition.

FRESH AND DRIED PEPPERS: Capsicum heat from peppers comes in many different forms. Fresh jalapeños, Fresnos, and habaneros provide fruity, fresh heat. Dried ancho and guajillo add a spicy, earthy, and smoky flavor when cooked.

FRESH AND AGED CHEESE: Fresh cheeses such as ricotta add creaminess to a dish. They are used as a filling in pastas. Aged cheeses such as Parmesan, Tomme, or Manchego add a salty umami bomb when grated over a dish.

SPRING

What's in Season?

Spinach, Fennel, Mint, Morels, Cherries, Chives, Arugula, Fava Beans, Spring Peas, Strawberries, Spring Onions, Wild Ramps, Radishes, Rhubarb, Dill, Carrots, Beets, Asparagus, New Potatoes

Spring is a time to begin and to start anew. After months of hibernating, we reemerge from our homes, shake out the cobwebs of the winter months, and look to a brighter year ahead. I love to step outside for a walk and take my time to watch the world come back to life around me.

When I was growing up, words like *seasonal, local,* and *organic* weren't part of my vocabulary. We certainly ate fresh food, grew a garden, and spent time on my grandparent's farm, yet the idea of supporting an "intentional food" movement had not become a common thought in our day-to-day lives. Now, I live for the farmers' market in the spring. While shopping at the market for nourishing fruits and vegetables, old friends emerge and relationships are rekindled. Our eyes are flooded with the beauty of the fruits, flowers, and vegetables teeming on the market tables. There's a crisp reenergizing feel to the morning air. It's a reminder that we are all connected. At the market, those beautiful greens in the back of my friend Anne's pickup truck revitalize me for another year.

Beginning in April, I venture to the outdoor farmers' markets again. The cold is mostly behind us for the year and it's a great way to get my family out of the house on the weekend. Shopping at the farmers' markets is a key way I plan my meals—both at the restaurants and at home. My favorite market on the planet happens to be right at home in Asheville, North Carolina, at the North Asheville Tailgate Market. The first ripe strawberries or the spicy arugula, eaten raw right at the market stall sends you to bliss. We've been missing this kind of explosive freshness since last year. The transition of seasons never fails to astonish me, and the world becomes lush whereas a month earlier there was snow and cold. Suddenly the market is filled with asparagus, new potatoes, fava beans, and peas. Our foragers are emerging from the forest with wild morel mushrooms and ramps!

If you pause and take a moment to recognize this return to life after winter, you'll end up feeling more connected to the land around you, and understand the true terroir of your community. Spring has taught me to pay attention and to be astonished. I begin to crave dishes that are lighter and less heavy than the slow-cooked winter braises, soups, and stews. It's a wonderful time when we can eat much more raw and fresh, but also enjoy dishes like roasted carrots or a hearth-baked flatbread.

As the season progresses toward May, my family spends more time outdoors in the beautiful Blue Ridge Mountains. May is my favorite time of year in the region. I plant a small garden at our family home, with my children helping to lend a hand and learn the cycle of nature. Dirt therapy always helps no matter what age you are.

Not only am I planting my own little home plot with produce my family will love, I get to be surprised by new tastes of the season every week. Our weekly CSA starts in May: a box full of that week's harvest, which keeps things creative and fun in the kitchen. For years, we've been supporting our friends Aaron and Anne Grier at Gaining Ground Farm where they grow some of the finest vegetables around on their biodynamic farm outside of Asheville. Each year, when I visit their farm, I'm filled with a renewed connection to my community—this wonderful place I call home. It's time to be outdoors, enjoying the fresh spring scent, firing up the grill, and spending time again in the open air with family and friends.

Bright Lights Chard and Goat Cheese Tart
WITH SPRING HERBS

SERVES 6 TO 8

In the spring, things tend to pick up around my house and around the restaurants. My kids love eggs, and I'm always looking for a way to sneak greens into their diet. For that reason, this recipe is one of my favorites. Bright Lights chard is a variety of leafy green Swiss chard. It is versatile in the kitchen, colorful, and full of nutrients. The tart shell can be prepared in advance, so you just have to sauté the vegetables and quickly prepare the filling for an impressive dish for the kids, or to impress your most discerning friends. You can sub out any other leafy greens you enjoy, such as spinach or kale, and you can replace the goat cheese with any other soft cheese such as ricotta or even pimento cheese. I like to serve the tart with a light side salad for a delicious, healthy meal.

TART DOUGH
- 1½ cups all-purpose flour, plus extra for rolling
- 1½ tablespoons chopped, fresh thyme
- ½ teaspoon kosher salt
- ¾ cup cold unsalted butter, diced
- 4 to 6 tablespoons ice water

FILLING
- 3 tablespoons extra virgin olive oil
- ¾ pound (about 3) leeks, white parts only, cleaned and julienned
- 1 pound Swiss chard, leaves cut into a wide chiffonade and stems diced
- 1 tablespoon minced garlic
- ½ teaspoon red pepper flakes
- 3 large eggs
- ½ cup heavy cream
- Zest from ½ lemon
- 1¼ teaspoons kosher salt
- ¼ teaspoon freshly ground black pepper
- One 6-ounce log fresh goat cheese
- ¼ cup fresh parsley leaves
- ¼ cup chopped fresh dill
- ¼ cup chopped fresh chives
- Violets for garnish

TART DOUGH

1. Place the flour, thyme, and salt into the bowl of a food processor and pulse five or six times, until blended. Add the butter and pulse until the mixture resembles coarse cornmeal.

2. Transfer the mixture to a medium bowl and add 4 tablespoons of the ice water. Combine thoroughly to make a shaggy wet dough. Squeeze a small amount in your hand. If the dough does not hold together, add the remaining ice water, 1 tablespoon at a time until it holds together.

3. Turn the dough out onto a floured counter and form into a disk. Wrap in plastic wrap and refrigerate for at least 1 hour and up to overnight.

4. Position a rack in the lower part of the oven and preheat the oven to 400°F.

5. Lightly flour a work surface and roll the dough into a 13-inch circle. Roll the dough onto the rolling pin, gently lift the dough into a 10-inch tart pan, and unroll. Gently press the dough into the tart pan so it fits snugly against the sides and bottom. Trim away the excess dough that overhangs. Prick the bottom of the dough a few times with the tines of a fork and cover with parchment paper.

6. Fill the parchment paper with pie weights or beans and bake until the edges of the crust are just beginning to brown, 25 to 30 minutes. Remove the pie weights and parchment and set aside to cool to room temperature.

FILLING

1. Place the olive oil in a large sauté pan and set over medium heat. Once the oil shimmers, add the leeks and Swiss chard stems and cook until softened, about 5 minutes. Add the garlic and red pepper flakes and continue cooking until aromatic, 1 to 2 minutes. Add the Swiss chard leaves and cook until the leaves are wilted and tender, about 5 minutes. Remove the pan from the heat and set aside to cool slightly.

2. Place the eggs, heavy cream, lemon zest, salt, and black pepper in a medium bowl and whisk to combine. Add the leek mixture and stir to thoroughly combine. Pour the mixture into the prepared tart shell and dot with the goat cheese. Place the tart into the oven and bake until the filling is set, about 25 minutes.

3. Remove the tart to a wire rack and cool to room temperature before slicing. Once cool, slice the tart and serve with a hefty topping of the mixed herbs and violets.

THOUGHTFUL TIP

Source the freshest eggs for the most flavor. Ask your farmer what they feed their chickens. A richer-colored yolk means a healthier, more nutritious egg. Chickens that graze naturally on grass, bugs, and seeds are well nourished and produce eggs that have bright orange yolks with a high percentage of nutrients and healthy fats.

Bright Lights Chard and Goat Cheese Tart
with Spring Herbs

Yukon Gold Focaccia Flatbread
with Cured Salmon, Crème Fraîche,
and Pickled Red Onions

Yukon Gold Focaccia Flatbread
WITH CURED SALMON, CRÈME FRAÎCHE, AND PICKLED RED ONIONS

SERVES 6 TO 8

Focaccia is one of my favorite breads—it's great for beginners and is extra delicious with copious amounts of olive oil drizzled on it. The addition of mashed potatoes in the dough creates a wonderfully light yet crispy flatbread. When cooking salmon (or any seafood for that matter), the source really matters. Wild Alaskan sockeye or king salmon are among my favorites. Recently, I was introduced to Bluehouse Salmon out of Florida, recognized as one of the only sustainable salmon farms on the planet with a "green rating" by Seafood Watch. You could substitute gravlax or smoked salmon and crème fraîche from your local grocery store or market. But once you make these recipes from scratch, you'll never go back to store-bought!

YUKON GOLD FOCACCIA

1 medium Yukon Gold potato

¾ cup warm water

¾ teaspoon active dry yeast

3 tablespoons extra virgin olive oil, plus extra for shaping

2¼ cups bread flour, plus extra for kneading

1 teaspoon kosher salt

1 teaspoon chopped thyme

¼ teaspoon sea salt

CURED SALMON

One 12- to 14-ounce skin on, salmon fillet, pin bones removed

1½ tablespoons freshly squeezed lemon juice

1 tablespoon vodka

½ bunch fresh thyme

½ cup kosher salt

½ cup sugar

1 tablespoon coarsely ground black pepper

TO SERVE

1 cup Pickled Red Onions (page 267)

1½ tablespoons drained capers

½ cup Crème Fraîche (page 275)

¼ teaspoon freshly ground black pepper

2 tablespoons chopped dill

2 tablespoons chopped mint

1 tablespoon chopped basil

1 tablespoon chopped chives

Extra virgin olive oil, as needed

YUKON GOLD FOCACCIA

1. Peel and chop the potato into six to eight uniform pieces. Place in a small saucepan, cover with water, and set over high heat. Bring to a boil and cook until the potatoes are tender and fall apart when poked with a fork. Drain off the liquid and mash the potato. Set aside to cool. Reserve ½ cup of mashed potatoes for the focaccia.

2. Place the ¾ cup warm water into the bowl of a stand mixer fitted with the dough hook. Sprinkle in the yeast and set aside until the mixture bubbles, about 2 to 3 minutes.

3. Add the ½ cup of potatoes and 2 tablespoons of the olive oil to the bowl. Mix on low speed until well combined, 15 to 20 seconds. Add the flour and kosher salt and mix until the dough comes together, 2 to 3 minutes. Increase to medium and mix for 3 to 4 minutes or until the dough pulls away from the sides of the bowl.

4. Turn the dough out onto a lightly floured counter. Lightly oil your hands and knead the dough two or three times, shaping it into a ball.

5. Lightly oil the bowl and return the dough. Cover the bowl with a towel or plastic wrap and set aside to rise in a warm place until the dough has doubled in size. Alternatively, place the covered dough in the refrigerator to ferment overnight.

6. Place a baking stone onto the center oven rack and preheat the oven to 425°F. Line a baking sheet with parchment paper and set aside.

7. Turn the dough out onto a lightly floured work surface and shape into a ball.

8. Transfer the ball to the prepared baking sheet and press out the dough to a 10-by-8-inch rectangle or oval. Use your fingertips to press dimples over the surface of the dough.

9. Drizzle with the remaining 1 tablespoon of olive oil over the surface of the focaccia and sprinkle with thyme and sea salt.

10. Slide the parchment paper with the dough off the baking sheet and onto the baking stone in the oven. Bake until the bread is golden in color and sounds hollow when you tap it, 20 to 25 minutes.

11. Remove from the oven and allow to cool for a few minutes before transferring the bread to a rack to cool completely. Use as desired.

CURED SALMON

1. Place a wire rack in a baking sheet and lay a 4-foot-long double layer of cheesecloth on top of the wire rack and set the salmon on the cheesecloth.

2. Combine the lemon and vodka in a small bowl and brush over the salmon. Scatter the thyme evenly on the salmon.

3. Combine the salt, sugar, and pepper in a small bowl. Sprinkle evenly over the salmon.

4. Wrap the excess cheesecloth over the salmon. Place three soup cans inside a 9-by-13-inch cake pan and set the pan on top of the salmon to weigh it down.

5. Refrigerate the salmon 18 to 24 hours, depending on the thickness of the salmon, until the salmon is cured. The salmon will deepen in color and take on a shine.

6. Gently remove the salmon from the cure and wipe clean. Wrap tightly with plastic wrap and refrigerate until ready to use, up to 2 weeks.

TO SERVE

1. Thinly slice the salmon and evenly distribute across the focaccia. Scatter the pickled red onions and capers over the salmon and top with dollops of the crème fraîche.

2. Garnish with the black pepper, dill, mint, basil, chives, and a drizzle of extra virgin olive oil. Slice and serve immediately.

Strawberry and Arugula Salad

WITH RED ONION MARMALADE AND CONFIT SHALLOT DRESSING

SERVES 4

After a long winter of serving kale and other hearty greens, this arugula salad is a welcome change. It's always a tough competition, but strawberries rank as my favorite fruit of the spring season. Bursting with sweetness and acidity, I like to eat them when they are so ripe they explode with flavor. The shaved fennel in this salad adds a nice crunch and brings a welcome counterbalance to the peppery arugula and sweetness from the strawberries and red onion marmalade. This is sure to be a showstopper around your family table. Pro Tip: If you have leftover red onion marmalade, save it to top off a sandwich at lunchtime.

RED ONION MARMALADE

4 medium red onions, diced small

3 cups sugar

2 cups balsamic vinegar

1 cup red wine vinegar

1 cup dry red wine

2 teaspoons kosher salt

CONFIT SHALLOT DRESSING

2 large shallots, peeled

4 garlic cloves, peeled

5 tablespoons canola oil

5 tablespoons extra virgin olive oil

3 tablespoons apple cider vinegar

1 teaspoon Dijon mustard

1 teaspoon honey

½ teaspoon chopped
   fresh rosemary

½ teaspoon chopped fresh thyme

Kosher salt, to taste

Freshly ground black
   pepper, to taste

TO SERVE

2 quarts arugula

12 ounces strawberries, stems
   removed and sliced

1 fennel bulb, thinly shaved
   and some fronds reserved

3 radishes, thinly sliced

Kosher salt, to taste

Freshly ground black
   pepper, to taste

½ cup coarsely chopped
   roasted almonds

½ cup chèvre cheese

RED ONION MARMALADE

1. Place the onions, sugar, balsamic vinegar, red wine vinegar, red wine, and salt in a large, heavy pot. Set over medium heat and bring to a simmer. Decrease the heat to medium-low and cook until the mixture has thickened to a jam consistency, stirring every 10 to 15 minutes, for about 2 hours. Taste and adjust the seasoning as needed. Set aside to cool.

CONFIT SHALLOT DRESSING

1. Place the shallots, garlic, canola oil, and olive oil in a small saucepan, set over medium-low heat and cook until the shallots are translucent and tender, about 25 minutes. Set aside to cool to room temperature. Once cool, strain out the shallots and garlic, reserving the infused oil and the shallots and garlic separately.

2. Transfer the reserved shallots and garlic to a blender and add the apple cider vinegar, Dijon, and honey. With the motor running on medium speed, slowly add

the reserved oil and process until pureed. Transfer to a small bowl and stir in the rosemary and thyme. Taste and season with salt and pepper as necessary.

TO SERVE

1. Place the arugula, strawberries, fennel, fennel fronds, and radishes in a large mixing bowl. Add enough vinaigrette to lightly coat the arugula. Season with salt and pepper, and gently toss to combine.

2. Spread a few tablespoons of the red onion marmalade around the exterior of four medium plates. Place the salad in the center and garnish with roasted almonds and dots of chèvre. Serve immediately.

Le Grand Aioli
WITH TARRAGON AND DILL AND SPRING CRUDITÉS

SERVES 6

As a child, I remember my mother making crudités for our school lunches, snack time, or a long car ride. I always complained about eating my vegetables, but you know what? Deep down I loved them. Later, during college, I majored in English and French. Traditional French cooking really took a hold on me through my studies. Le Grand Aioli is my vegetarian version of the traditional aioli, and it uses the freshest ingredients of the spring season. Classic and delicious. *Allons-y* to the farmers' market to find some beautiful produce to adorn your table for this highlight of spring.

1 cup Duke's Mayonnaise

1 tablespoon Confit Garlic (page 272)

½ teaspoon Dijon mustard

1 tablespoon finely chopped tarragon

1 tablespoon finely chopped dill

½ teaspoon lemon zest

1 tablespoon freshly squeezed lemon juice

2 dashes Frank's RedHot

¼ teaspoon kosher salt, plus extra to taste

12 fingerling potatoes, boiled

1 cup green beans, blanched

1 bunch asparagus, blanched

12 radishes, leaves on and halved

2 heads Little Gem lettuce, leaves pulled apart

1 cucumber, sliced

12 spring onions, roasted

½ cup sugar snap peas

1 bunch baby carrots, with tops

1 cup pea tendrils

1 cup sorrel leaves

1. Place the mayonnaise, confit garlic, mustard, tarragon, dill, lemon zest, lemon juice, and hot sauce into a food processor and pulse 8 to 10 times or until the ingredients are fully incorporated. Taste, and adjust the seasoning with salt as necessary.

2. Arrange the potatoes, green beans, asparagus, radishes, lettuce leaves, cucumber, spring onions, sugar snap peas, and carrots on a large serving platter and garnish with the pea tendrils and sorrel leaves.

3. Place the aioli in a bowl and serve with the vegetables.

THOUGHTFUL TIP

Don't get me wrong, what I'm about to say will inevitably start a battle. Yes: eggs, lemon juice, and oil are used to make aioli. *But* you can also make aioli with store-bought mayonnaise. I live in the South, and Duke's Mayonnaise reigns supreme. It changed my life and will change yours. Thank me later.

Wild Ramp and New Potato Bisque
WITH PINE NUT DUKKAH AND MINT PISTOU

SERVES 4

Ramps, how I love thee. *Allium tricoccum.* Wild leeks. Ramson. Wild garlic. Bear's garlic. At heart, I'm a mountain man and forager from West Virginia. I've learned to love ramps, and I yearn for them each spring. I plan my work schedule around foraging trips into the forest to explore my ramp patches, and I harvest them to use throughout the year. Ramps are a beloved ingredient among chefs as they are found only in the wild, and for only a few weeks of the whole year. When I asked one old-timer about when to forage for ramps, he said, "Tax Day is Ramp Day around here." And I think he's right. Mid-April is when the mountains in Appalachia begin to turn green again with life, and if you look hard enough you might be able to find this elusive allium delicacy hiding among the trees.

PINE NUT DUKKAH

- ¼ cup pine nuts
- ¼ cup pistachios
- 1 tablespoon benne or sesame seeds
- 1 tablespoon sunflower seeds
- 1 teaspoon coriander seeds
- 1 teaspoon cumin seed
- 1 teaspoon fennel seed
- 1 teaspoon kosher salt
- ½ teaspoon ground sumac
- ½ teaspoon freshly ground black pepper

MINT PISTOU

- 2 tablespoons almonds
- ½ cup lightly packed, chopped mint leaves
- ¼ cup lightly packed, chopped flat-leaf parsley
- ½ teaspoon lemon zest
- 1 teaspoon freshly squeezed lemon juice
- ½ teaspoon kosher salt, to taste
- ½ cup extra virgin olive oil

WILD RAMP AND NEW POTATO BISQUE

- 2 tablespoons diced bacon
- 1 tablespoon unsalted butter
- 3 cups rough chopped wild ramps
- ¼ teaspoon red pepper flakes
- 2 cups peeled and medium-diced new potatoes
- 1 quart Vegetable Stock (page 273)
- ⅓ cup heavy cream
- ⅓ cup whole milk
- 2 tablespoons honey
- Kosher salt, to taste

PINE NUT DUKKAH

1. Place the pine nuts, pistachios, benne seeds, sunflower seeds, coriander seeds, cumin seeds, fennel seeds, salt, sumac, and pepper in a medium sauté pan. Set over medium heat and cook, moving continually, until aromatic and slightly toasted, 6 to 8 minutes. Be careful not to burn.

2. Place the mixture in a food processor and pulse three to four times until roughly chopped. Set aside. Store any unused dukkah in an airtight container for 2 to 3 weeks.

MINT PISTOU

1. Place the almonds in a small sauté pan, set over medium heat, and cook, stirring occasionally, until lightly toasted, about 4 minutes. Set aside to cool, and then roughly chop.

2. Place the toasted almonds, mint, parsley, lemon zest, lemon juice, and salt in a food processor and pulse until a rough paste forms, five or six times.

3. With the machine running, slowly add the olive oil. Taste and adjust the seasoning with salt as necessary. Set aside until ready to use.

WILD RAMP AND NEW POTATO BISQUE

1. Place the bacon in a large, heavy-bottom saucepan or Dutch oven, set over medium heat, and cook until crisp and golden brown, 5 to 6 minutes. Remove the bacon from the pan with a slotted spoon and drain on a paper towel. Set aside and reserve.

2. Add the butter, ramps, and red pepper flakes to the pan and cook until the ramps have wilted and are tender, about 5 minutes.

3. Increase the heat to medium-high, add the potatoes, reserved bacon, and vegetable stock and bring to a boil. Reduce the heat to low and simmer 20 to 25 minutes, until the potatoes are tender.

4. Add the heavy cream, milk, and honey and stir to combine. Taste and adjust seasoning with salt as necessary. Simmer for 2 to 3 minutes to heat through.

5. Remove from the heat and set aside to cool slightly. Transfer the mixture in batches to a blender and carefully puree until smooth. Pour the soup back into a clean pot and set over low heat to keep warm until ready to serve.

6. Serve immediately in bowls garnished with a sprinkle of the dukkah and a drizzle of the pistou.

THOUGHTFUL TIP

You don't have to get lost in the woods to find wild ramps. Check out the local farmers' markets between mid-April to mid-May to find this garlicky wild delicacy. Make sure to ask how they were harvested. If the roots are still attached it means they were pulled from the ground in an unsustainable manner. Ramps take 7 years to grow from seed to mature plant, and it's important to harvest them sustainably by leaving the roots in the ground. You can also preserve this seasonal specialty. Check out my recipe for Pickled Ramps (page 265) in Foundation Recipes.

Wild Ramp and New Potato Bisque
with Pine Nut Dukkah and Mint Pistou

Roasted Carrots with Benne Seed Za'atar, Preserved
Lemon Yogurt, and Carrot Top Pistou

Roasted Carrots

WITH BENNE SEED ZA'ATAR, PRESERVED LEMON YOGURT,
AND CARROT TOP PISTOU

SERVES 4

My friend and chef, Steven Satterfield from Atlanta, said it best when talking about sustainability and vegetables: We need to use them from root to leaf. That's the plan here when cooking these super tender spring carrots. Carrots can undoubtedly become a forgetful ingredient, but here they are the star of the show. Taste the whole plant in this dish: sweet roasted carrots as a foundation, bitter and earthy carrot top as a pistou. Eating the tops by themselves can be a little rough, but with the addition of almonds, garlic, parsley, and a glug of good olive oil they turn into an inspiring addition to top a plate of roasted carrots. Look for the rainbow-colored carrots at the market to add even more color onto your plate.

CARROT TOP PISTOU

- 1 bunch (about 1½ cups) carrot tops, roughly chopped
- ½ cup loosely packed, chopped parsley
- 2 garlic cloves, minced
- 2 tablespoons roughly chopped almonds
- 1½ tablespoons freshly squeezed lemon juice
- 3 tablespoons extra virgin olive oil
- ½ teaspoon Aleppo pepper
- Kosher salt, to taste

PRESERVED LEMON YOGURT

- ½ cup whole-fat plain yogurt
- 2 tablespoons mayonnaise
- 1 tablespoon minced Preserved Lemons (page 269)
- 1 garlic clove, minced
- 1 teaspoon freshly squeezed lemon juice
- ½ teaspoon Aleppo pepper
- Kosher salt, to taste

BENNE SEED ZA'ATAR

- 2 tablespoons minced thyme
- 2 tablespoons benne seeds, may substitute sesame seeds
- 2 teaspoons ground sumac
- ½ teaspoon sea salt

ROASTED CARROTS

- 1 pound carrots, scrubbed and peeled if desired
- 2 tablespoons canola oil
- 2 tablespoons freshly squeezed lemon juice
- 2 tablespoons unsalted butter
- Kosher salt, to taste
- Freshly ground black pepper

CARROT TOP PISTOU

1. Place the carrot tops, parsley, garlic, almonds, and lemon juice into a food processor and process until a rough paste has formed. With the motor running, slowly add the olive oil until well incorporated, 1 to 2 minutes. Transfer to a small bowl, add the Aleppo pepper, stir to combine, and taste. Taste and adjust seasoning with salt and pepper as necessary. Set aside until ready to use.

PRESERVED LEMON YOGURT

1. Place the yogurt, mayonnaise, preserved lemon, garlic, lemon juice, and Aleppo pepper in a small bowl and whisk to combine. Taste and adjust seasoning with salt and pepper as necessary. Set aside until ready to use.

BENNE SEED ZA'ATAR

1. Place the thyme, benne seeds, sumac, and salt into a small bowl and stir to combine. Set aside until ready to use.

ROASTED CARROTS

1. Place the carrots and oil in a large bowl and toss to combine.

2. Place a large sauté pan over medium-high heat for 3 to 4 minutes, until hot.

3. Add the carrots to the hot pan and cook, stirring occasionally, until golden and tender, 15 to 20 minutes, depending on the size of the carrots. If necessary to prevent overcrowding the pan, cook in two batches.

4. Remove the pan from the heat, add the lemon juice and butter, and toss to coat. Taste and season with salt and pepper as necessary.

5. Spoon the yogurt onto a serving platter and using the back of your spoon, spread into a circle. Top with the carrots, drizzle with the pistou, and sprinkle with the za'atar. Serve immediately.

THOUGHTFUL TIP

Who doesn't love the runny, gooey goodness of a soft-cooked egg yolk? It's a free, unctuous sauce that helps provide healthy protein and depth of flavor to any dish. I can't imagine a world without eggs. Here, it's a gorgeous and delicious addition that brings richness to the roasted asparagus.

Roasted Asparagus
WITH POACHED FARM EGGS AND GREEN GODDESS DRESSING

SERVES 4

Any idea how I can get *more* spring flavor on a plate? We source our asparagus from Riverview Organic Farm in Mills River, North Carolina, where the multi-generational Cole family grows vegetables with integrity. Why? They sell us their asparagus only when it's at its peak. When putting this dish together I wanted to let the ingredients shine. All of these items are friends on the plate, but Benton's Smoky Mountain Country Hams are my choice for layering a deep, rich, smoky, porky goodness with the roasted asparagus. It's a winner every time.

½ cup Panko bread crumbs

2 tablespoons extra virgin olive oil

1 teaspoon chopped thyme

Kosher salt, to taste

1 bunch asparagus, ends trimmed

1 tablespoon canola oil

2 quarts water

2 tablespoons white vinegar

4 large eggs

8 tablespoons Green Goddess Dressing (page 273)

Aleppo pepper, to taste

½ cup chopped Pickled Rhubarb (page 265)

4 ounces country ham, thinly shaved

¼ cup chive flowers

1. Place the bread crumbs and the oil in a small sauté pan, set over medium heat, and cook until toasted, 3 to 4 minutes. Add the thyme and a pinch of salt and stir to combine. Place on a paper towel lined–plate to drain. Set aside until ready to use.

2. Heat a large sauté pan or cast-iron skillet over high heat.

3. Toss the asparagus in the canola oil and place into the pan. Cook, stirring occasionally, until the asparagus is charred on all sides, 2 to 3 minutes. Season with salt to taste and set aside.

4. Place the water in a medium saucepan, set over medium-high heat, bring to a simmer, and add the white vinegar.

5. Crack the eggs one by one into the simmering water. Cook until the eggs are soft poached, about 3 minutes. Remove the eggs from the water and place on a paper towel–lined plate.

6. Spread 2 tablespoons of green goddess dressing on each of the four plates. Place the roasted asparagus over the dressing and sprinkle with the fried bread crumbs.

7. Place a poached egg on top of each plate and garnish with the Aleppo pepper, pickled rhubarb, country ham, and chive flowers. Serve immediately.

Pea and Ricotta-Stuffed Morel Mushrooms

WITH ROMESCO SAUCE

SERVES 4

Mushrooms always remind me of my grandfather. When I was a kid, we would make weekend trips to his rural farm. My pawpaw would take me on walks through the garden and forest. He would always pick wild herbs like ginseng, and he'd pull ramps and grab mushrooms from the forest floor. Honestly, I thought he was a little crazy for doing this, but as I've grown older I've learned that if you know what you are doing, foraging can actually yield safer, fresher, and more delicious foods than what you find at the grocery store. And better yet, your foray through the forest provides an adventure, probably with someone close to you, and together you score the ingredients for the night's dinner.

ROMESCO SAUCE

3 tablespoons olive oil

1 cup large-dice ciabatta or crustless white bread

5 tablespoons slivered almonds

3 garlic cloves, chopped

½ teaspoon red pepper flakes

12 ounces plum tomatoes, peeled, large diced

5 ounces roasted red bell peppers

2 tablespoons sherry vinegar

2 teaspoons smoked paprika

1 teaspoon sugar

½ teaspoon kosher salt, plus extra to taste

Pinch freshly ground black pepper, plus extra to taste

STUFFED MORELS

4 tablespoons extra virgin olive oil, plus extra for serving

1 tablespoon minced shallots

1 teaspoon minced garlic

Pinch red pepper flakes

¼ cup dry white wine

1 cup blanched green peas

⅔ cup drained Ricotta (page 275)

2 tablespoons grated Parmesan cheese

1 teaspoon finely chopped mint

¼ teaspoon lemon zest

Kosher salt, to taste

Freshly ground black pepper, to taste

16 morel mushrooms, cleaned

½ cup pea tendrils

ROMESCO SAUCE

1. Preheat the oven to 350°F.

2. Place the olive oil in a medium sauté pan, set over medium heat, and when the oil shimmers, add the bread and almonds. Cook, stirring frequently, until they are just beginning to brown, 3 to 4 minutes. Add the garlic and red pepper flakes, and cook until aromatic, about 1 minute.

3. Transfer the mixture to the bowl of a food processor and add the tomatoes, bell peppers, vinegar, smoked paprika, sugar, and salt. Puree until smooth. Taste and adjust the salt and pepper to taste.

4. Transfer the mixture to a medium baking dish, place in the oven, and bake until the edges of the sauce are beginning to caramelize, 15 to 20 minutes.

5. Remove from the oven, stir, and set aside to cool.

STUFFED MORELS

1. Place 2 tablespoons of the olive oil in a small sauté pan, set over medium-high heat, and when the oil shimmers add the shallots, garlic, and red pepper flakes. Cook, stirring frequently, until aromatic, 2 to 3 minutes. Add the wine and cook at a simmer, stirring occasionally, until reduced to a glaze, 4 to 5 minutes. Set aside to cool to room temperature.

2. Increase the oven temperature to 400°F.

3. Place the green peas, ricotta, Parmesan, mint, lemon zest, and cooled shallot glaze into the bowl of a food processor and puree until incorporated. Taste and add salt and pepper to taste.

4. Transfer the mixture to a piping bag or a gallon zip-top bag.

5. Pipe the puree into the mushrooms through the hollow stems, completely filling each mushroom with the puree.

6. Toss the filled mushrooms in the remaining 2 tablespoons of olive oil and season with salt and pepper. Place the mushrooms on a parchment-lined sheet tray and roast in the oven until they are beginning to become golden in color and the filling is hot, 10 to 12 minutes.

7. Divide the romesco sauce among four plates. Top with four mushrooms per plate. Garnish with the pea tendrils. Serve immediately.

THOUGHTFUL TIP

When foraging for wild mushrooms (or any wild-grown ingredient for that matter), it's always best to go with a guide, to learn from another human, in person, and to follow up with multiple authoritative sources to verify your wild harvest is safe to eat. Then go on and enjoy the spoils of your foraging treasure hunt. You earned it!

Fava Beans and Charred Spring Onions

WITH WATERCRESS, FETA, AND SHERRY THYME VINAIGRETTE

SERVES 4

Fava beans (also known as broad beans) are the king of beans in the spring. They have a smoother flavor and are sweeter and richer than most other beans. They are a chore to peel—to some, it's a little confusing figuring out how to get the actual bean out of the pod. Fava beans, when in their tough pods, look like an overgrown sweet pea. The beans have to be peeled twice. So, you will have to buy a lot more beans than you might think for your recipe. One pound of unpeeled beans will give you roughly ⅓ cup of favas.

SHERRY THYME VINAIGRETTE

2 tablespoons aged sherry vinegar

1 teaspoon minced shallots

¼ teaspoon minced garlic

¼ teaspoon honey

¼ teaspoon Dijon mustard

6 tablespoons extra virgin olive oil

1½ teaspoons thyme leaves

½ teaspoon kosher salt, plus extra to taste

Freshly ground black pepper, to taste

FAVA BEANS AND SPRING ONIONS

1 tablespoon canola oil

8 spring onions, trimmed

3 cups peeled fava beans (see Thoughtful Tip)

2 teaspoons freshly squeezed lemon juice

Kosher salt, to taste

4 cups watercress

¼ cup crumbled feta cheese

2 teaspoons Aleppo pepper

SHERRY THYME VINAIGRETTE

1. Place the vinegar, shallots, garlic, honey, and mustard in a small bowl and whisk to combine.

2. Slowly add the oil, while whisking continually. Add the thyme, salt, and pepper and whisk to combine. Taste and adjust seasoning as desired. Set aside until ready to use or refrigerate in an airtight container for up to 5 days.

FAVA BEANS AND SPRING ONIONS

1. Add the canola oil to a large cast-iron skillet and set over medium-high heat. Once the oil shimmers and almost smokes, add the spring onions, laying them down away from you to keep from splashing the oil. Cook the onions until charred on all sides, 5 to 6 minutes.

2. Decrease the heat to medium and add the fava beans. Cook, stirring continually, until tender, 2 to 3 minutes. Remove from the heat, add the lemon juice, and season with salt and Aleppo pepper. Taste and adjust the seasoning as necessary. Transfer the onions and fava beans to a large shallow bowl and cool slightly.

3. In the meantime, place the watercress in a large bowl and toss with half of the vinaigrette. Taste and season with salt and pepper as needed.

4. Spoon the fava beans across a medium platter and arrange the charred scallions over the beans.

5. Spoon more of the vinaigrette over the fava beans and scallions. Sprinkle the feta cheese on top. Arrange the watercress over the beans and sprinkle with the Aleppo pepper. Serve immediately.

THOUGHTFUL TIP

How to peel and prepare fava beans:

1. First, remove the beans from the tough, exterior pods (much like you would when shelling peas). Simply run a finger up the seam of the pod, split it open, and remove the beans. There will be about four or five beans per pod.

2. At this point you'll notice that the bean has a thick white skin around it, which also needs to be peeled off.

3. Place the fava beans in boiling salted water and blanch them for about 30 seconds. Remove the beans from the boiling water and submerge them in ice water to stop them from cooking. This step softens the second skin, making it easier to remove.

4. Next, with your fingers, squeeze the bean out from its skin.

5. Now the fava beans have been peeled, and you can use them for your recipes.

Fava Beans and Charred Spring Onions with
Watercress, Feta, and Sherry Thyme Vinaigrette

Mac and Cheese with Smoked Cheddar Mornay, Spring Peas, and Aged Ham

Mac and Cheese

WITH SMOKED CHEDDAR MORNAY, SPRING PEAS, AND AGED HAM

SERVES 4

Mac and cheese can be found on the menu at most Southern restaurants, or on the table for many family celebrations. It's rich, cheesy, gooey, and hits all the high notes. It brings us back to our childhood in one delicious bite. This mac and cheese came about from a family meal I served years ago while working the line and coming up in the restaurant industry. I didn't have time to make a traditional flour-based roux, so I just used the reduction method. It turned out to be a hit with my teammates. Since then, it's made its rounds in my restaurants. I love the addition of the green spring peas and the country ham. Ham and peas are like two old friends, and when they invite mac and cheese over, it's a real party.

MORNAY SAUCE

1 tablespoon olive oil

1 tablespoon minced shallot

½ teaspoon minced garlic

2 tablespoons white wine

½ cup heavy cream

3 ounces cream cheese

2 ounces applewood smoked Cheddar, shredded

¾ ounce shredded Parmesan cheese

1¼ ounces chèvre goat cheese

½ teaspoon honey

¾ tablespoon Frank's RedHot

1 teaspoon Worcestershire sauce

Kosher salt, to taste

Freshly ground black pepper, to taste

MAC AND CHEESE

2 slices Pullman bread, crusts removed and left out to dry overnight

2½ tablespoons extra virgin olive oil

2 teaspoons chopped fresh thyme

¼ teaspoon kosher salt

½ cup, diced country ham (Benton's Smoky Mountain Country Hams is best)

½ cup blanched green peas

½ cup heavy cream, plus extra if needed

4 cups elbow macaroni, cooked al dente

MORNAY SAUCE

1. Place the olive oil in a medium saucepan and set over medium heat. Once the oil shimmers, add the shallots and garlic, and sauté until the shallots are translucent, about 5 minutes. Add the wine and cook, stirring frequently, until it reduces to a syrup, about 5 minutes.

2. Add the heavy cream and reduce by half.

3. Reduce the heat to low and whisk in the cream cheese, Cheddar, Parmesan, goat cheese, honey, hot sauce, and Worcestershire sauce. Whisk until the cheeses have all melted. Taste and season with salt and pepper. Set aside to cool.

MAC AND CHEESE

1. Place the bread in a food processor and pulse until crumbs. Place 1½ tablespoons of olive oil in a sauté pan set over medium heat, add the bread crumbs, and cook, tossing frequently, until golden brown, 7 to 8 minutes. Be careful not to burn.

2. Remove from the heat, add the thyme and salt, and stir to combine. Transfer to a paper towel–lined plate to drain. Set aside until ready to use.

3. Add the remaining 1 tablespoon of olive oil to a medium sauté pan and set over medium heat. Add the country ham and cook, stirring occasionally, until golden and crisp, 5 to 6 minutes. Add the green peas and stir to combine.

4. Add the heavy cream and Mornay sauce and bring to a light simmer. Add the cooked macaroni, stir to combine, and decrease the heat to medium-low. Continue to cook, stirring frequently, until the mixture is heated through. It should be creamy, not dry. Add more cream if needed to adjust consistency.

5. Serve immediately, in bowls, topped with the herbed bread crumbs.

THOUGHTFUL TIP

There are country hams, and then there are *country* hams. I suggest that you take the time to seek out an artisan country ham producer in your region. In the South, hams are produced akin to prosciuttos from Italy. One of my all-time favorites comes from the great Allan Benton of Benton's Smoky Mountain Country Hams in Madisonville, Tennessee. The smoky goodness of his cured pork will forever change your life.

Crispy Soft-Shell Crabs
WITH GREEN GARLIC AIOLI

SERVES 4

Feeling crabby? I certainly am when soft crabs come into season in the Carolinas. Fried, grilled, sautéed . . . they are delicious and crispy and one of my favorite bites of the spring. Dredging the crabs in the seasoned flour allows for a big crunch when biting into them, and it also allows for the sweet flavor of the crabmeat to shine through. Green garlic is the fresh version of garlic before it's been hung to cure and dry to use later in the year. Use green garlic as you would cured garlic from the grocery store, and notice the fresher flavor.

Serve soft-shell crabs with a side salad or use as the protein on a sandwich with the green garlic aioli, lettuce, and tomato. So good!

GREEN GARLIC AIOLI

½ cup loosely packed basil

½ cup loosely packed spinach

1 tablespoon canola oil

¼ cup chopped green garlic

1 tablespoon freshly squeezed lemon juice

1 teaspoon Frank's RedHot

¾ cup Duke's Mayonnaise

Kosher salt, to taste

Freshly ground black pepper, to taste

CRAB

1 cup all-purpose flour

1½ teaspoons kosher salt, plus extra as needed

1 teaspoon freshly ground black pepper

1 teaspoon smoked paprika

½ teaspoon cayenne pepper

4 jumbo soft-shell crabs, cleaned (see Thoughtful Tip)

½ cup canola oil

4 lemon wedges, for serving

AIOLI

1. Set a small saucepan over high heat, add 2 inches of water, and bring to a boil. Fill a small bowl with ice water and set aside.

2. Add the basil and spinach and blanch until just wilted, about 10 seconds. Immediately transfer to the ice water to stop the cooking. Allow to cool completely. Transfer the basil and spinach to a paper towel or kitchen towel and wring out the water. Once dry, roughly chop.

3. Place the canola oil in a small sauté pan, set over medium heat, add the green garlic, and sauté about 3 minutes or until tender. Transfer the green garlic to a small food processor.

4. Add the spinach, basil, lemon juice, and hot sauce and puree. Transfer the mixture to a small bowl. Fold in the mayonnaise until fully incorporated. Adjust the seasoning with salt and pepper. Set aside until ready to use.

CRAB

1. Line a plate or sheet pan with paper towels and set aside.

2. Place the flour, salt, black pepper, smoked paprika, and cayenne pepper in a shallow wide bowl or pie pan and whisk to combine.

3. Dredge the crabs on both sides in the flour mixture and set aside.

4. Heat the canola oil in a tall-sided sauté pan set over medium heat. Working with one or two at a time, making sure not to overcrowd the pan, fry the soft-shell crabs until golden on the bottom side, about 3 minutes.

5. Gently flip the crabs over, using tongs, flipping away from you to not splash the oil. Cook until golden on the bottom side, about 2 to 3 more minutes, and remove to the prepared plate or sheet tray and season with salt. Repeat until all the crabs are cooked.

6. Serve with the green garlic aioli and lemon wedges.

THOUGHTFUL TIP

What is a soft-shell crab? It's a kitchen term for when blue crabs (or really any crab) molt between seasons, lose their old exoskeleton, and grow a new one. The crabs are harvested during this molting period, and so the entire crab can be eaten, rather than having to cook the crustacean and discard the shell. Make sure to clean away the mouth, gills, and abdominal cover before cooking.

Crispy Soft-Shell Crabs with Green Garlic Aioli

Whole Stuffed Rainbow Trout
with Lemon Butter and Grilled Ramps

Whole Stuffed Rainbow Trout
WITH LEMON BUTTER AND GRILLED RAMPS

SERVES 4

Since I've lived in Asheville, I've really gotten into fly-fishing. Being able to get away from it all for a few hours, and to be knee-deep in a cold mountain stream, helps me to reset my mind and body. I certainly love to catch fish, and the methodic act of casting, and mending my line as it floats downstream, is an act of being one with nature. Roasted trout with wild ramps and lemon butter is sure to please even your pickiest eater. And if you want to take this dish to another level, stuff the ramps into the trout, or wrap the trout in the whole ramps so the wild leek flavor can infuse into the fish while cooking it.

LEMON BUTTER

1 lemon, halved

1 cup dry white wine

3 small shallots, sliced

1 tablespoon thinly sliced fresh ginger

2 garlic cloves, peeled

2 thyme sprigs

1 fresh bay leaf

½ teaspoon whole black peppercorns

¼ cup heavy cream

½ cup unsalted butter, cubed

Kosher salt, to taste

RAINBOW TROUT AND RAMPS

Two 1-pound whole rainbow trout, cleaned

5 tablespoons canola oil

Kosher salt, to taste

Freshly ground black pepper, to taste

2 lemons, 1 sliced and 1 cut into 4 wedges

10 thyme sprigs

16 ramps, may substitute spring onions, trimmed

LEMON BUTTER

1. Place the lemon, wine, shallots, ginger, garlic, thyme, bay leaf, and peppercorns into a small saucepan, set over medium heat, and bring to a simmer. Cook, stirring frequently, until the mixture reduces to a light syrup consistency, 7 to 8 minutes.

2. Add the cream, stir to combine, and continue cooking, stirring frequently until the mixture reduces by about two-thirds. Whisk in the butter until melted. Taste and season with salt as necessary. Pour through a fine mesh strainer, discard the solids, and keep the butter in a warm place until ready to use. May be stored at room temperature for up to 4 hours.

RAINBOW TROUT AND RAMPS

1. Preheat an oven to 400°F and line a sheet tray with parchment paper.

2. Place the cleaned trout on the sheet tray and rub thoroughly with 3 tablespoons of the canola oil. Season the inside and outside of the fish with the salt and pepper. Place the lemon slices and thyme into the cavity of the fish. Optional: Truss the fish with butcher's twine to hold the fish together and keep the ingredients inside the cavity.

3. Roast until the skin is crisp and the flesh is just cooked through and tender, about 20 minutes.

4. While the fish is cooking, heat a grill or a grill pan on high heat.

5. Toss the trimmed whole ramps in the remaining 2 tablespoons of canola oil and season with salt. Grill the ramps on all sides until lightly charred, about 6 minutes.

6. Place the trout on a platter and garnish with the grilled ramps. Serve with the lemon butter and lemon wedges.

THOUGHTFUL TIP

While I hope you are able to grab your fishing pole and make it out to your nearest stream to catch your dinner, you can also find rainbow trout at your local grocer or fishmonger. When sourcing farmed rainbow trout, I opt for Sunburst Trout Farms from my friends, the Easons, who have been growing their delicious mountain trout in the cold waters below the Shining Rock Wilderness in Canton, North Carolina, for over three generations.

Slow Roasted Pork Shoulder

WITH CRISPY SMASHED NEW POTATOES, ASPARAGUS CREAM, AND GREEN STRAWBERRY RELISH

SERVES 6 TO 8

You're probably asking yourself, *What is a green strawberry and why would you cook with it?* Every spring, I ask our berry farmers to harvest the "green" or underripe strawberries. At this stage, the raw strawberries are bitter with little to no sweetness, but they have a wonderful deep strawberry flavor when cooked. I apply a bread-and-butter-style pickle to the strawberries to make the relish, and then use it like you would a cucumber pickle relish with traditional Southern pulled pork. This recipe kicks it up a notch and turns the simple Southern staple into a more refined dish.

PORK BUTT RUB

½ cup kosher salt

¼ cup light brown sugar

2 tablespoons mustard powder

1 tablespoon dried basil

1 tablespoon garlic powder

1 tablespoon dried marjoram

1 tablespoon dried oregano

1 tablespoon paprika

1 tablespoon smoked paprika

1 tablespoon dried rosemary

1 tablespoon dried thyme

½ tablespoon freshly ground black pepper

¾ teaspoon ground cumin

PORK SHOULDER

One 8-to-10-pound skin-on, bone-in pork shoulder

1½ cups Pork Butt Rub

GREEN STRAWBERRY RELISH

2 cups Pickled Green Strawberries (page 267)

½ cup strained pickling liquid from Pickled Green Strawberries (page 267)

3 shallots, sliced

ASPARAGUS CREAM

1 bunch cooked asparagus, cut into 2-inch pieces

¼ cup water

1 tablespoon Confit Garlic (page 272)

1 teaspoon freshly squeezed lemon juice

1 teaspoon honey

½ teaspoon kosher salt, plus extra to taste

¼ cup extra virgin olive oil

CRISPY SMASHED NEW POTATOES

2 pounds new potatoes, cleaned

1 teaspoon kosher salt, plus extra to taste

½ cup canola oil

Freshly ground black pepper, to taste

PORK BUTT RUB

1. Place the salt, brown sugar, mustard, basil, garlic powder, marjoram, oregano, paprikas, rosemary, thyme, black pepper, and cumin in a bowl and whisk to combine.

PORK SHOULDER

1. Place the oven rack in the middle of the oven and preheat to 250°F.

2. Season the pork shoulder liberally with the pork butt rub, making sure to get all sides of the meat.

3. Line a sheet tray with aluminum foil and set a wire rack inside of it. Lay a small piece of parchment paper in the center of the rack and place the pork on top. Roast the pork until a knife inserted into the pork has little resistance, about 8 hours.

4. Remove the pork from the oven and tent with aluminum foil. Set aside to rest for at least 15 minutes and up to 1 hour.

5. Increase the oven temperature to 500°F and return the pork to the oven and cook for 10 minutes, until the skin begins to become golden and crisp. Set aside until ready to serve.

GREEN STRAWBERRY RELISH

1. Strain the strawberries and cut into quarters. Strain and reserve ½ cup of the pickling liquid, removing any pickling spices.

2. Place the shallots and the pickling liquid into a small saucepan, set over medium-high heat, and reduce by two-thirds. Add the strawberries and set aside to cool. Refrigerate until ready to use.

ASPARAGUS CREAM

1. Place the asparagus, water, confit garlic, lemon juice, honey, and salt into a blender and process until pureed. With the blender running, slowly drizzle in the olive oil until a cream is formed. Taste and adjust the seasoning as needed. Set aside until ready to use.

CRISPY SMASHED NEW POTATOES

1. Place the potatoes and salt into a large saucepan and cover with cold water by 2 inches. Set over medium-high heat and bring to a simmer. Cook until the potatoes are fork-tender, about 30 minutes. Strain the potatoes and spread them on a sheet pan to cool to room temperature. Once cool, gently smash each potato using the palm of your hand.

2. Place the canola oil in a large cast-iron skillet and set over medium-high heat. Once the oil shimmers, add the potatoes, in batches if necessary, and cook until browned, 3 to 4 minutes per side. Remove the potatoes to a paper towel–lined plate to drain. Season with salt and pepper to taste.

TO SERVE

1. Spread a spoonful of the asparagus cream across each plate and top with potatoes and sliced pork. Spoon the green strawberry relish over the pork and serve.

THOUGHTFUL TIP

Pork shoulder, aka pork butt, is one of the most versatile cuts of pork. Slow roast it, or smoke it, for a lip-smacking version of Southern pulled pork. Grind it, and you can make sausage, pâté, terrines, and a million other charcuterie recipes. You will find dishes around the globe that incorporate this cut of meat. Think Mexican pork carnitas, Japanese chashu for ramen, or West African pork and peanut stew.

Asparagus and Rice Middlin' Risotto

Years ago, when I was in graduate school at the University of South Carolina, I was cooking at a local restaurant and teaching culinary arts at the university. During this time, I was introduced to a visionary man by the name of Glenn Roberts. He had recently started a new grain company called Anson Mills, and he was scouring the South for heirloom seeds and working with farmers to plant, grow, and harvest heirloom grains such as Carolina Gold Rice, Farro Piccolo, and Cherokee Blue Corn. Glenn introduced me to a byproduct of hulling rice: rice middlins' (aka rice grits). They are the broken pieces of rice, leftover from hulling dried rice. While they are not the whole rice grain, like the preferred Arborio from Italy, these bits and pieces work perfectly for risotto as they exude their starch during the cooking process making for a creamy, delicious pot of rice.

1 bunch asparagus, woody ends trimmed

5 cups Vegetable Stock (page 273)

3 tablespoons unsalted butter

4 small shallots, minced

1 teaspoon minced garlic

1 pinch red pepper flakes

1½ cups Carolina Gold Rice Grits

¾ cup Carpano Dry vermouth

1 fresh bay leaf

1 small bunch thyme, bundled with kitchen twine

¾ cup grated Parmesan cheese

½ teaspoon kosher salt, plus extra to taste

¼ teaspoon ground white pepper, plus extra to taste

3 radishes, thinly sliced

3 tablespoons chiffonade basil

4 tablespoons extra virgin olive oil

1. Fill a large bowl with ice water and set aside.

2. Bring a medium pot of water to a boil and season with salt so it tastes like the ocean.

3. Add the asparagus and cook until just tender, about 3 minutes.

4. Transfer the asparagus to the ice water to stop the cooking. Once cool, drain and cut the asparagus into 1-inch pieces. Set aside until ready to use.

5. Bring the vegetable stock to a simmer in a small saucepan. Decrease the heat to low to keep it warm.

6. Place a medium saucepan over medium heat and add the butter. Once the butter begins to foam, add the shallots, garlic, and red pepper flakes and stir to combine. Cook until the shallots are translucent and aromatic, about 3 minutes.

7. Stir in the rice and cook for another 2 minutes, until the grains are coated with butter.

8. Add the vermouth and stir to combine. Cook until the vermouth has reduced by three-fourths. Reduce the heat to medium-low and ladle in 1 cup of vegetable stock. Add the bay leaf, thyme, salt, and white pepper and stir to combine.

9. Cook the rice at a low simmer, until the liquid is beginning to evaporate and the rice begins to look dry. Add another cup of vegetable stock and stir to fully incorporate.

10. Repeat again once the liquid begins to evaporate and the rice begins to look dry. Stir repeatedly to keep the rice from sticking.

11. Continue to cook the rice like this, adding stock as needed, until the rice is fully cooked and tender to the tooth when chewed, about 20 minutes.

12. Add the Parmesan and stir to combine. Taste and adjust the seasoning with salt and white pepper. Add the asparagus and fold to combine.

13. Evenly divide the risotto into bowls and top with the radishes, basil, and olive oil.

THOUGHTFUL TIP

You can make this dish vegan by skipping the dairy and using cashew or almond cream in lieu of the butter and cheese. We serve a rendition of this version on our menu at The Market Place, and most folks don't even know we just served them a vegan dish.

Cornmeal and Olive Oil Cake

WITH WHIPPED CRÈME FRAÎCHE AND STRAWBERRY PRESERVES

I love the depth of the cornmeal and olive oil in this cake: a little savory, a little sweet. It translates well to each season, and you can substitute different preserves throughout the year to garnish the dessert. Spring is the time for strawberry preserves. In the summer, I love to make peach and blackberry preserves and, in the fall, a star anise–spiked pear butter hits the spot. Give this recipe a try and turn it into a surefire favorite for your friends and family.

Canola oil for the pan

1 cup stone-ground cornmeal

¾ cup all-purpose flour

1½ teaspoons baking powder

½ teaspoon kosher salt

2 large eggs

2 egg whites

1 cup sugar

¼ cup extra virgin olive oil, plus extra for drizzling

2 tablespoons unsalted butter, melted and cooled slightly

1 cup Crème Fraîche (page 275)

2 tablespoons lemon zest (about 5 lemons)

2 tablespoons freshly squeezed lemon juice

Powdered sugar for garnish

½ cup Strawberry Preserves (page 269)

1. Place an oven rack in the center of the oven and preheat the oven to 350°F.

2. Line the bottom of an 8-inch round cake pan with a parchment paper round. Lightly brush the sides and bottom of the pan with canola oil.

3. Place the cornmeal, flour, baking powder, and salt into a medium bowl and whisk to combine.

4. Place the eggs, egg whites, and sugar in the bowl of a stand mixer fitted with the whisk attachment and whisk on medium-high speed until creamy and pale yellow in color, 3 to 4 minutes. Add the olive oil, butter, ½ cup of the crème fraîche, lemon zest, and lemon juice and whisk on low speed until well combined.

5. Stir the dry ingredients into the wet ingredients until well combined.

6. Pour the cake batter into the prepared cake pan, place in the oven, and bake 30 to 35 minutes, until a toothpick inserted into the center of the cake comes out clean.

7. Remove the cake from the oven to a cooling rack. Cool the cake in the pan for 15 minutes. Run a butter knife around the edge of the pan to loosen the cake and invert it onto a rack to completely cool.

8. Whisk the remaining ½ cup crème fraîche to soft peaks.

9. Serve slices of cake with a drizzle of olive oil, a sprinkle of powdered sugar, a tablespoon of strawberry preserves, and a dollop of the whipped crème fraîche.

Pickled Ramp Dirty Martini

MAKES 2
COCKTAILS

All your hipster friends are doing it. Go for it. Take those beloved pickled ramps and make a dirty martini! It's wild, it's fun, and you'll be the talk of the cocktail party with your foraged food knowledge. All jokes aside, this is one delicious spring drink, and my go-to when processing ramps at our restaurants to preserve for the year.

Ice
1 ounce liquid from Pickled Ramps (page 265)
5 ounces vodka, such as Belvedere
2 splashes dry vermouth, such as Carpano Dry
2 Pickled Ramps (page 265)

1. Place two martini glasses in the freezer for at least 20 minutes before making the cocktails.
2. Fill a cocktail shaker halfway with ice and add the pickling liquid, vodka, and vermouth.
3. Cover and shake hard for 30 seconds.
4. Strain into the chilled martini glasses. Garnish with the pickled ramps and serve immediately.

THOUGHTFUL TIP

While martini traditionalists often scoff at a shaken martini (most prefer stirred), bruising the ice really helps to balance the pungency of the ramps in this drink. So go ahead and go full James Bond . . . shaken, not stirred.

Spring Champagne Cocktail

Crème de violette is a light and floral liquor that originates from France with nuances of spring violet flowers. As the weather warms up, we love to host happy hours at home with our neighbors while the kids play outside. As the season is springing into action, and more sunshine and warmth are on the way, my mind is on new cocktails for the season. This simple, yet effervescent Champagne cocktail is made with just three easy ingredients, which gives this sparkling cocktail a beautiful floral essence and the fragrance of spring. This is a great cocktail for big events or small gatherings. Prep the cocktail in advance by pouring the liqueur and lemon juice into the glasses, and then add the Champagne (or sparkling wine) when you are ready to serve.

2 ounces crème de violette
1 ounce freshly squeezed lemon juice
7 ounces dry sparkling wine or Champagne
Viola flowers for garnish

1. Pour 1 ounce of the crème de violette and ½ ounce of the lemon juice into each of two Champagne flutes.

2. Top each glass with 3½ ounces sparkling wine.

3. Garnish each glass with viola flowers and serve immediately.

DEEP THOUGHTS
OCEAN STEWARDSHIP

One early morning at The Market Place Restaurant, I was receiving our seafood delivery from one of our fishermen who had just driven up from the Carolina coast. That morning, I was expecting 60 pounds of beautiful wild caught black grouper for our menu at the restaurant. I noticed, however, that over the past few years, rather than getting two large, whole fish (typically about 30 pounds each), I was now receiving a much smaller size of the grouper. So I started asking questions: Why aren't my fishermen able to catch the larger fish I wanted for my menus? Why are these fish so small? What's happening in the ocean to cause the change to this species?

These questions led me to reach out to my friends at the Monterey Bay Aquarium's Seafood Watch program. These folks are where the buck stops with ocean stewardship and sustainability. Their brilliant scientists and industrious team work hand in hand with the National Oceanic and Atmospheric Administration (NOAA) to create sustainability ratings on all species of seafood. After many emails and phone calls (and a few trips to the aquarium itself), I had the tools I needed to become a more aware customer, restaurateur, and eater. I began using the Seafood Watch website for seafood sustainability ratings and asking our fishermen and fishmongers about other species of fish we could serve that were not as overfished.

Living in the mountains away from the coast, most of the fish I grew up with were trout, catfish, or smallmouth bass from the freshwater rivers and streams running through these valleys. My colleague Paul Greenberg wrote in his book, *Four Fish*, that most of us are only eating salmon, sea bass, cod, and tuna, and it was time for me to learn more about other species.

Being a thoughtful cook, I had to get outside of my comfort zone. As I studied more about the ocean, I learned about the effects of climate change on the ocean waters and how warming water temperatures, ocean plastics, and ocean acidification are dramatically affecting the seafood species we love to eat. Climate change has also caused a shift in seafood migration, which is causing overfishing. While I'm not much of a scientist or mathematician, the equation does not create a very good outcome for our planet or for the ocean.

But what can we all do to help and to make change? We can become stewards of the ocean. Ask your seafood purveyor or fishmonger where their seafood comes from and how it has been caught. When you go out to eat, ask the waiter the same questions. Use websites like Seafood Watch to check on the sustainability rating of the fish you like to regularly eat. Become a *thoughtful* eater.

While there are certainly many fish in the sea, we need to protect our oceans and create an environment to help them flourish, so that we may help feed our planet for generations to come.

SUMMER

What's in Season?

Blueberries, Basil, Blackberries, Cilantro, Chanterelles, Corn, Cucumbers, Eggplant, Beans, Melons, New Potatoes, Okra, Peaches, Peppers, Plums, Salmon, Squash, Tomatoes, Watermelon

It's summertime! The fireflies are lighting up the night as they float across the grass in my backyard, their blinking a reminder to cherish the dog days of summer. The kids are out of school and we're trying to figure out adventures for each week. We move up to higher elevations to escape the heat, hike in the woods, and explore the lakes and streams to cool off in a swimming hole and take respite from humid Southern afternoons. The days are long and filled with discovery and wanderlust.

Having mastered their bicycles, my kids zip around the neighborhood, learning their own way. Besides spending time with family, we are opening our eyes to nature, growing our relationship with the earth, and learning about the summertime bounty from the garden. Blueberries, tomatoes, basil, and more arrive. The sunshine and warmth change the way I approach my cooking in the summer months: fresh, bright flavors without much pomp and circumstance.

I go to the farmers' market and see old friends, picking up Purple Cherokee tomatoes and zucchini still warm from the earth. I stop by the cheesemonger and grab some fresh mozzarella. A fisherman has driven up from the coast with dayboat shrimp destined for the hot coals on my grill. Searching for the best ingredients is an adventure unto itself, along with the people you meet and the flavors you find. This time of year we're searching for the best, ripest ingredients, so ripe you have to wipe off your chin after you take a bite. Tomatoes that are bright in color, heavy for their size, and bursting with flavor. That's what I love about summer cooking. We can truly cook in the moment and let our spontaneity as cooks come out.

Once we've visited the local markets, we gather our family and friends for an outdoor evening feast. The kids run and march to the beat of their own drum, and the adults put the finishing touches on a much-needed soiree. We eat and drink and catch up with one another. We're making tarts with fresh farm eggs, Swiss chard, and local chèvre; tomato and cucumber salads; roasted corn and peach succotash; and thick rib-eye steaks charred on the grill with chanterelles foraged from the forest around us. It's simple cooking, letting the ingredients shine. All we need are some fresh herbs and some seasoning and a laid-back cocktail to wash it all down. Summer's here and it's time to fire up the grill and unwind!

Zucchini Fritters

WITH HOT HONEY

SERVES 4

When summer yellow squash and zucchini arrive, they arrive in abundance. We're always looking for ways to use them! Panfried and roasted, or cooked into zucchini bread, are some of my favorites. This recipe is a straightforward winner—light and crispy with just the right hint of heat and sweet. We love the flowers, too. Ask your farmer about available zucchini or squash blossoms.

12 ounces zucchini (about 2), seeded and shredded

1 teaspoon kosher salt, plus extra to taste

1½ cups all-purpose flour

¾ teaspoon paprika

½ teaspoon baking powder

½ teaspoon granulated sugar

Canola oil, for frying

¾ cup whole milk, room temperature

2 large room-temperature eggs, slightly beaten

1½ tablespoons melted unsalted butter, slightly cooled

1 clove Confit Garlic, smashed (page 272)

½ cup wildflower honey

1½ teaspoons Kashmiri chili powder

Pinch sea salt

1. Place a rack in a sheet tray and set aside.

2. Place the shredded zucchini into a colander and sprinkle with ½ teaspoon of the salt and toss to combine. Set aside in the sink to drain for 15 minutes.

3. Rinse the zucchini with cold water and place into cheesecloth. Wring dry and reserve.

4. Place the flour, remaining ½ teaspoon of salt, paprika, baking powder, and sugar in a bowl and whisk to combine. Place 1½ inches of canola oil in a large, heavy-bottom saucepan or Dutch oven. Set over medium-high heat and bring the oil to 350°F.

5. Place the zucchini, milk, eggs, butter, and confit garlic into a separate bowl and stir to combine.

6. Add the dry ingredients to the wet ingredients and fold together using a rubber spatula, just until combined.

7. Scoop the fritter mixture, using a 1½ tablespoon scoop, into the oil, holding the scoop as close to the oil as you can to avoid splashing. Fry 6 to 8 fritters at a time, until cooked through or until a cake tester inserted into the fritter comes out clean, 3 to 5 minutes.

8. Repeat until all the fritter dough has been fried.

9. Transfer the cooked fritters to the prepared sheet tray and season with additional salt to taste.

10. Place the honey, chili powder, and sea salt in a small mixing bowl and whisk to combine.

11. Place the fritters onto a platter and drizzle liberally with the hot honey. Serve immediately.

THOUGHTFUL TIP

Whenever you are going to deep-fry an ingredient, it's always best to fill the oil about half-way up the side of a pot or fryer, leaving about 4 inches of open air above the oil so that there is no danger of a spillover. This also helps contain the splattering and makes cleanup easier. Use enough oil so that you can submerge a small batch of food completely.

Tomato Pie

SERVES 6 TO 10

On a hot summer day in my hometown in West Virginia, 12-year-old me, "Billy," was sitting outside my friend's house. My friend's father pulled two German Johnson tomatoes off the vine and began cooking bacon for traditional BLTs. My request for a simple bacon and lettuce version was flatly rejected—he was a man who had grown up in these fertile hills, and he knew what was best for his daughter's friend. "Son, it's July," he said. After I dutifully sat down and ate my first real BLT, an immediate love of all-things-tomato hit little Billy like, well, a tomato to the face. Food memories, like this one, are pivotal points in my life. That was the moment for heirloom tomatoes, which are the star ingredients in this dish.

CORNMEAL PÂTE BRISÉE

- 1 cup all-purpose flour, plus extra for rolling
- ⅓ cup stone-ground cornmeal
- 1 teaspoon kosher salt
- 4 ounces cold unsalted butter, cubed
- ½ cup ice water, strained

TOMATO PIE

- 8 large plum tomatoes, sliced ¼ inch thick
- 1 tablespoon olive oil
- ½ teaspoon kosher salt
- ¼ teaspoon freshly ground black pepper
- 2 cups plus 2 tablespoons grated Parmesan cheese
- 1½ cups Duke's Mayonnaise
- 1½ tablespoons whole-fat buttermilk
- 1½ tablespoons Frank's RedHot
- 1 large egg
- 1 tablespoon chiffonade basil
- 3 cloves mashed Confit Garlic (page 272)
- 2 teaspoons Worcestershire sauce
- ¼ cup grated, aged Cheddar cheese

CORNMEAL PÂTE BRISÉE

1. Place the flour, cornmeal, and salt into the bowl of a stand mixer fitted with the paddle attachment. Combine on low speed for 30 seconds.

2. Add the butter. Starting on low speed, mix until the mixture resembles small peas, 2 to 3 minutes.

3. Add the water and mix on low speed until a dough comes together. The dough will feel wet.

4. Remove the dough from the bowl, wrap in plastic, and refrigerate for 1 hour.

5. Dust the counter and rolling pin with flour and roll the dough to a round, slightly larger than a 10-inch tart pan. Carefully roll the dough around the rolling pin and transfer to the pan and unroll. Carefully press the dough into the edges of the pan and remove any dough that hangs over. Prick the surface of the dough all over with the tines of a fork. Place in the freezer for 15 minutes.

6. Preheat the oven to 400°F. Place parchment paper on top of the crust and use dried beans, rice, or pie weights to weigh down. Bake until slightly browned around the edges and the bottom of the crust is just beginning to lose its shine, 20 to 25 minutes. Remove the parchment and pie weights and set aside.

TOMATO PIE

1. Decrease the oven to 350°F. Set a rack in a sheet tray.

2. Place the sliced tomatoes on the rack, drizzle with the olive oil, and season with the salt and pepper.

3. Bake until the tomatoes are shriveled and lightly browned, 50 to 60 minutes.

4. Place 2 cups of the Parmesan, mayonnaise, buttermilk, hot sauce, egg, basil, garlic, and Worcestershire sauce into a mixing bowl and whisk to combine.

5. Sprinkle the Cheddar evenly across the bottom of the par-baked tart shell.

6. Evenly spread one-third of the tomatoes over the bottom of the tart pan.

7. Evenly spread half of the mayonnaise mixture over the tomatoes.

8. Top with another third of the tomatoes and evenly spread the remaining mayonnaise on top. Place the remaining third of the tomatoes on top. Sprinkle with the remaining 2 tablespoons of Parmesan.

9. Increase the oven temperature to 375°F. Place the tart on a sheet tray and bake until the mixture is set, the tart is light gold, and a wooden skewer inserted into the tart comes out clean, 30 to 35 minutes.

10. Cool completely before cutting and serving.

Tomato Pie

Country Ham Wrapped Peaches
with Stracciatella and Candied Hazelnuts

Country Ham Wrapped Peaches

WITH STRACCIATELLA AND CANDIED HAZELNUTS

SERVES 4

Peaches, especially South Carolina peaches, are one of my favorite stone fruits. When they're ripe they are a true delicacy of the season. I like them so ripe that when you eat them you need a towel nearby to wipe up the juices. This dish was born out of my love for salty and sweet flavor combinations. The country ham and homemade stracciatella cheese work like a charm with the sweet fruits, and the addition of bourbon barrel-aged maple syrup and candied hazelnuts make a dish that you'll be craving all season long.

¾ cup granulated sugar

3 tablespoons water

1 cup blanched hazelnuts

1 teaspoon sea salt

½ teaspoon smoked paprika

4 ripe peaches, pits removed and cut into one-sixths

6 ounces thinly sliced country ham (preferably Benton's Smoky Mountain Country Hams)

2 tablespoons blended oil

1 batch Stracciatella (page 276)

5 tablespoons bourbon barrel-aged maple syrup

1 cup pea shoots

2 tablespoons extra virgin olive oil

1. Line a sheet tray with a nonstick silicone mat. Set aside.

2. Place the sugar and water into a small saucepan, set over high heat, and stir gently to dissolve the sugar. Cook until the mixture turns amber in color, 4 to 5 minutes

3. Remove the pan from the heat, add the hazelnuts, salt, and smoked paprika, and stir to evenly coat.

4. Transfer the candied hazelnuts to the prepared sheet tray and quickly spread the nuts until they are no longer touching each other. Set aside to cool completely.

5. Break the candied nuts into smaller pieces, transfer to a food processor, and process until lightly crumbled. Set aside at room temperature until ready to use.

6. Wrap each slice of peach with a slice of country ham.

7. Line a sheet tray with paper towels and set aside.

8. Place a large cast-iron skillet over medium heat and add the blended oil.

9. Place the peaches into the pan, in batches if necessary, and cook until the ham is golden and crispy on one side, 4 to 5 minutes. Transfer, crispy side up, to the prepared sheet tray. Repeat until all the peaches are cooked.

10. Spread a large spoonful of the stracciatella on each of the four plates. Arrange the peach slices over the cheese. Top each plate with a drizzle of maple syrup, a sprinkle of hazelnuts, pea shoots, and a drizzle of olive oil. Serve immediately.

THOUGHTFUL TIP

The best peaches have some "give" to the skin of the fruit when you squeeze them. But don't squeeze too hard or it will bruise the peach! If a peach is too firm, let it sit out on the counter for another day or two to ripen. Look at the shape: A peach will become more round as it ripens. And also smell the peach—it should smell sweet. If there is no smell, it's not ready to be enjoyed!

Fresh Watermelon

WITH TOASTED BENNE SEEDS AND FETA CHEESE

SERVES 8

Watermelon is a quintessential summer ingredient. Grab one from the farmers' market and let it ripen on the kitchen counter, then slice and enjoy. It's one of nature's easy-to-use delicacies. There are many types of watermelon, and one of the best is the Sugar Baby. It's dark green on the outside with bright, sweet magenta flesh on the inside. Watermelon is high in antioxidants, making it a sweet way to pack in good nutrition. This recipe is a riff on the Hispanic spice, Tajín. Here we're building the salty, spicy, and zesty flavors ourselves and using a unique Turkish dried pepper called urfa biber that has a smoky, raisin-like, and peppery taste.

1 small to medium watermelon, cut into 16 equal wedges
2 tablespoons toasted benne seeds
2 tablespoons urfa biber
Lime zest from 2 limes
1 teaspoon sea salt, plus extra as desired
1½ cups crumbled feta cheese

1. Place two wedges of watermelon on each of the eight plates.

2. Sprinkle the wedges with equal amounts of benne seeds, urfa biber, lime zest, salt, and feta cheese. Serve immediately.

Tomato Sandwiches

WITH CONFIT GARLIC AIOLI, HEIRLOOM TOMATOES, AND BASIL

<u>SERVES 4</u>

You're probably thinking, *Why is there a tomato sandwich recipe in this book?* Once I learned the beauty of a tomato sandwich as a teenager, I knew this was peak summer bliss. The simplicity of good white bread with mayonnaise, vine-ripe heirloom tomatoes, salt, pepper, EVOO, and basil is the quintessential summer treat. As for tomato varieties, some are sweet and some are acidic, and some fall right in the middle. For this life-altering sandwich, I like to combine super ripe and sweet Sungold tomatoes (each is like a little piece of candy) with slices of Mountain Magic tomatoes, which have medium sweetness and acidity. Don't get me wrong, I love Purple Cherokee, Green Zebra, and Mortgage Lifter tomatoes, but this combo is sure to please even the pickiest connoisseur. And let's be real, this is the sandwich you eat leaning over the sink, blissing out in the moment.

CONFIT GARLIC AIOLI

1 cup mayonnaise

4 cloves mashed Confit Garlic (page 272)

1 teaspoon freshly squeezed lemon juice

½ teaspoon kosher salt, plus extra as needed

¼ teaspoon freshly ground black pepper, plus extra as needed

TOMATO SANDWICHES

2 pounds heirloom tomatoes, such as Sungold and Mountain Magic, cut into ¼-inch slices

Kosher salt, to taste

Freshly ground black pepper, to taste

2 tablespoons extra virgin olive oil

3 tablespoons chiffonade basil

8 slices Pullman bread

CONFIT GARLIC AIOLI

1. Place the mayonnaise, confit garlic, lemon juice, salt, and pepper into a mixing bowl and whisk to combine. Taste and adjust seasoning as necessary. Set aside until ready to use or refrigerate for up to 1 week.

TOMATO SANDWICHES

1. Lay the tomatoes on a cutting board or platter and evenly sprinkle with salt, pepper, and olive oil.

2. Lay the slices of bread across a cutting board and liberally slather with the aioli. Arrange the tomato slices across four of the bread slices and scatter the basil on top. Top with the remaining bread, cut each sandwich in half, and serve immediately.

Saving seeds is a tradition that's been passed down for millennia. It provides us a way to grow food and save vegetable and fruit varieties that we love and that are also resistant to environmental stressors. One way to save tomato seeds is to cut a tomato in half (use a favorite tomato variety), scoop out all the seeds, and place them into a bowl. You can set aside the rest of the tomato for eating or cooking. Add about ½ cup of water to the bowl and let it sit at room temperature for 3 days. A film will form on top of the water. Remove the film, add another ½ cup of water, and gently stir the seeds. Good seeds will sink to the bottom, so carefully pour off the water and floating pulp. Repeat this fill-stir-and-pour process two or three times until you have clean seeds. Then drain off the water and lay the seeds on towels to completely dry. Next, place the dry seeds into an airtight container and put the container in the freezer. When the next season rolls around, use those saved seeds to grow your favorite tomato variety.

Tomato Sandwiches with Confit Garlic Aioli, Heirloom Tomatoes, and Basil

Grilled Summer Squash with Blistered
Sungold Tomatoes and Garlic Chili Crisp

Grilled Summer Squash

WITH BLISTERED SUNGOLD TOMATOES AND GARLIC CHILI CRISP

SERVES 4

The temperature is rising outside, so we might as well bring the heat to what we are eating. When you're on the go all day and need to get dinner on the table, the grill is your friend. That's where this flavorful side dish comes in. This is one of my go-tos when squash are plentiful in our garden or the weekly CSA box. Here we are simply grilling fresh squash and dressing it with a homemade spicy garlic chili crisp. This stuff is all the rage currently, but it's worth the hype: spicy, garlicky, crunchy, and full of flavor and umami. You'll want to put it on everything from your eggs in the morning to an afternoon popcorn snack to a dinnertime bowl of soup that needs an extra kick. The recipe makes more than you'll need for this meal, so enjoy the extra and kick it up a notch!

GARLIC CHILI CRISP

1⅔ cups blended oil

6 tablespoons minced garlic

3 tablespoons minced shallots

9 dried arbol chilies, roughly chopped

2 dried ancho chilies, roughly chopped

1 dried guajillo chili, roughly chopped

4 tablespoons peeled, chopped fresh ginger

2 tablespoons tamari

1 tablespoon Aleppo pepper

2 whole star anise

1 cinnamon stick

1 tablespoon sugar

1 teaspoon ground cardamom

1 teaspoon cumin seeds

4 tablespoons dried minced garlic

1 teaspoon mushroom powder

Kosher salt, to taste

SQUASH

1½ to 2 pounds summer squash, cut in half lengthwise

3 tablespoons extra virgin olive oil

1 teaspoon kosher salt, plus extra to taste

¼ teaspoon freshly ground black pepper, plus extra to taste

1 cup Sungold tomatoes

1 lemon, cut in half

GARLIC CHILI CRISP

1. Place the oil in a large sauté pan and set over medium heat. Once the oil shimmers, add the garlic and shallots, and cook, stirring frequently, until golden and crisp, 2 to 3 minutes Watch carefully to prevent burning. Remove the garlic and shallots from the pan using a slotted spoon and transfer to a paper towel–lined plate to drain.

2. Add the arbol, ancho, and guajillo chilies and cook until crisp and aromatic, 2 to 3 minutes. Remove the chilies from the pan with the slotted spoon and transfer to the plate to drain.

3. Decrease the heat to low and wait 3 to 4 minutes to allow the oil to cool slightly. Very carefully place the ginger, tamari, Aleppo pepper, star anise, cinnamon stick, sugar, cardamom, cumin, and garlic into the oil and simmer 10 to 12 minutes to infuse the oil. Strain through a fine mesh strainer and reserve the oil.

4. Roughly chop the fried shallots and garlic and transfer to a mixing bowl. Finely chop the fried chilies and add them to the mixing bowl. Add the reserved oil and mushroom powder. Taste and adjust the seasoning with salt as necessary. Transfer to an airtight container and keep at room temperature for up to 6 months.

SQUASH

1. Preheat a grill to medium-high heat.

2. Place the squash in a large bowl and add the oil, salt, and pepper and toss to evenly coat. Allow any excess oil to drain from the squash and place cut side down onto the hot grill. Cook until the squash has grill marks, 2 to 3 minutes. Turn the squash 90 degrees and continue to cook 2 to 3 minutes. Turn the squash 90 degrees one last time and cook, until the squash is golden brown, 2 to 3 minutes. Remove the squash to a platter and set aside.

3. Place a sauté pan over high heat and heat 4 minutes. Place the tomatoes in the pan and cook until charred on one side, about 4 minutes. Turn the tomatoes and cook on the other side until charred, about 4 minutes.

4. Transfer the tomatoes to the platter with the squash. Generously spoon the garlic chili crisp over the vegetables, squeeze the lemon juice over the vegetables, and serve immediately.

THOUGHTFUL TIP

Chili crisp is definitely spicy, so start with a little and work your way up. It's addictive, and you'll be surprised how much your tolerance will grow and how much more of it you'll want to spoon on everything you eat. I love to stir it into mayonnaise to spice up a sandwich at lunchtime. It's also a winner spooned over top of fried chicken. Thank me later!

Roasted Street Corn

WITH JALAPEÑO LIME BUTTER, FRESH PEACHES, AND CORIANDER CREAM

SERVES 4

My summers growing up were spent running through the field at my grandparents' farm. One of my most vivid memories was when my grandmother asked me to go and fetch some corn from the field for dinner. I remember waddling back to the house with my arms filled with corn piled up to my nose. We sat on the front porch and shucked the corn while a pot of salted water came to a boil. After the corn was boiled for a few minutes until tender, we slathered it down with softened butter and a sprinkle of salt. This is a memory ingrained so deep in my mind, I can still taste the sweetness of the corn and the deep flavor of butter. This recipe is a little more involved than the dish from my mawmaw's house; it showcases a riff on Mexican-style street corn that is spicy, smoky, unctuous, bright, and fun to eat. Peaches are a favorite snack, and their addition to the sautéed corn brings this dish to life.

CORIANDER CREAM

2 tablespoons finely chopped cilantro

2 teaspoons finely chopped jalapeño

Juice from ½ lime

1½ teaspoons coriander seed, toasted and ground

½ cup Greek yogurt

½ cup mayonnaise

Kosher salt, to taste

ROASTED STREET CORN

6 ears corn, shucked

2 tablespoons blended oil

1 red onion, small dice

1 red bell pepper, small dice

1 tablespoon minced garlic

2 peaches, pitted and cut into large dice

4 tablespoons Jalapeño Lime Butter (see page 272)

2 tablespoons freshly squeezed lime juice

½ teaspoon kosher salt, plus extra to taste

Freshly ground black pepper, to taste

¼ cup roughly chopped cilantro

1 lime, cut into 4 wedges

CORIANDER CREAM

1. Place the cilantro, jalapeño, lime juice, and coriander seed into a blender or small food processor and process until smooth, 1 to 2 minutes. Transfer to a bowl, add the yogurt and mayonnaise and stir to combine. Taste and adjust the seasoning with salt as needed. Set aside.

ROASTED STREET CORN

1. Preheat a grill to high. Place the corn on the grill and cook until slightly charred on all sides, about 10 minutes. Set aside until cool enough to handle.

2. Cut the corn away from the cob and place into a large bowl.

CONTINUES →

3. Place the oil in a large sauté pan and set over medium-high heat. Once the oil shimmers, add the onions and cook until translucent, 2 to 3 minutes. Add the bell pepper and garlic and cook, stirring continually, until the garlic is aromatic, 3 to 4 minutes. Add the corn and cook until heated through, 2 to 3 minutes.

4. Add the peaches, jalapeño lime butter, lime juice, and salt and toss to combine and heat through. Taste and adjust seasoning with salt and pepper as necessary.

5. Transfer to a large bowl and garnish with the cilantro.

6. Serve the corn with a dollop of the coriander cream and a lime wedge.

THOUGHTFUL TIP

Save your corn cobs, throw them into a zip-top bag, and store them in your freezer for later. Add the cobs to a homemade vegetable stock, or "milk" them by scraping your knife down the side of the cob to release the juices to use as a thickener for a soup (think cornstarch). You can also use the cobs the same way you would wood chips for smoking poultry or vegetables, as they impart a sweet, mellow, smoky flavor.

White Gazpacho, Cucumbers, Green Grapes, and Almonds

SERVES 4

Let's face it, some days we need a quick and easy go-to for lunch or a weeknight summer meal that requires little thought. This is a riff on a traditional Spanish Andalusian gazpacho that is one of the least complex and most user-friendly food preparations ever. It's a breeze to whip up in the blender, and you can make it a few hours ahead or a day in advance of when you are planning to serve it. The za'atar spice can be made in advance, too, and can also be used to sprinkle on cooked vegetables, salads, seafood, or poultry. The chilled soup is a true star on hot days, and it's a vibrant showcase for the summer season's abundance of cucumbers. The bread absorbs the flavors of the vegetable stock and provides depth to the soup, and as a bonus, it's a great way to use up day-old bread!

3 slices white bread, toasted, crusts removed and cubed

1 cup Vegetable Stock (page 273)

½ cup sliced, toasted almonds

2 garlic cloves

1½ cups seedless green grapes plus 16 cut in half

2 small cucumbers (about 3 cups), peeled and seeded

⅓ cup white wine vinegar

1½ teaspoons honey

2 tablespoons extra virgin olive oil, plus extra for serving

½ teaspoon kosher salt, plus extra to taste

Freshly ground black pepper, to taste

¼ cup slivered almonds, toasted

1. Place the bread in a medium bowl and set aside. Place the stock into a small saucepan, set over medium heat, and bring to a simmer. Once simmering, pour the stock over the bread and set aside to cool.

2. Place the almonds and garlic into the bowl of a food processor and pulse until combined. Add the bread and any extra stock to the processor along with the 1½ cups grapes and cucumbers. Pulse until it is a rough puree, 10 to 15 times. Add half of the vinegar and all the honey and pulse to combine. Taste and add the remaining vinegar if necessary. With the motor running, slowly add the olive oil. Taste and adjust the seasoning with salt and pepper as needed. Refrigerate until cold.

3. To serve, divide the mixture among four bowls. Top with the halved green grapes and almonds. Drizzle with additional olive oil and serve immediately.

Indian Okra and Tomato Stew
WITH CILANTRO AND CUCUMBER RAITA

SERVES 4

When I was growing up, many of my friends were of Indian heritage. So when I went to their homes, I was introduced to dishes such as dal, khichdi, and many other amazing treats that opened my eyes to the food and culture of the Indian subcontinent. It's no wonder that when I met my wife, Jenny, who was born in Ahmedabad in the state of Gujarat in India, that I instantly fell in love. She is a great cook, and between her and her family, they introduced me to some of their favorite dishes, mostly vegetarian and all delicious! I've lived all over the United States, but have spent much of my time in the southeastern part of the country. While in South Carolina I was introduced to the slimy vegetable known as okra. At first, I abhorred this vegetable and had no idea why anyone would ever want to eat it. But thanks to dishes like gumbo, fried okra, Limpin' Susan, and Southern okra and tomato stew, I soon learned to love it! This dish is inspired by my wife's bhindi (okra) masala recipe. It's similar to okra and tomato stew from the South, but the flavor jumps right off the plate! This is a wonderful side dish, but you can make it a meal with the addition of cucumber raita, fresh cilantro, and a bowl of jasmine rice. Serve with rice or whole wheat roti.

CUCUMBER RAITA

1 cup plain Greek yogurt

½ medium cucumber (about 1 cup), peeled, seeded, and diced

1 garlic clove, minced

1 tablespoon chopped cilantro

2 teaspoons chopped mint leaves

1½ teaspoons freshly squeezed lime juice

¼ teaspoon toasted, ground cumin

¼ teaspoon garam masala

Pinch cayenne pepper

Kosher salt, to taste

INDIAN OKRA AND TOMATO STEW

¼ cup extra virgin olive oil

1 medium yellow onion, thinly sliced

¼ teaspoon cayenne pepper

½ teaspoon ground turmeric

1 teaspoon kosher salt, plus extra to taste

¼ teaspoon freshly ground black pepper, plus extra to taste

1 teaspoon minced garlic

2 plum tomatoes, diced

1 pound okra, sliced

½ cup chopped cilantro

2 tablespoons freshly squeezed lime juice

1 teaspoon garam masala

4 lime wedges, for serving

CUCUMBER RAITA

1. Place the yogurt, cucumber, garlic, cilantro, mint, lime juice, cumin, garam masala, and cayenne pepper in a small bowl and stir to combine. Taste and adjust seasoning with salt as necessary. Refrigerate until ready to use.

CONTINUES →

1. Place the olive oil in a large sauté pan, set over medium-high heat, and add the onions. Cook, stirring occasionally, until translucent, about 7 minutes. Add the cayenne, turmeric, salt, and black pepper, stir to combine, and cook until fragrant, 1 to 2 minutes. Add the garlic and cook 30 seconds. Add the tomatoes, stir to combine, and cook for another minute. Add the okra, stir to combine, and cook for 2 minutes.

2. Cover and continue cooking, stirring occasionally, until the okra is just tender, 6 to 7 minutes. Remove from the heat, add half of the cilantro, the lime juice, and the garam masala and stir to combine.

3. Divide the okra between four serving bowls and garnish each with a dollop of raita, the remaining cilantro, and serve with a lime wedge.

THOUGHTFUL TIP

Okra is thought to be of African origin, brought to the United States three centuries ago by enslaved people (the word *okra* is derived from the West African word *nkruma*). By the late 1700s, the plant was gaining widespread popularity in the United States and Americans were enthusiastically cooking with it. Okra is grown in tropical and warm temperate climates, and it's usually available from May to October. Look for brightly colored pods, and choose okra that is no longer than 4 inches in length. Too long, and it gets tough.

Fairy Tale Eggplant

WITH BENNE SEEDS, GREEN TAHINI, AND PICKLED FRESNO PEPPER RELISH

SERVES 4

Eggplant that's been roasted in the oven has a creamy interior with a crispy outer skin that I crave. This vegetable is a good medium to showcase any flavor it encounters. In this dish, we jazz up nutty, earthy tahini with fresh herbs to bring out the sesame and herbal notes. It's light, tangy, and cooling and brings just the right balance to the roasted eggplant. We're garnishing the dish with benne seeds, which are the African relative of sesame seeds. You'll discover their flavor is much more pronounced than standard sesame seeds. We contrast these flavors with a bright pickled Fresno pepper relish that brings a note of heat and acid to leave you craving for more. This is the eggplant dish you never knew you loved!

EGGPLANT

- 1 pound fairy tale eggplant, cut in half lengthwise
- 3 tablespoons extra virgin olive oil
- 1 teaspoon kosher salt, plus extra to taste
- ¼ teaspoon freshly ground black pepper, plus extra to taste
- 1 tablespoon toasted benne seeds or sesame seeds

GREEN TAHINI

- ½ cup tahini
- 3 ounces water, plus extra if necessary
- ¼ bunch parsley, roughly chopped
- ¼ bunch basil, roughly chopped
- 2 tablespoons freshly squeezed lemon juice
- ½ teaspoon toasted, ground cumin seed
- ½ teaspoon minced garlic
- Kosher salt, to taste
- Freshly ground black pepper, to taste

PICKLED FRESNO RELISH

- ½ cup drained, seeded, and diced Pickled Fresno Peppers (page 267)
- 2 tablespoons sliced green onion
- 1 tablespoon chopped chives
- One 1-inch piece orange peel, minced
- 1½ tablespoons extra virgin olive oil, plus extra as needed
- 1 tablespoon pickling liquid from Pickled Fresno Peppers (page 267), plus extra as desired
- Kosher salt, to taste
- Freshly ground black pepper, to taste

EGGPLANT

1. Preheat the oven to 425°F. Place the eggplant into a bowl and toss with the oil, salt, and pepper.

2. Arrange the eggplants cut side up on a sheet tray in a single layer, making sure not to overcrowd the tray. Roast the eggplant 30 to 35 minutes, until it begins to become golden in color and the flesh is tender. Keep warm.

CONTINUES →

GREEN TAHINI

1. Place the tahini, water, parsley, basil, lemon juice, cumin, and garlic into a blender and puree until the mixture is smooth and green in color. Add additional water as needed to create a smooth, dressing-like consistency. Taste and add salt and pepper as desired. Refrigerate for up to 1 week.

PICKLED FRESNO RELISH

1. Place the Fresno peppers, green onions, chives, orange peel, olive oil, and pickling liquid in a small mixing bowl and stir to combine. Taste and adjust the seasoning with salt, pepper, additional pickling liquid, and olive oil to taste. Refrigerate for up to 2 weeks.

TO SERVE

1. Place the roasted eggplant onto a platter and drizzle with the green tahini. Sprinkle the pickled Fresno relish over the eggplant and drizzle with additional olive oil as desired. Sprinkle with benne seeds and serve immediately.

Sockeye Salmon Crudo

WITH JIMMY NARDELLO PEPPERS, PINE NUT ZA'ATAR, AND CHARRED TORPEDO ONIONS

SERVES 4

After reading through the recipe, you might be wondering what a Jimmy Nardello pepper is. Well, it isn't your cousin from New Jersey who works in waste management. It is a sweet Italian frying pepper that was brought to the United States in the late 1800s, and it lends itself to slicing and eating raw, or roasting over an open flame for more depth of flavor. In this recipe, the Nardello pepper adds some sweet crunch to a light raw seafood dish that's perfect for summertime. *Crudo* is the Italian word for "raw," and here we use wild Alaskan sockeye salmon sliced thinly and dressed with grapefruit juice and good EVOO for an appetizer with explosive flavor.

2½ tablespoons ground sumac

2 tablespoons toasted pine nuts

1½ tablespoons toasted benne seeds or sesame seeds

1½ tablespoons fresh thyme leaves

2 teaspoons sea salt

½ cup ruby red grapefruit juice

1 pound sockeye salmon, pin bones removed

1 torpedo onion, no tops, cut into ¼-inch rings

4 tablespoons extra virgin olive oil

½ teaspoon sea salt

2 Jimmy Nardello peppers, sliced into rings

12 cherry tomatoes, quartered

1 ruby red grapefruit, cut into supremes

1 cup purslane

1. Combine the sumac, pine nuts, benne seeds, thyme, and 1 teaspoon of the salt in a small mixing bowl and stir to combine. Transfer to an airtight container until ready to use. Will keep for up to 1 month at room temperature.

2. Place the grapefruit juice in a small saucepan, set over medium-high heat, and cook until reduced by half, 4 to 5 minutes. Transfer to a small container, cover and refrigerate until cold.

3. Place the salmon into the freezer until firm to the touch, 15 to 20 minutes.

4. Place a small cast-iron pan over high heat, until very hot, 4 to 5 minutes. Place the torpedo onion rings in the pan so they are flat and cook until the onions are completely charred on one side, 4 to 5 minutes. Transfer the onions to a small bowl, cover with plastic wrap, and set aside to steam for 5 minutes. Remove the plastic and separate the onions into smaller rings. Set aside to cool.

5. Remove the salmon from the freezer and set on a cutting board, skin side down. Use a very sharp knife to cut through the flesh, as close to one end of the fillet as possible. Stop before slicing through the skin. Rotate the blade so it's parallel between the flesh and the skin. Holding on to the skin with your other hand, slice away from you, using a back-and-forth motion, while pulling the skin

CONTINUES →

toward you. You should completely remove the skin. Trim the fillet of any uneven edges, and cut it into two long pieces, using the natural seam in the center of the fillet as a guideline.

6. Hold a knife at a 45-degree angle to the fish and slice the fish as thinly as possible without the fish falling apart (about ⅛ inch thick). Transfer the fish to each of the four plates. If not serving immediately, transfer the fish to a plate and cover with plastic wrap and hold under refrigeration until needed.

7. Spoon 1 tablespoon of the reduced grapefruit juice and 1 tablespoon of extra virgin olive oil over the fish on each plate. Sprinkle with the remaining teaspoon of sea salt.

8. Garnish each plate with onions, peppers, tomatoes, grapefruit, and purslane. Sprinkle ½ teaspoon of the za'atar over the fish on each plate and serve immediately.

THOUGHTFUL TIP

Not all salmon are the same! Much of the Atlantic salmon we see in restaurants and grocery stores has been farm raised. While many varieties are being sustainably farm raised nowadays, there are many more that are not. During the summer months each year, sockeye salmon run by the tens of millions in Bristol Bay, Alaska. Sockeye are leaner than their king salmon counterparts, deeper in ruby red color, have a wonderful flavor, and are packed with super healthy fish oil. This is one of the best, and healthiest, fish in the sea!

Cornmeal Fried Catfish

WITH BUTTER BEAN AND BOILED PEANUT STEW, GREEN TOMATO
CHOWCHOW, AND HERB AIOLI

SERVES 4

When I'm feeling nostalgic, I love cooking this dish in my old cast-iron pan. It renews my appreciation for the way cast iron evenly distributes heat like nothing else. This time of year, the beans and field peas start taking charge and I can't get enough of them. Butter beans, aka lima beans, are a favorite type of broad bean. As a kid, I hated them because I was told by my peers that I was supposed to. As I grew up, and the lima beans of my youth began to be cooked with flavor, I found out that I had been lied to all along! Butter beans are delicious! Here we're pairing some serious Southern flavors: cornmeal-fried catfish, butter bean and boiled peanut stew, chowchow, and herb aioli. This is some real South in your mouth!

CHOWCHOW

¼ head green cabbage, cored and finely chopped

½ cup seeded, diced green bell pepper

½ cup seeded, diced red bell pepper

½ cup diced yellow onion

¼ cup diced green tomatoes

1 tablespoon minced garlic

1 tablespoon kosher salt

½ cup sugar

⅓ cup apple cider vinegar

¼ cup water

½ teaspoon yellow mustard seeds

¼ teaspoon mustard powder

¼ teaspoon red pepper flakes

¼ teaspoon celery seeds

¼ teaspoon ground ginger

¼ teaspoon ground turmeric

HERB AIOLI

½ cup mayonnaise

1 tablespoon mashed Confit Garlic (page 272)

2 teaspoons finely chopped basil

2 teaspoons finely chopped chives

2 teaspoons finely chopped parsley

½ teaspoon freshly squeezed lemon juice

¼ teaspoon kosher salt, plus extra to taste

Pinch freshly ground black pepper, plus extra to taste

Pinch cayenne pepper

Pinch paprika

BOILED PEANUT STEW

2 tablespoons blended oil

¼ cup diced yellow onion

¼ cup peeled and diced carrot

¼ cup diced celery

2 tablespoons seeded, diced red bell pepper

2 garlic cloves, minced

½ teaspoon kosher salt, plus extra to taste

Pinch red pepper flakes

½ cup dry white wine

2 cups butter beans, blanched

½ cup shelled, boiled peanuts

1 bay leaf

2 cups Vegetable Stock (page 273)

2 tablespoons unsalted butter

2 tablespoons chopped parsley

1½ teaspoons Frank's RedHot

1½ teaspoons freshly squeezed lemon juice

¼ teaspoon freshly ground black pepper, plus extra to taste

CATFISH

1 cup whole-fat buttermilk

1 tablespoon Frank's RedHot

4 catfish fillets

¾ cup cornmeal

½ cup all-purpose flour

1 teaspoon garlic powder

1 teaspoon freshly ground black pepper

1 teaspoon paprika

½ teaspoon cayenne

½ teaspoon celery seeds

½ teaspoon kosher salt

⅓ cup canola oil

CONTINUES →

CHOWCHOW

1. Place the cabbage, bell peppers, onion, tomatoes, and garlic in a large mixing bowl. Sprinkle with the salt and toss to combine. Cover and refrigerate overnight.

2. Drain and discard the liquid from the vegetables.

3. Place the sugar, vinegar, and water in a heavy saucepan, set over medium-high heat, and bring to a boil. Cook, stirring occasionally, until the sugar dissolves, about 2 minutes. Add the mustard seeds, mustard powder, red pepper flakes, celery seeds, ginger, and turmeric and stir to combine.

4. Add the drained vegetables, stir to combine, and return to a boil. Reduce the heat to maintain a low simmer and cook, stirring occasionally, until the relish is thick and saucy, 35 to 45 minutes. Refrigerate until ready to use.

HERB AIOLI

5. Place the mayonnaise, confit garlic, basil, chives, parsley, salt, pepper, cayenne, paprika, and lemon juice into a small bowl. Whisk to combine. Taste and adjust seasoning as necessary.

BOILED PEANUT STEW

1. Place the blended oil in a heavy-bottom saucepan and set over medium-high heat. Once the oil shimmers, add the onions, carrots, and celery and cook, stirring occasionally, until the onions are translucent, 4 to 5 minutes.

2. Add the bell pepper, garlic, salt, and red pepper flakes; stir and cook for another 30 seconds.

3. Add the wine, deglaze the pan, and cook until the wine reduces by half. Add the butter beans, boiled peanuts, bay leaf, and stock. Bring to a boil, and then reduce to a simmer and cook until the butter beans are tender, 20 to 25 minutes.

4. Add the butter, parsley, hot sauce, lemon juice, and black pepper. Taste and adjust the seasoning as necessary. Keep warm until ready to serve.

CATFISH

1. Place the buttermilk and hot sauce into a shallow pan and whisk together. Add the catfish, spoon the mixture over so the fillets are covered, and refrigerate for 30 minutes.

2. Place the cornmeal, flour, garlic powder, black pepper, paprika, cayenne, celery seeds, and salt in a shallow pan and stir to combine.

3. Set a large cast-iron pan over medium heat and add the oil.

4. Lift the catfish out of the buttermilk and allow the excess buttermilk to drip off. Transfer to the pan with the dry ingredients and dredge the fillets on each side.

CONTINUES →

5. Gently place the breaded catfish fillets into the hot oil, placing them away from you to make sure you don't splash hot oil. You may have to do this in two batches to avoid overcrowding the pan.

6. Fry the catfish until golden brown, 3 to 4 minutes. Gently flip the fish and cook on the other side until just cooked through, firm and golden brown on the second side, 3 to 4 minutes. Place the fish on a paper towel–lined sheet tray to drain.

7. Divide the stew between each of four bowls and top with a tablespoon of chow-chow. Place the catfish on top and garnish with a dollop of the aioli. Serve immediately.

THOUGHTFUL TIP

Boiled peanuts are one of my favorite Southern roadside snacks. Years ago I was snacking on a bag of them as I crisscrossed the low country, and started thinking about how their texture was similar to a cooked bean. The experiments soon began, and I started using them in soups and stews to add a nutty depth of flavor, and a lot of nostalgia!

Garlic and Herb Grilled Shrimp
WITH DILL YOGURT

SERVES 4

This is a dinner party favorite. Grilled shrimp skewers are easy to knock out while getting things ready for guests to arrive, and they are without fail a winner with kids as well as adults. It's a simple dish to put together, and you can easily ramp up the recipe if you are having more people over to join in the festivities. I always like to make the marinade right before grilling the shrimp so the flavors are robust, but it can be made in advance, if needed. Don't marinate the shrimp for too long, or you'll end up with ceviche, as the acid in the marinade denatures the proteins and "cooks" the shrimp instead of adding flavor and tenderizing the seafood. You'll love the char from the fire on the shrimp and the garlicky, herbal notes that come through from the marinade.

DILL YOGURT
- ½ cup Greek yogurt
- ¼ cup finely chopped dill
- 1 tablespoon mayonnaise
- ½ teaspoon lemon zest
- 1 tablespoon freshly squeezed lemon juice
- ½ teaspoon kosher salt, plus extra to taste
- ¼ teaspoon paprika
- Freshly ground black pepper to taste
- 1 tablespoon extra virgin olive oil

SHRIMP
- ¼ cup extra virgin olive oil
- 1 tablespoon minced garlic
- 1 tablespoon finely chopped parsley
- 1 tablespoon finely chopped basil
- 1 teaspoon lemon zest
- ½ tablespoon freshly squeezed lemon juice
- ½ tablespoon orange zest
- ¼ teaspoon freshly ground black pepper
- ¼ teaspoon red pepper flakes
- ½ teaspoon paprika
- ½ teaspoon kosher salt
- 1 pound (21/25 count) shrimp, peeled and deveined
- Blended oil for the grill
- 1 lemon, cut into wedges
- 10 to 20 dill sprigs

DILL YOGURT

1. Place the yogurt, dill, mayonnaise, lemon zest, lemon juice, salt, and paprika into a small bowl and whisk to combine. Taste and adjust seasoning as needed with black pepper and salt. Transfer to a serving dish, drizzle with olive oil, cover and refrigerate until ready to use.

SHRIMP

1. Soak 12, 6-inch skewers in warm water for 30 minutes.

2. Place the olive oil, garlic, parsley, basil, lemon zest, lemon juice, orange zest, black pepper, red pepper flakes, ¼ teaspoon of the paprika, and salt in a medium bowl and whisk to combine. Remove one-quarter of the marinade for use after grilling.

CONTINUES →

3. Add the shrimp to the bowl and gently toss to coat with the marinade. Refrigerate 20 to 25 minutes. While the shrimp are marinating, preheat a grill to medium-high heat (about 450° F).

4. Skewer the shrimp, two per skewer, through the tail end and head end of the shrimp to make a "half-moon." Place the skewers onto a sheet tray and spoon the marinade over the shrimp. Sprinkle the shrimp with kosher salt.

5. Brush the grill with the blended oil. Lay the skewers on the grill and cook until golden, 3 to 4 minutes. Turn the skewers over and grill until just cooked through, 2 to 3 minutes.

6. Remove the shrimp to a serving platter and sprinkle with the remaining paprika. Spoon the reserved marinade over the shrimp, garnish with the lemon wedges and dill, and serve with the yogurt.

THOUGHTFUL TIP

While it's easy to get frozen shrimp, or shrimp that's already been shelled, go with the biggest, most beautiful head-on shrimp you can find. I like to do this same recipe and cook the shrimp with the shells still on, as it protects the flesh and adds even more flavor. The shrimp are equally great shelled, but it's important that you do it yourself so you know you're getting the freshest, sweetest shrimp you can find! And don't throw away the heads after grilling the shrimp! They're delicious and full of keratin, a vitamin that is great for healthy skin, nails, and hair. If you do peel your shrimp, save the shells for shrimp stock by placing them into a zip-top bag and storing them in the freezer.

Pan-Roasted Golden Tilefish

WITH RICE PIRLOU, LADY PEAS, ROASTED EGGPLANT,
AND ROASTED CHERRY TOMATO RELISH

SERVES 4

Seared fish is one of my favorite preparations, specifically when it's snapper, grouper, and their cousin: golden tilefish. Here I pair this golden tilefish (which is a Seafood Watch Best Choice) with a low country rice pirlou featuring fresh lady peas, roasted eggplant, and a lemony, herbal cherry tomato relish. I came up with this relish while I was playing around in the kitchen, and I love not only how simple it is to make, but how big of a flavor punch it packs! To get your fish skin crispy, give the tilefish fillets a good pat with a paper towel to dry them off, and use a sharp knife to gently score the fish skin two times across the width of the fillet to keep the skin from curling up while cooking. Cook the fish skin side down, until the skin begins to crisp up and naturally releases from the pan. So good!

ROASTED CHERRY TOMATO RELISH

1 pint cherry tomatoes

¼ cup extra virgin olive oil

2 tablespoons julienne shallots

2 tablespoons thinly sliced garlic

¼ teaspoon red pepper flakes

2 tablespoons chopped parsley

2 tablespoons diced chives

2 tablespoons chopped basil

2 tablespoons freshly
  squeezed lemon juice

½ teaspoon kosher salt,
  plus extra to taste

¼ teaspoon freshly ground
  black pepper, to taste

RICE PIRLOU

2 slices bacon, small dice

1 cup diced yellow onion

½ cup diced celery

½ cup diced carrots

¼ cup diced red bell pepper

2 garlic cloves, minced

Pinch red pepper flakes

¾ cup Carolina Gold Rice

2½ cups Shrimp Stock (page 274)

2 thyme sprigs

1 bay leaf

½ teaspoon kosher salt,
  plus extra to taste

1 cup blanched lady peas

¼ teaspoon freshly ground black
  pepper, plus extra to taste

1 tablespoon freshly
  squeezed lemon juice

1 tablespoon unsalted butter

1 tablespoon roughly
  chopped parsley

TILEFISH

Four 6-ounce skin-on
  golden tilefish fillets

½ teaspoon kosher salt,
  plus extra to taste

¼ teaspoon freshly ground black
  pepper, plus extra to taste

2 tablespoons blended oil

2 tablespoons unsalted butter

3 garlic cloves

4 thyme sprigs

ROASTED CHERRY TOMATO RELISH

1. Place a medium sauté pan over high heat and heat 4 to 5 minutes, until the pan is very hot. Add the tomatoes and do not stir. Cook until the tomatoes are golden brown, blistered, and starting to burst, 6 to 7 minutes. Transfer the tomatoes to a medium bowl and set aside.

CONTINUES →

2. Reduce the heat to medium-high and return the pan to the heat. Add 2 tablespoons of the olive oil, the shallots, garlic, and red pepper flakes to the pan. Cook until the shallots are translucent and aromatic, about 2 minutes. Transfer to the bowl with the tomatoes and stir to combine. Set aside to cool slightly. Add the remaining olive oil, parsley, chives, basil, lemon juice, salt, and pepper and stir to combine. Taste and adjust the seasoning as necessary. Set aside at room temperature until ready to use.

RICE PIRLOU

1. Place the bacon in a medium heavy pot or Dutch oven, set over medium heat, and cook until crispy, 3 to 4 minutes. Remove the bacon to a paper towel–lined dish to drain.

2. Add the onion, celery, and carrots and cook until the vegetables are just beginning to become tender, 4 to 5 minutes. Add the bell pepper, garlic, and red pepper flakes and cook for 1 minute. Add the rice and cook, stirring continually, for 1 minute. Add the shrimp stock, stir to combine, and scrape any bits from the bottom of the pan.

3. Add the thyme, bay leaf, and salt and stir to combine. Bring the rice to a simmer, stirring occasionally, until most of the liquid is absorbed and the rice is cooked, about 18 minutes. Decrease the heat if needed to maintain a simmer. The rice should be creamy, not dry, and fluffy like a pilaf.

4. Remove the rice from the heat and add the lady peas. Cover the pot and steam for 5 minutes. Remove the thyme and bay leaf and add the black pepper.

5. Add the reserved bacon, lemon juice, butter, and parsley. Adjust seasoning as needed. Keep warm.

TILEFISH

1. Preheat the oven to 400°F.

2. Score the skin of the tilefish with a sharp knife, making sure to not slice into the flesh. Pat the fish dry with a paper towel and season the skin side of the fish with salt and pepper.

3. Place the oil in an oven-safe sauté pan large enough to hold all the fish and set over medium-high heat. Once the oil shimmers, carefully place the fish into the pan, skin side down. Press down on the top of the fish with a fish spatula to make sure the fish is searing evenly. Lightly season the top of the fish with additional salt and cook until the skin is crispy on the bottom, about 3 minutes. Place the pan into the oven and cook until just cooked through and tender, 3 to 4 minutes for a 1-inch-thick fillet.

4. Remove the pan from the oven and place the pan back on the burner over high heat. Add the butter, garlic, and thyme. As the butter melts and foams, gently baste each piece of fish four or five times. Remove the fish from the pan and keep warm until ready to serve.

5. Place a portion of the rice pirlou into four dinner bowls. Top the rice with the tilefish, spoon the tomato relish over each piece of fish, and serve immediately.

THOUGHTFUL TIP

Pirlou, perloo, or pilau . . . whatever the spelling, this is a rice dish that originates from West Africa. One-pot rice dishes like this are found around the globe, but the origins of low country pirlou resonate with a dish known as jollof rice from Senegal. Over two centuries ago, Charleston, South Carolina, was the entry point for almost 40 percent of the African slaves who entered the United States, and the low country cuisine from this region reflects those African roots. Even the rice that this dish originated with is African, brought over the Atlantic Ocean by slaves. This variety of rice was once one of the most well-known and revered across the planet. The rice, which came to be known as Carolina Gold Rice, was from an industry that was almost lost around the time of the Civil War. It was resurrected about 20 years ago by a farmer and historian named Glenn Roberts. Many varieties of pirlou exist, but most of them are cooked with seafood, primarily shrimp, oyster, and crab.

Grilled Rib Eye
WITH BOURBON CHANTERELLES AND SAUCE VERTE

SERVES 4

I'm a carnivore at heart. Don't get me wrong, I love my vegetables, but I also love a perfectly grilled rib eye from time to time! Rib eyes are the king of the beef family, and when cooking them I don't get too fussy with marinades or rubs, as I want the deep beef flavor to shine through after cooking. What I do love with grilled steaks, or any grilled meat for that matter, is a tangy, herbal, umami-packed *sauce verte* (French for "green sauce"). It's a simple blend of garlic, herbs, capers, lemon juice, some white anchovy for depth, ground pepper, and lots of olive oil: you can't go wrong! Finish the dish with a ragout of chanterelles cooked in bourbon and you're ready for a feast!

SAUCE VERTE

½ cup chopped parsley

¼ cup chopped chervil

¼ cup chopped chives

1 shallot, coarsely chopped

1 tablespoon capers, rinsed

2 teaspoons freshly
   squeezed lemon juice

1 garlic clove

½ teaspoon minced
   white anchovies

½ teaspoon kosher salt,
   plus extra to taste

¼ teaspoon freshly ground black
   pepper, plus extra to taste

½ cup extra virgin olive oil

BOURBON CHANTERELLES

2 tablespoons blended oil

4 shallots, peeled and quartered

4 garlic cloves, thinly sliced

¼ teaspoon red pepper flakes

2 pounds chanterelle mushrooms,
   torn into bite-size pieces

½ teaspoon kosher salt,
   plus extra to taste

¼ teaspoon freshly ground black
   pepper, plus extra to taste

1 cup bourbon

3 tablespoons unsalted butter

2 tablespoons chopped parsley

GRILLED RIB EYE

Two 16-ounce, 1½-inch thick,
   rib-eye steaks, trimmed

2 tablespoons blended oil

1 teaspoon kosher salt,
   plus extra to taste

¼ teaspoon freshly ground black
   pepper, plus extra to taste

SAUCE VERTE

1. Place the parsley, chervil, chives, shallot, capers, lemon juice, garlic, anchovies, salt, and pepper in a food processor and process to a coarse puree. With the motor running, very slowly add the oil until thoroughly combined. Taste and adjust the seasoning as desired. Refrigerate until ready to serve.

BOURBON CHANTERELLES

1. Place the blended oil in a large cast-iron skillet and set over medium-high heat. Once the oil shimmers, add the shallots and cook until lightly caramelized, 4 to 5 minutes. Add the garlic and red pepper flakes, and cook until the garlic is slightly caramelized and aromatic, 1 to 2 minutes.

2. Add the mushrooms, salt, and pepper and cook, stirring occasionally, until the mushrooms are tender, 4 to 5 minutes.

CONTINUES →

3. Carefully add the bourbon and deglaze the pan. If using an open flame burner, tilt the pan forward to flambé the bourbon. Cook until the bourbon has reduced by half, 5 to 6 minutes. Add the butter and parsley, stir to combine, and cook until the butter has melted. Taste and adjust the seasoning as needed. Remove from the heat and keep warm until ready to serve.

GRILLED RIB EYE

1. Place the rib eyes on a sheet tray, rub with the oil, and season with the salt and pepper. Set aside and bring to room temperature, about 1 hour.

2. Preheat a grill to 500°F.

3. Place the steaks on the grill and cook for about 5 to 6 minutes on the first side. Turn the steaks 90 degrees and cook for another 2 to 3 minutes. Flip the steaks and cook on the other side for another 4 to 5 minutes, or until the steaks are golden brown and the internal temperature reaches 130°F. Remove from the grill and rest for 5 to 10 minutes.

4. Slice the steaks into ¼-inch-thick slices and place on a platter. Spoon the sauce verte across the steaks and serve with the chanterelles.

THOUGHTFUL TIP

Chanterelle mushrooms are a forest floor superstar during the summer months. They grow abundantly across the United States, and you can typically find them in the warmer months. On the East Coast they grow around hardwood forests, near oak, maple, poplar, or birch trees; and on the West Coast they are found near coniferous forests of Douglas fir and various pines. The bright yellow of chanterelles should light up against the green of summer. Once you find a patch you'll think you've found the yellow brick road (of mushrooms, that is). When you're out foraging, it's always best to learn from another human, in person, and to follow up with multiple authoritative sources to ensure your safety. Happy foraging!

Billy D's Fried Chicken

WITH NASHVILLE HOT DIP AND WHITE BARBECUE SAUCE

SERVES 4

This is the recipe where the cult following began for my fried chicken. I grew up as "Billy," and when I went to culinary school my friends asked me if I thought I was going to be Chef Boyardee, which later morphed into Chef Billy D (like my Instagram handle). I grew up eating fried chicken, and when I had the opportunity to open my own fried chicken restaurant, it was a no-brainer to call it Billy D's Fried Chicken. Everyone has their own unique take on fried chicken. Some brine, some don't. Some use bread crumbs and others make a batter. Some like Nashville hot or Korean-style. Honestly, I can't think of a piece of fried chicken I don't like! Deep down, this is a simple recipe, but the attention to detail is what makes it unique and special. Use the best chicken you can find, and make sure it's free-range and hormone-free. When you're frying, make sure not to overcrowd the deep fryer (or pot). Work in batches to ensure that the chicken cooks evenly. Bone-in fried chicken can be cooked a few hours ahead and warmed through in the oven if you're cooking for a crowd.

CHICKEN BRINE

4 cups water

1 cup apple cider vinegar

⅔ cup kosher salt

⅓ cup sugar

1 teaspoon coriander seed

1 bay leaf

1 teaspoon whole black peppercorns

1 teaspoon yellow mustard seeds

1 bunch thyme

CHICKEN

One 4- to 5-pound whole chicken, fryer size, cut into 8 pieces

Canola oil for frying

1 tablespoon plus ½ teaspoon kosher salt

1 tablespoon freshly ground black pepper

1 teaspoon dried thyme

½ teaspoon cayenne pepper

½ teaspoon paprika

2 cups whole-fat buttermilk

2 large eggs

2 cups all-purpose flour

2 tablespoons nonfat dry milk

½ teaspoon garlic powder

NASHVILLE HOT DIP

¼ cup red pepper flakes

1 cup blended oil

½ teaspoon chili powder

¼ teaspoon kosher salt

Pinch cayenne pepper

BARBECUE SAUCE

1 cup mayonnaise

4 teaspoon sugar

2 teaspoons apple cider vinegar

2 teaspoons water

1 teaspoon Worcestershire sauce

1 teaspoon freshly squeezed lemon juice

1 teaspoon Frank's RedHot

½ teaspoon garlic powder

½ teaspoon onion powder

½ teaspoon kosher salt

½ teaspoon freshly ground black pepper

CHICKEN BRINE

1. Place the water, vinegar, salt, sugar, coriander, bay leaf, peppercorns, mustard seeds, and thyme into a small saucepan, set over medium-high heat, and stir until the salt and sugar have dissolved. Set aside to cool to room temperature. Strain the brine through a fine mesh strainer and refrigerate until ready to use.

CONTINUES →

2. Place the chicken pieces into a 1-gallon zip-top bag, add the brine, and seal. Place the bag into a large bowl and refrigerate 30 minutes.

3. Remove the chicken from the brine, rinse under cold water, and pat dry. Place the chicken on a sheet tray lined with a cooling rack and refrigerate uncovered, for at least 2 hours and up to overnight so the chicken dries completely.

NASHVILLE HOT DIP

1. Place the red pepper flakes in a small saucepan and cover with the oil. Set over medium-high heat and bring to 165°F. Remove from the heat and set aside to cool slightly. Add the chili powder, salt, and cayenne pepper and stir to combine. Set aside until ready to use or store in an airtight container, at room temperature, for up to 2 weeks.

BARBECUE SAUCE

1. Place the mayonnaise, sugar, cider vinegar, water, Worcestershire sauce, lemon juice, hot sauce, garlic powder, onion powder, salt, and black pepper into a medium bowl and whisk to combine. Refrigerate in an airtight container until ready to use and up to 2 weeks.

CHICKEN

1. Place 1½ inches of oil into a large, heavy pot or Dutch oven, set over medium-high heat, and bring to 325°F. (Or heat a deep fryer to 325°F, per the fryers instructions.)

2. Place 1 tablespoon of the kosher salt, the black pepper, dried thyme, cayenne pepper, and paprika into a small bowl and stir to combine. Set aside.

3. Place the buttermilk and eggs into a large bowl and whisk to combine.

4. Place the flour, powdered milk, garlic powder, 2 tablespoons of the seasoning blend, and the remaining ½ teaspoon of kosher salt in a medium bowl and whisk to combine.

5. Season the chicken on all sides with the remaining seasoning blend. Place the chicken, one piece at a time, in the flour mixture and turn to evenly coat. Shake off excess and return to the rack inside the sheet tray.

6. Transfer all the chicken to the bowl with the buttermilk and egg mixture.

7. Spoon ¼ cup of the buttermilk mixture into the flour mixture and using your fingertips, rub together until the texture is coarse like wet sand. One piece at a time, remove the chicken from the buttermilk, allowing excess buttermilk to drip off. Place the chicken into the wet flour mixture and turn to coat well, pressing the mixture into the chicken to adhere as much of the flour on each piece as possible. Return the chicken to the prepared sheet tray and repeat until all the chicken has been coated.

8. Prepare a clean sheet tray with a rack and set aside.

9. Working in batches, carefully place two or three pieces of chicken at a time into the hot oil and cook until the chicken reaches an internal temperature of 165°F, 8 to 10 minutes.

10. Carefully remove the chicken from the fryer and place on the clean, prepared sheet tray and allow to drain. Repeat until all chicken is cooked.

11. If desired, dip the chicken in the Nashville hot dip as soon as it comes out of the oil and then place on prepared sheet tray. Serve warm with the barbecue sauce.

THOUGHTFUL TIP

Some like it *hot!* I've added my recipe for the Nashville Hot Dip. If you like it a little spicy (a 5 out of 10 on the hotness scale), dip the fried chicken into the hot oil as soon as it comes out of the deep fryer, place it on a sheet tray with a rack to strain out the oil, and then season it with salt. If you like it spicier, spoon more of the hot oil over the chicken, or try using spicier chiles in the spice blend.

Grilled Plums
WITH SPICED MASCARPONE

SERVES 4

Sometimes the best desserts are the simplest. Since you've already got your grill fired up this summer, why not make a casual dessert that everyone is sure to love? And what's even better is that you can whip up this recipe in no time at all. Stone fruit was made for the grill. Charring sweet, ripe stone fruit like plums or peaches really sets off their flavor. Top each plum with a spoonful of wildflower honey, a dollop of spiced mascarpone, and some crunchy hazelnuts and you're ready to look like a star when you bring this dessert to the table.

1 cup mascarpone cheese, room temperature

¼ cup heavy cream, room temperature

¼ cup plus 1 tablespoon wildflower honey

½ teaspoon ground sumac

¼ teaspoon freshly ground black pepper

¼ teaspoon ground cloves

¼ teaspoon kosher salt

4 black plums, cut in half and pitted

2 tablespoons canola oil

¼ cup toasted, finely chopped hazelnuts

½ bunch lemon balm

1. Place the mascarpone in a small bowl, add the heavy cream a little at a time, and slowly whisk to combine. Add 1 tablespoon of the honey, the sumac, black pepper, cloves, and salt and gently whisk to combine. Set aside until ready to use.

2. Heat a grill, or grill pan, over high heat.

3. Place the plums and the oil in a small bowl and toss to combine. Place the plums onto the grill and cook until they have golden brown grill marks, 2 to 3 minutes. Turn the plums 90 degrees and grill for another 2 minutes.

4. Divide the plums among four plates and drizzle with the remaining ¼ cup of wildflower honey. Place a dollop of the mascarpone on each plum, sprinkle on the hazelnuts and lemon balm, and serve immediately.

Peach and Blackberry Crisp
WITH ALMOND CRUMBLE AND PEACH ICE CREAM

<u>SERVES 6</u>

When peaches start to ripen and blackberries plump up on the vine, I can't stop thinking about how I'm going to use these decadent warm-weather fruits in everything—especially dessert! Here, we are going full peach and blackberry in this not-so-traditional fruit crisp recipe.

ALMOND CRUMBLE
1 cup all-purpose flour
1 cup almond flour
1 cup light brown sugar
1 teaspoon baking powder
½ teaspoon kosher salt
½ teaspoon ground cinnamon
1 cup unsalted butter, melted

PEACH AND BLACKBERRY CRISP
½ cup unsalted butter
4 medium peaches (about 5 cups), pitted and chopped large
½ cup light brown sugar
1 teaspoon ground cinnamon

½ teaspoon ground green cardamom
3 cups blackberries
½ cup Blackberry Preserves (page 269)
Peach Ice Cream (page 276)

ALMOND CRUMBLE

1. Heat the oven to 400°F.

2. Place the all-purpose flour, almond flour, brown sugar, baking powder, salt, and cinnamon in a medium bowl and whisk to combine. Add the melted butter and stir until just combined. Do not overmix.

3. Evenly spread the mixture onto a parchment-lined sheet tray and bake, stirring every 5 minutes, until lightly golden brown in color, 10 to 15 minutes. Remove from the oven and set aside to cool. Store in an airtight container at room temperature for up to 1 week.

PEACH AND BLACKBERRY CRISP

1. Heat the oven to 400°F.

2. Place the butter into a large cast-iron pan and set over medium heat. When the butter begins to foam and starts to brown, add the peaches and cook just until they start to become tender, about 4 minutes. The peaches should still have texture and bite. Turn off the heat and add the brown sugar, cinnamon, and cardamom and stir to combine. Add the whole blackberries and blackberry preserves, and stir to fully incorporate.

3. Top with the almond crumble and place into the oven. Bake 15 to 20 minutes, until the crumble is beginning to brown and the mixture is hot and beginning to bubble around the edges of the pan.

4. Remove from the oven and allow to cool 15 to 20 minutes before serving with Peach Ice Cream.

THOUGHTFUL TIP

If you prefer your peaches peeled, I recommend using the classic French technique of concasse. Bring a pot of water to a boil. Using a sharp paring knife, slice an X through the bottom of the peach, and then place the peaches into the boiling water for 30 seconds. Remove the peaches with a slotted spoon and place them into a bowl of ice water. The skin should gently peel off. You may then cut the peach in half to remove the pit and cut the peaches as needed.

Grey's Hound Cocktail

MAKES 2

COCKTAILS

Break out the vodka and try this riff on a classic greyhound recipe! While Gin and Juice became popular in the 1990s, this is the OG cocktail where it all started. In the 1930s, bartender Harry Craddock published his recipe for a similar drink in *The Savoy Cocktail Book*. It called for gin and grapefruit juice over ice. In 1945, *Harper's Magazine* published a similar recipe replacing the gin for vodka and called the drink a greyhound. The magazine attributed the drink to a chain of restaurants owned by Greyhound bus line. At our flagship restaurant, The Market Place, we mix it up by adding fresh rosemary, which pairs incredibly with ripe grapefruit.

½ cup sugar

½ cup boiling water

5 rosemary sprigs

Ice

4 ounces Grey Goose vodka

4 ounces freshly squeezed ruby grapefruit juice

2 pieces ruby grapefruit peel

1. Place the sugar in a small container, add the boiling water, and stir to dissolve the sugar. Add 3 of the rosemary sprigs, stir, and set aside to come to room temperature. Remove the rosemary sprigs and discard. There will be more simple syrup than you'll need for this cocktail. Refrigerate the syrup in a covered container for up to 1 month.

2. Place ice into two old-fashioned glasses and set aside.

3. Place ice into a mixing cup and add the vodka, grapefruit juice, and 1 ounce simple syrup. Stir to combine.

4. Strain into the prepared glasses and garnish with a sprig of rosemary and a grapefruit peel. Serve immediately.

THOUGHTFUL TIP

While the vodka-based cocktail has become the namesake for this drink, try making it with other spirits. Tequila and mezcal are also excellent with grapefruit juice and make for a wonderful drink!

Peach and Jalapeño Margarita

MAKES 2
COCKTAILS

Fresh peaches blitzed into a puree and accented with a hint of spice from the jalapeño give this drink a 10 on the craveability scale! In the mixology world, I dabble in multilayered cocktails, but honestly I lean more toward easy drinking and crushable cocktails . . . especially on a hot day. While this recipe serves two drinks, it can be easily scaled to make a pitcher when inviting friends over for a party.

½ cup hot water
½ cup sugar
1 jalapeño
Ice

½ cup black sea salt
3 ounces reposado tequila
2 ounces peach puree
1 ounce Cointreau

1 ounce freshly squeezed
    lemon juice
1 ounce freshly squeezed lime juice
2 peach slices

1. Place the water and sugar into a small saucepan and set over medium-high heat. Cook, stirring occasionally, until the sugar dissolves. Remove from the heat. Cut the jalapeño in half, crosswise, and place one-half into the sugar syrup and set aside to cool to room temperature.

2. Cut the remaining half of the jalapeño into four rings and set aside until ready to use.

3. Strain the simple syrup into another container. Discard the jalapeño. You will have more jalapeño simple syrup than needed. Refrigerate for up to 1 month.

4. Wet the rims of two old-fashioned glasses with water and dip into the black sea salt. Fill the glasses three-quarters of the way with ice.

5. Place additional ice in a cocktail shaker and add the tequila, peach puree, Cointreau, lemon juice, lime juice, and 2 ounces of the jalapeño simple syrup. Shake vigorously and strain into the old-fashioned glasses. Garnish each glass with a peach slice and two jalapeño rings. Serve immediately.

DEEP THOUGHTS

PRESERVATION

One of the beautiful things about our planet is the abundance of food and fresh water available to create an ecosystem suitable for plants and animals to live in harmony. Life has been able to sustain itself through good times, bad times, and even catastrophes because of the resilience of Mother Nature, and the resilience of our own species. In short, we are adaptable. Our world has evolved for millions of years due to our location in the solar system, our unique atmosphere, and our fertile land and seas. The cycle of life and death creates symmetry in our world and provides balance in our natural habitat.

While our species chases the cycle of life, we find ourselves constantly working on self-preservation, and on a betterment of one's self, to give ourselves a shot of having a better life while we're here on this planet. We evolve. Our nearest act of self-preservation is through food. We all need sustenance and calories each day to fuel our bodies for what's ahead. Humans have learned to build fire, hunt, gather, save seeds, farm, fish, cook, and preserve the bounty of our gardens and forests.

As a child I recall playing hide-and-go-seek in the garden and canning shed, with my sisters, on my grandmother Jane's farm. I was a kid from suburbia, and her canning shed, dark and dank, always seemed so odd to me. Why would she spend all of this time to growing a huge garden just to put vegetables into glass jars and keep them in a shed with a dirt floor? Needless to say, as a child I wasn't much of a fan of canned green beans and sour corn.

I learned so much from those formative days playing in the barn and chasing chickens. My grandmother was a sustainability guru before her time. She realized that in order to sustain her family, she needed to take care of the land around her, not to harm the soil, and to be thankful for the bounty her farm provided. So she cooked: a lot. She shucked beans and corn, saved the drippings from side meat and bacon, and canned, pickled, cured, fermented, and dehydrated every last vegetable and fruit that grew on her land.

Preservation of food is a vast conversation that we'll need to discuss in another book. Experts like Sandor Katz and David Zilber have been leading the charge to teach cooks about these important preservation fundamentals. Civilization has been preserving food with salt, smoke, and acid for thousands of years to feed our communities. For me, it's the flavor we can create through these techniques, as well as the tradition and heritage that we can honor, that I focus on in my cooking.

As the world around us continues to get faster and to modernize, I believe that in order for us to take a step forward we need to take a step backward and appreciate the preservation techniques that our ancestors created. As our society builds things faster and more efficiently, it's important to remember to take a look back at the fundamentals that have helped guide us to this point in humanity. Without understanding the journey taken before us, it's hard to see the light in the future.

Reach out to your family, ask your mother and grandmother for their family recipes, read their old cookbooks, and take a moment to use their time-tested recipes to pickle or ferment vegetables from the grocery store or garden. And, like me, you'll be able to open a jar of sunshine to help warm your spirit when you need it.

FALL

What's in Season?

Apples, Pears, Carrots, Celery, Cauliflower, Sunchokes, Kale, Swiss Chard, Pumpkin, Winter Squash, Broccoli, Kohlrabi, Brussels Sprouts, Parsnips, Persimmons, Wild Mushrooms

I love to watch the seasons cross from summer into fall, when the autumn weather begins to cool down and the leaves begin to change color and the fruits and vegetables flourish in the harvest season. It's always the most beautiful time of year. Our kids are headed back to school and life seems to get more scheduled after the laissez-faire attitude of summer. As the kids are sharpening their pencils and packing up their backpacks, I'm finding inspiration in the crossroads of the seasons.

When I was a younger cook, I was always so overwhelmed by the amount of produce this time of year. Heirloom tomatoes and winter squash at the market in the early days of fall, followed by wild maitake and chicken of the woods mushrooms that our foragers triumphantly brought through the kitchen door. Abundance from the land is so inspiring.

As the days begin to grow shorter, I like to light a fire outside and snuggle up with a soup that warms the soul, or savor a slowly roasted piece of pork that falls off of the bone. As the fire burns, a bourbon cocktail helps keep me warm from the inside out. Our cooking tends to slow down like we do as the days turn to night, always earlier than expected. It's time to move away from the quick cooking we do in the summer and plan ahead for dishes that are cooked low and slow on the stovetop or in the oven. As the foliage changes to fire engine red and vibrant orange and yellow, I notice the food I'm cooking is beginning to do the same: roasted pumpkin and winter squash, beautiful sides of wild salmon, and corn bread made with freshly ground heirloom corn.

In September and October, the weather in the Carolinas is idyllic, and we spend as much time as we can outdoors chasing our children around the yard and through the forests. November brings cooler weather and shorter days, and the knowledge that winter is coming. The holidays are ahead, but for now we'll bask in the fall glow.

Cast-Iron Monkey Bread
WITH CARAMEL SAUCE AND WALNUTS

SERVES 8

Monkey bread is warm, sticky, and gooey in all the right ways, and I haven't met anyone yet who can say no to this special treat. I like to serve it like a coffee cake for breakfast, for an interactive afternoon snack, or as a fun dessert for a party or with the kids. When I'm in a pinch and am craving it, I use biscuit dough, but I prefer a yeast-based version that makes the dough softer. The vanilla-cinnamon sugar can go on just about anything, but it adds the right notes of sweetness to this treat. Serve it with hot chocolate, coffee, or tea and you're going to have a lot of happy friends and family.

CINNAMON COATING
¾ cup light brown sugar
1 vanilla bean, split and scraped
2 teaspoons ground cinnamon

CARAMEL SAUCE
2 cups heavy cream
3 ounces water
1½ cups sugar

3 ounces unsalted butter
1 teaspoon ground cinnamon
1 teaspoon vanilla extract

MONKEY BREAD
1 cup whole milk
¼ cup canola oil
¼ cup sugar

1½ teaspoons dry active yeast
2 cups plus ¼ cup all-purpose flour
¼ teaspoon baking powder
¼ teaspoon baking soda
¼ teaspoon kosher salt
⅓ cup melted unsalted butter
   plus 2 tablespoons unmelted
1 cup chopped, toasted walnuts

CINNAMON COATING
1. Place the brown sugar, vanilla bean paste, and cinnamon in a small bowl and toss to combine. Set aside until ready to use.

CARAMEL SAUCE
1. Place the heavy cream in a small saucepan, set over medium heat, and bring just to a bare simmer, about 5 minutes. Remove from the heat and set aside.

2. Place the water and sugar into a medium saucepan, set over medium-high heat and cook, without stirring, until the sugar has turned a deep amber hue, 7 to 8 minutes.

3. Carefully add the warm cream to the sugar mixture and whisk to combine. The mixture will bubble up vigorously, so be careful. Continue to cook and whisk until the mixture is smooth, about 2 minutes. Remove from the heat, and whisk in the butter, cinnamon, and vanilla extract. Set aside and keep warm.

MONKEY BREAD
1. Place the milk, oil, and sugar in a small saucepan, set over medium heat and stir until the sugar dissolves. Remove from the heat and set aside to cool to 110°F.

CONTINUES →

Sprinkle the yeast over the milk mixture and set aside for 10 minutes, or until it becomes bubbly, indicating the yeast has been activated.

2. Add 2 cups of the flour and whisk to combine. Transfer to a mixing bowl, cover, and set aside in a warm place for 1 hour or until the dough has doubled in size.

3. Add the remaining ¼ cup flour, baking powder, baking soda, and salt, and mix well into the dough until no dry ingredients are visible. At this point the dough is ready to bake or may be covered and refrigerated for up to 24 hours.

4. Rub a 10-inch cast-iron pan thoroughly with the 2 tablespoons of the butter.

5. Remove the dough to a work surface and use a bench scraper to divide the dough into ¾-ounce pieces, about 30 in total. Roll each piece into a small ball.

6. Dip each dough ball into the ⅓ cup of melted butter and then into the cinnamon-sugar mixture. Place the dough balls into the prepared cast-iron skillet and cover with plastic wrap in a warm place until the dough becomes puffy, about an hour.

7. Preheat the oven to 350°F.

8. Place the pan on the middle rack of the oven and bake for 25 to 30 minutes, until the top is golden brown and the sugar is bubbling around the sides of the pan.

9. Remove the pan from the oven and allow to cool for 10 minutes. Turn the monkey bread out onto a serving platter. Drizzle with caramel sauce and garnish with walnuts.

THOUGHTFUL TIP

Monkey bread is said to have started as a riff on a dessert from Hungarian immigrants to the United States in the 1800s, but it gained its fame from silent film actress ZaSu Pitts and her neighbor Ann King who named the bread after the neighborhood children who couldn't keep their hands off the fresh, warm treats: meddling little "monkeys." I sure know that this dish appeals to all ages, and young and old won't be able to keep their hands off this delicious treat!

Shrimp and Grits

WITH APPALACHIAN TOMATO GRAVY AND COUNTRY HAM

SERVES 4TO 6

Tomato gravy technically isn't a gravy, in the sense of combining meat drippings with butter and flour and milk. But make no mistake, it's gravy! While fresh shrimp and stone-milled grits are the stars of the show, the tomato gravy plays the key supporting role. Cooked slow and low, it comes out hot and silky from the pan. This sauce works really well with breakfast staples, but it sings when it's featured in this take on a traditional Southern dish. After years of living in the low country of South Carolina, I fell in love with shrimp and grits. As much as I love the traditional version made with andouille and bacon, I prefer this version with its tangy tomato gravy that has just the right amount of spice and acid to cut through the richness of the grits and to stand up to, and complement, the sautéed shrimp.

TOMATO GRAVY

1 tablespoon olive oil

½ cup medium-dice yellow onion

½ cup medium-dice fennel bulb

2 teaspoons minced garlic

1 teaspoon red pepper flakes

1 tablespoon tomato paste

¼ cup white wine

One 16-ounce can San Marzano tomatoes

½ cup water

¼ cup heavy cream

1 teaspoon honey

½ teaspoon kosher salt, plus extra to taste

¼ teaspoon ground cumin

¼ teaspoon ground fennel seeds

¼ teaspoon smoked paprika

¼ teaspoon freshly ground black pepper, plus extra to taste

GRITS

1 tablespoon blended oil

¼ cup minced onion

1 tablespoon minced garlic

4 cups water

1 cup Anson Mills yellow stone-ground grits

1 cup heavy cream, room temperature

4 ounces grated applewood smoked Cheddar

1 jalapeño, seeded and brunoise-cut

1 tablespoon Frank's RedHot

½ teaspoon kosher salt, plus extra to taste

¼ teaspoon freshly ground black pepper, plus extra to taste

SHRIMP

2 tablespoons canola oil

½ cup julienned country ham

2 pounds (16/20 count) shrimp, peeled and deveined

¼ teaspoon kosher salt, plus extra to taste

Pinch freshly ground black pepper, plus extra to taste

½ cup red bell pepper, julienned

2 tablespoons julienned shallot

1 teaspoon minced garlic

Pinch red pepper flakes

2 tablespoons unsalted butter

1 tablespoon freshly squeezed lemon juice

1 tablespoon roughly chopped parsley

Kosher salt, to taste

Freshly ground black pepper, to taste

2 tablespoons thinly sliced chives

TOMATO GRAVY

1. Place the olive oil in a medium saucepan and set over medium-high heat. Once the oil shimmers, add the onions and fennel, and cook until translucent, 4 to 5 minutes. Add the garlic and red pepper flakes, and cook until aromatic, 1 to 2 minutes. Add the tomato paste and cook, stirring frequently, for 30 seconds.

2. Deglaze the pan with the white wine, scraping any fond from the bottom of the pot, and reduce by half, 8 to 10 minutes. Add the tomatoes and water, bring to a simmer, and cook until the entire mixture has reduced by half, about 30 minutes. Stir occasionally to help break down the tomatoes.

3. Add the heavy cream, stir to combine, and cook for another 10 minutes. Add the honey, salt, cumin, fennel seeds, smoked paprika, and pepper and stir to combine.

4. Remove from the heat and cool for 15 minutes before transferring to a blender and processing until smooth. Taste and adjust the salt and pepper as necessary.

GRITS

1. Place the oil in a medium saucepan and set over medium-high heat. Once the oil shimmers, add the onion and cook until translucent, 2 to 3 minutes. Add the garlic and cook until aromatic, 1 minute. Add the water, increase the heat to high heat, and bring to a boil. Add the grits in a slow, steady stream while whisking continually. Bring to a simmer, stirring constantly. Once simmering, decrease the heat to low and cook, stirring frequently, for about 1 hour.

2. Add the heavy cream and cook, stirring continually, for 5 minutes. Add the Cheddar, jalapeño, hot sauce, salt, and pepper and stir until the Cheddar has melted. Taste and adjust seasoning as necessary. Keep warm until ready to serve.

SHRIMP

1. Place the oil into a large sauté pan and set over medium heat. Add the ham and cook, stirring frequently, until crisp, but still tender, 3 to 4 minutes. Remove from the pan with a slotted spoon and transfer to a paper towel–lined plate. Set aside.

2. Increase the heat to medium-high and add the shrimp to the pan. Season the shrimp with the salt and pepper. Cook the shrimp until golden on one side, 2 to 3 minutes. Flip the shrimp and add the bell pepper, shallot, garlic, and red pepper flakes and cook for 1 minute. Add the butter, lemon juice, and parsley along with the reserved country ham and stir to combine. Cook for another minute to heat through.

TO SERVE

1. Place a cup of grits into each bowl and top with 2 tablespoons of tomato gravy. Add the shrimp and country ham mixture and garnish with sliced chives. Serve immediately.

THOUGHTFUL TIP

When cooking grits, fresh is best. When corn is milled, it releases its essential oils that hold much of the flavor. So when I buy grits from wonderful millers like Farm & Sparrow, Anson Mills, and Marsh Hen Mill, I put them into the refrigerator or freezer immediately until I plan to use them, to keep that beautiful flavor of the stone-ground heirloom corn fresh.

Foraged Mushroom Toast

WITH BLACK PEPPER RICOTTA AND PICKLED RAMPS

SERVES 8

Fall is a high time for wild mushrooms. Getting outside to forage provides time to reset the mind and body, and any forest adventure can turn into a treasure hunt for fungi! In the fall, some of my favorite varieties such as chicken of the woods, maitake, and oyster mushrooms grow steadily until the first hard freeze. You can certainly substitute cultivated varieties like button, shiitake, and portobello if you don't have the opportunity to forage or source from a trustworthy source. In this recipe the mushroom ragout is the perfect complement to the black pepper ricotta and sourdough toast.

6 tablespoons blended oil

2 pounds wild mushrooms, medium diced

4 medium shallots, sliced

2 tablespoons thinly shaved garlic

1 teaspoon kosher salt, plus extra to taste

½ teaspoon red pepper flakes

½ cup bourbon

½ cup Vegetable Stock (page 273)

¼ cup unsalted butter

¼ cup chopped herbs, (equal parts parsley, chive, and basil)

Pinch freshly ground black pepper, plus extra to taste

One sourdough boule, cut into eight 1-inch thick slices, reserve the rest for another use

1 cup Ricotta (page 275)

½ cup Pickled Ramps, cut into rings (page 265)

2 tablespoons parsley leaves

2 tablespoons basil leaves

2 tablespoons sliced chives

1. Place 4 tablespoons of the blended oil into a large sauté pan, set over medium-high heat. Once the oil shimmers, add the mushrooms and shallots, and cook until they begin to caramelize, 8 to 10 minutes. Add the garlic, salt, and red pepper flakes and cook until aromatic, 1 to 2 minutes.

2. Deglaze the pan with the bourbon and cook, stirring occasionally, until the liquid reduces to a glaze, about 1 minute. Add the vegetable stock and reduce by three-fourths, about 3 minutes.

3. Add the butter, herbs, and pepper, and stir to combine. Taste and adjust seasoning as necessary. Keep warm.

4. Turn the oven on broil.

5. Brush each of the eight slices of sourdough bread with the remaining 2 tablespoons of the blended oil and lightly sprinkle with salt. Place the toast on a sheet tray and broil in the oven until golden brown, 3 to 4 minutes.

6. Spoon 2 tablespoons of the ricotta onto each of the eight toasts and top with mushrooms, ramps, parsley, basil, and chives. Season with additional salt as necessary. Serve immediately.

Wild mushrooms can grow abundantly around many parts of the world. Most people think that foragers have to trek miles and miles into the forest on a fungal treasure hunt, but wild mushrooms can grow just about anywhere, including your own backyard. But don't just pick and eat any wild mushroom! While there are many varieties of edible mushrooms, there are also many poisonous look-alikes. Always make sure to learn about mushroom foraging from another human being, in person, and make sure to follow up with multiple authoritative sources to confirm your harvest.

Roasted Corn Chowder

WITH CHARRED CORN AND CRAB SALAD

SERVES 6

As the summer fades into fall, I hold on to fresh, sweet corn as long as I can until the cooling weather signals it's time to make this corn chowder recipe. The crossing of seasons during the fall harvest brings in the last of fresh corn before we have to wait another year for corn season. The fresh lump crab enhances the corn and adds just the right juxtaposition to make this soup sing in the bowl. You'll be hanging on to corn season as long as you can, too!

CORN CHOWDER

6 ears yellow corn

1 cup heavy cream

1 cup whole milk

2 bay leaves

1 tablespoon white peppercorns

1 tablespoon unsalted butter

1½ teaspoons minced garlic

1½ teaspoons minced shallot

½ cup minced bacon

1½ cups small dice onion

1 cup small-dice celery

½ cup white wine

1 quart Chicken Stock (page 274)

1 cup peeled and small-dice Yukon gold potatoes

½ cup small-dice red bell pepper

½ cup small-dice yellow bell pepper

1 teaspoon honey

2 teaspoons Frank's RedHot

1 teaspoon Worcestershire sauce

½ teaspoon kosher salt, plus extra to taste

½ teaspoon ground white pepper, plus extra to taste

CHARRED CORN AND CRAB SALAD

¾ cup (about 1 large ear) yellow corn kernels, cut off the cob

2 tablespoons thinly sliced scallions

2 tablespoons small-dice red bell pepper

8 ounces jumbo lump crab

1 tablespoon freshly squeezed lemon juice

2 tablespoons extra virgin olive oil

½ teaspoon kosher salt, plus extra to taste

¼ teaspoon cayenne pepper

CORN CHOWDER

1. Cut the kernels from the cobs and reserve both. Place the corn cobs, heavy cream, milk, bay leaves, and peppercorns into a medium saucepan, set over medium heat, and bring to a simmer. Cook until the liquid is reduced by one-fourth, about 15 minutes. Remove from the heat. Strain and reserve the heavy cream mixture.

2. Place the butter in a large sauté pan, set over medium heat. Add the reserved kernels and cook, stirring occasionally until tender, 6 to 8 minutes. Add the garlic and shallots and cook until aromatic, about 1 minute. Reserve two-thirds of the mixture. Place the remaining third into a food processor and puree. Set aside

3. Place the bacon in a medium heavy-bottomed pot or Dutch oven, set over medium heat, and cook until it has rendered its fat, 5 to 6 minutes. Add the onions and celery, and cook until tender, 3 to 4 minutes. Add the wine and deglaze the pan, scraping up any bits of fond on the bottom of the pan. Reduce the wine by half. Add the cooked corn kernels, corn puree, and the chicken stock, bring to a simmer and cook for 30 minutes.

4. Add heavy cream mixture and potatoes and bring to a simmer. Cook until the potatoes are tender, about 15 minutes. Add the red and yellow bell peppers, honey, hot sauce, Worcestershire, salt, and pepper and stir to combine. Taste and adjust seasoning as necessary.

CHARRED CORN AND CRAB SALAD

1. Heat a small sauté pan over high heat and when it's very hot, add the corn and cook until charred, 1 to 2 minutes. Transfer to a plate and set aside to cool completely.

2. Place the charred corn, scallions, red bell pepper, crab, lemon juice, olive oil, salt, and cayenne pepper into a small bowl and toss to combine. Taste and adjust the seasoning as necessary.

3. Serve the soup garnished with the corn and crab salad.

THOUGHTFUL TIP

I always save my corn cobs, as they're packed with flavor. Throw them into a zip-top bag and save them in the freezer until you have enough to fill a small stockpot. Then in the colder months use the cobs to make a batch of corn stock to use for soups like this one.

Charred Radicchio

WITH PRESERVED LEMON VINAIGRETTE

SERVES 4

As I get older, I've noticed that I am starting to like bitter food and drink more than before. I've started drinking black coffee (who needs sugar and cream?), I love the sharp bite of negronis, and I like my salad greens bitter! Enter radicchio: bitter, biting, and maybe a little disgruntled. Maybe that's what happens with age? Nonetheless, they've become one of my favorite salad greens. When you combine them with the tart green apples, earthy pecans, and mellow preserved lemon vinaigrette, you create a quartet made in heaven.

PRESERVED LEMON VINAIGRETTE

- 4 tablespoons finely chopped Preserved Lemon rind (page 269)
- 2 garlic cloves
- ⅓ cup freshly squeezed lemon juice
- ¼ cup white balsamic vinegar
- 1 tablespoon honey

- ¼ teaspoon kosher salt, plus extra to taste
- ¾ cup extra virgin olive oil
- Freshly ground black pepper, to taste

RADICCHIO

- 2 heads radicchio, quartered
- 1 tablespoon extra virgin olive oil
- ½ teaspoon kosher salt, plus extra to taste

- Pinch freshly ground black pepper, plus extra to taste
- 1 green apple, seeded and thinly sliced
- ½ cup toasted pecans
- ⅓ cup thinly shaved red onion
- 2 tablespoons julienned Preserved Lemon rind (page 269)
- 2 tablespoons oregano leaves

PRESERVED LEMON VINAIGRETTE

1. Place the lemon rind, garlic, lemon juice, vinegar, honey, and salt into a blender and puree until smooth, 1 to 1½ minutes. With the motor running, slowly add the olive oil until well combined. Taste and adjust seasoning with salt and pepper.

RADICCHIO

1. Preheat a grill, grill pan, or cast-iron skillet on the stovetop, to high heat.

2. Gently rub the radicchio with the olive oil and season with salt and black pepper. Sear each wedge of radicchio on one side until charred, 3 to 4 minutes. Remove to a plate and cool completely.

3. Cut each quarter of radicchio into 2-inch pieces and transfer to a mixing bowl. Add the apple, pecans, red onion, and ½ cup of the vinaigrette and toss to coat. Taste and season with additional salt and pepper as desired.

4. Equally divide the salad among four plates and garnish with the lemon rind and oregano leaves. Serve immediately.

THOUGHTFUL TIP

Fortunately for us, the more bitter we get (when eating salad greens), the healthier we find ourselves. Bitter salad greens, like radicchio, are jam-packed with vitamins A, C, and K, as well as potassium, calcium, iron, and magnesium. I always try to sneak them into family salads at home for dinner, but bitter greens such as chicory, puntarella, dandelion greens, mustard greens, arugula, and nettle also work great for a quick sauté, stir-fries, or as a filling for stuffed pastas.

Braised Romano Beans
WITH ROASTED TOMATO SAUCE

SERVES 6

These tender braised Romano beans with berbere-spiced tomato sauce make an easy and incredibly flavorful side dish, as well as a meal unto themselves. Topped with smoky bacon, rich crème fraîche, and mint leaves, this dish will leave you coming back for seconds. I love this riff on traditional Italian-style braised flat beans. It's great to use the last tomatoes of the year in early fall for this dish, or if you've been planning ahead, pull 2 quarts of canned tomatoes out of your larder to use in place of fresh.

1 tablespoon extra virgin olive oil

8 ounces bacon, cut into lardons

1 cup diced yellow onion

¾ cup peeled and diced carrots

¾ cup diced celery

½ teaspoon kosher salt, plus extra to taste

1 tablespoon minced garlic

¼ teaspoon red pepper flakes

2 pounds plum tomatoes, medium dice

1 cup water

2 tablespoons berbere spice (see Thoughtful Tip)

1 teaspoon freshly squeezed lemon juice

Freshly ground black pepper, to taste

1½ pounds Romano beans, strings removed and broken in half

¾ cup Crème Fraîche (page 275)

¼ cup mint leaves, torn

1. Preheat the oven to 400°F.

2. Place the oil in a large heavy-bottom pot or Dutch oven. Add the bacon, set over medium heat, and cook, stirring frequently, until the bacon renders its fat and is crisp, 6 to 8 minutes.

3. Remove the bacon to a paper towel–lined plate to drain. Set aside.

4. Increase the heat to medium-high and add the onions, carrots, celery, and salt. Cook, stirring frequently, until the onions are translucent, 4 to 5 minutes. Add the garlic and red pepper flakes and cook until aromatic, about 2 minutes.

5. Add the tomatoes, water, and berbere spice. Stir to combine and bring to a simmer, about 5 minutes. Continue cooking until the tomatoes are tender and falling apart, about 15 minutes. Add the lemon juice and taste. Adjust the seasoning with salt and black pepper. Add the beans and stir to combine.

6. Cover the pot with a lid and place in the oven. Bake, stirring once, halfway through, until the beans are tender, 25 to 30 minutes.

7. Remove from the oven and garnish with the bacon, crème fraîche, and mint leaves, and serve immediately.

Berbere spice is a traditional spice blend from Ethiopia and is the backbone of their cuisine. It consists of red chile peppers, ginger, and fenugreek with the addition of warm spices such as cardamom, coriander, cumin, allspice, black peppercorns, cloves, cinnamon, and some lesser-known indigenous spices such as ajwain, korarima, and long pepper. The ingredients in this spice blend impart warmth, earthiness, spiciness, and sweetness to slow-cooked dishes like these braised Romano beans.

Cauliflower and Apple Salad

WITH GREEN PEPPERCORN AND MUSTARD DRESSING AND SOFT HERBS

SERVES 6 TO 8

Cauliflower is one of the unsung heroes during the colder months. It's great roasted, stewed, or even pureed. I love it in salads, too. Unlike the big chunks of cauliflower florets found at your local salad bar, this recipe calls for shaving it thin. When cut this way, the cauliflower keeps some crunch while highlighting the tenderness of this cruciferous vegetable. I was inspired by a recipe from Chef Michael Symon, and I couldn't get enough of his technique of shaving the cauliflower thin for salads and slaws. I think you'll enjoy this version with a tangy whole-grain mustard and apple cider dressing.

GREEN PEPPERCORN AND MUSTARD DRESSING

- ¼ cup chopped, pickled green peppercorns
- 3 tablespoons apple cider vinegar
- 2 tablespoons whole grain mustard
- 1 tablespoon wildflower honey
- 1 teaspoon minced garlic
- ½ cup extra virgin olive oil
- Kosher salt, to taste
- Freshly ground black pepper, to taste

SALAD

- 1 small head cauliflower, thinly sliced
- 1 Granny Smith apple, julienned
- 1 cup thinly shaved red onion
- 1 cup julienned carrot
- 1 cup thinly shaved fennel
- ½ cup thinly sliced scallions
- ½ cup dried cherries
- ½ cup roasted, salted pistachios
- Kosher salt, to taste
- Freshly ground black pepper, to taste
- 2 cups arugula
- 8 ounces feta, crumbled
- ½ cup roughly chopped mint
- ½ cup roughly chopped flat-leaf parsley

GREEN PEPPERCORN AND MUSTARD DRESSING

1. Place the green peppercorns, vinegar, mustard, honey, and garlic in a large bowl and whisk to combine. Slowly add the olive oil while whisking continually. Taste and adjust seasoning with salt and pepper.

SALAD

1. Add the cauliflower, apple, onion, carrot, fennel, scallions, cherries, and pistachios to a large bowl. Toss to combine. Taste and adjust seasoning with salt and pepper. Set aside for 5 minutes.

2. Add the arugula, feta, mint, and parsley and toss to combine. Serve immediately or refrigerate for up to 6 hours before serving.

Cauliflower comes in all shapes and sizes: purple, green, 'Cheddar', white, Romanesco, caulilini, and more. When preparing cauliflower, cut off the surrounding leaves (if they're fresh, they can be cooked, too), and remove the stem base with a chef's knife. If you're looking for florets, cut them off one by one, aiming to keep them the same size so they cook evenly while being boiled or roasted. And if you're going for a raw approach, cut the cauliflower in half and lay the flat side down, so you have a firm surface to work from when slicing the vegetable thin.

Kale Salad

WITH ROASTED BEETS AND GINGER MISO DRESSING

SERVES 4 TO 6

I live in Asheville, and we love our salad greens here! While kale might be considered a trendy vegetable by some, and thought to be overrated by others, I think it's truly wonderful. Plus it's really healthy for you. The ginger miso dressing adds a nice punch to the salad, and the sliced pears provide a sweet and crunchy counterbalance. After trying this salad, you'll be putting kale back into the rotation more often!

GINGER MISO DRESSING

1 cup (about 4 small) peeled and roughly chopped carrots

¼ cup grapeseed oil

¼ cup rice wine vinegar

3 tablespoons yellow or white miso

1 tablespoon dark sesame oil

One 1-inch piece ginger, peeled and thinly

1 tablespoon sesame seeds

1 teaspoon honey

Kosher salt, to taste

Freshly ground black pepper, to taste

ROASTED BEETS AND SALAD

4 medium red beets, cleaned

2 tablespoons extra virgin olive oil

6 cups baby kale

½ cup thinly sliced red onion

½ cup thinly sliced radish

1 pear, cored and thinly sliced

1 cup roasted, salted walnuts

Kosher salt, to taste

Freshly ground black pepper, to taste

2 ounces Pecorino cheese, grated

GINGER MISO DRESSING

1. Place the carrots, oil, vinegar, miso, sesame oil, ginger, sesame seeds, and honey in a food processor and puree until smooth, 1 to 2 minutes. Taste and season with salt and pepper to taste. Transfer to an airtight container and refrigerate for up to 1 week.

ROASTED BEETS AND SALAD

1. Preheat the oven to 400°F.

2. Place the beets and the olive oil in an ovenproof dish and toss to coat. Cover with a tight-fitting lid or aluminum foil. Cook until tender, 45 to 50 minutes.

3. Remove from the oven and set aside until cool. Use a paper towel to rub off the exterior skin of the beets and discard. Cut the beets into quarters and set aside.

4. Place the baby kale into a medium mixing bowl, add the dressing, and gently massage to help tenderize the kale. Add the beets, red onion, radish, pear, and walnuts and toss to combine. Taste and adjust the seasoning with salt and pepper to taste.

5. Divide the salad equally among four plates. Top with Pecorino and serve immediately.

THOUGHTFUL TIP

When making a kale salad, make sure to "massage" your greens. This helps tenderize the greens and makes them much easier to eat.

Charred Broccolini

WITH SUNCHOKE MISO AND CURED EGG YOLK

SERVES 4 TO 6

It's cruciferous season! Break out the broccoli, cabbage, cauliflower, collard greens, turnips, and kale. Nowadays every restaurant has charred or fried Brussels sprouts on their menus. What do we like about it? The char and crispiness! Well, it's actually the caramelization of the natural sugars in the vegetable that we love, as it deepens the flavor and provides more texture. Here, we char the longer, leaner version of broccoli and pair it with a sweet, nutty, creamy sunchoke miso sauce and add an umami bomb with the shaved and cured egg yolk to make a delicious side dish that's going to change your mind about broccoli.

SUNCHOKE MISO

- ½ pound sunchokes, peeled and large dice
- 1 teaspoon kosher salt
- ¼ cup white or yellow miso
- 1 tablespoon freshly squeezed lemon juice
- 1 teaspoon honey

BROCCOLINI

- Salt for the pot of water
- 1½ pounds broccolini, trimmed
- 2 tablespoons canola oil
- 1 tablespoon shaved garlic
- ¼ teaspoon red pepper flakes
- Kosher salt, to taste

- Freshly ground black pepper, to taste
- 3 tablespoons unsalted butter
- 2 tablespoons freshly squeezed lemon juice
- 2 grated Cured Egg Yolks (page 272)

SUNCHOKE MISO

1. Place the sunchokes and the salt into a medium saucepan, cover with water, set over medium-high heat, and bring to a simmer. Cook until the sunchokes are very tender, about 20 minutes.

2. Strain the sunchokes, reserving 1 cup of the cooking water. Place the sunchokes in a blender, add ½ cup of the cooking water and puree until smooth. Add the miso, lemon juice, and honey and puree until smooth. Add additional liquid as needed to create a consistency like crepe batter. Remove from the blender and set aside to cool.

BROCCOLINI

1. Set a large pot of water over high heat, season with salt to taste like the ocean, and bring to a boil. Add the broccolini and cook until al dente, 4 to 5 minutes. Do not overcook.

2. Strain the broccolini and transfer to a large bowl of ice water to stop the cooking and cool completely. Drain and set aside.

CONTINUES →

3. Place a large cast-iron skillet over medium-high heat, add the canola oil, and when the oil shimmers, add the broccolini, in batches if necessary, and cook until charred, 3 to 4 minutes.

4. Turn the broccolini over, add the garlic and red pepper flakes, and continue cooking for 1 more minute.

5. If cooking in batches, add the butter and lemon juice to the last batch and then toss with all the broccolini. Season to taste with salt and pepper, and remove from the heat.

6. Drizzle the miso mixture over the broccolini, top with the cured egg yolks, and serve immediately.

Roasted Acorn Squash

WITH HAZELNUT PICADA, WILDFLOWER HONEY, AND CHILE

SERVES 4

Acorn squash is easy to work with and simple to cook. Prepping them to cook couldn't be easier, and a simple oven roast provides for a tender, sweet, and savory side dish. Just slice it open, scoop out the seeds, and cut it into crescent moons, and you're ready to cook it in the oven. Acorn squash roasts to a golden hue and is downright delicious on its own, but with the addition of the sweet and spicy honey glaze and the nutty picada it becomes addictive. You're going to love this simple and flavorful side dish.

HAZELNUT PICADA

2 tablespoons extra virgin olive oil

½ cup hazelnuts

3 cloves garlic, minced

¼ teaspoon red pepper flakes

⅓ cup toasted bread crumbs

¼ cup rough-chopped parsley

Zest from 1 small lemon

½ teaspoon kosher salt,
   plus extra to taste

Pinch freshly ground black
   pepper, plus extra to taste

ROASTED ACORN SQUASH

2 acorn squash, seeds removed
   and cut into one-sixths

2 tablespoons extra virgin olive oil

½ teaspoon kosher salt,
   plus extra to taste

Pinch freshly ground black
   pepper, plus extra to taste

½ cup wildflower honey

2 Fresno peppers, brunoise-cut

1 tablespoon freshly
   squeezed lemon juice

1 teaspoon minced garlic

½ teaspoon Aleppo pepper

½ teaspoon sea salt

HAZELNUT PICADA

1. Place 1 tablespoon of the olive oil in a large sauté pan and set over medium heat. Once the oil shimmers, add the hazelnuts, garlic, and red pepper flakes, and cook until aromatic, about 1 minute. Set aside to cool.

2. Transfer the mixture to a food processor and add the bread crumbs, parsley, lemon zest, and salt and pepper and process by pulsing until roughly chopped and thoroughly incorporated. With the processor running, drizzle in the remaining tablespoon of olive oil. Taste and adjust the seasoning with salt and pepper.

ROASTED ACORN SQUASH

1. Preheat the oven to 400°F.

2. Toss the acorn squash with the olive oil, salt, and pepper. Place the squash in an even layer on a sheet tray, making sure to leave space between the pieces and not overcrowd the pan. Roast until the squash are golden brown and tender, 45 to 50 minutes.

CONTINUES →

3. Place the honey, Fresno peppers, lemon juice, garlic, Aleppo pepper, and sea salt in a small bowl and toss to combine.

4. Place the squash on a serving platter, drizzle with the honey mixture, and sprinkle the picada on top. Serve immediately.

THOUGHTFUL TIP

Not all squash are made the same. Summer squash deserve a quick roast or sauté to bring out their natural flavors. Winter squash and pumpkins need a little more TLC . . . that is, *time, love,* and *cooking*! Cooking these squash slowly in an oven not only helps to tenderize the hard flesh, but also brings out their natural sweetness. Once you master acorn squash, try them all. Your local farmers' market has more varieties than you could imagine.

Candy Roaster Squash Soup
WITH BLUE CHEESE AND PUMPKIN SEEDS

SERVES 6 TO 8

There are winter squash and pumpkins, and then there are candy roaster squash! This oblong and banana-looking winter squash is one of the most flavorful and unique squash in the country. Known for having a sweet flesh, it lends itself to being baked or roasted, and it works as an amazing base for this fall soup. The addition of ginger and nutmeg helps to build flavor and accentuate the season. If you are having trouble finding candy roasters, you can always use a substitute like red kuri, blue hubbard, dutch fork, or butternut squash. The addition of creamy and funky blue cheese and crunchy, earthy pepitas (aka pumpkin seeds) adds a creaminess and a crunch. Use both as garnishes, or try the soup by itself.

One 4- to 5-pound candy roaster squash or other pumpkin

1 tablespoon olive oil

2 teaspoons kosher salt, plus extra to taste

¼ teaspoon freshly ground black pepper, plus extra to taste

3 tablespoons unsalted butter

1 cup diced onions

½ cup diced celery

½ cup diced leeks

1 tablespoon minced garlic

2 teaspoons minced ginger

½ cup white wine

1 bay leaf

3 cups Vegetable Stock (page 273)

½ cup heavy cream

2 teaspoons wildflower honey

Pinch of nutmeg

¼ cup blue cheese, crumbled (optional)

¼ cup roasted and salted pumpkin seeds (optional)

1. Preheat the oven to 425°F. Line a sheet tray with parchment and set aside.

2. Cut the squash in half and remove the seeds and fibrous strings. Score the flesh of the squash every 2 to 3 inches, with a sharp knife. If the squash is very large, cut into smaller pieces so it will fit on the sheet tray. Drizzle with the olive oil and season with 1 teaspoon of the salt and the pepper.

3. Place the squash on the prepared sheet tray, flesh side down, and roast about 1 hour, or until the flesh is tender when pierced with a knife.

4. Remove from the oven and set aside until cool enough to handle. Separate the flesh from the skin. Discard the skin and place the flesh in a blender to puree. Set aside.

5. Melt the butter in a large heavy-bottom pot and set over medium-high heat. Add the onions, celery, leeks, garlic, and ginger and sauté until the onions and leeks are translucent, 5 to 6 minutes.

6. Add the wine and cook, stirring occasionally, until reduced by half. Add the squash, bay leaf, and vegetable stock and stir to combine. Reduce the heat to low and simmer until the vegetables are tender, 30 to 35 minutes.

7. Add the heavy cream and stir to combine. Set aside to cool slightly. Discard the bay leaf.

8. Transfer to a blender and carefully puree until completely smooth. Add the remaining teaspoon of salt, honey, and nutmeg. Taste and adjust seasoning as desired.

9. Garnish with the blue cheese and pumpkin seeds, if using, and serve immediately.

THOUGHTFUL TIP

Candy roaster squash is an heirloom variety and is indigenous to the Appalachian Mountains of western North Carolina where the Cherokee tribes originally bred and proliferated this squash varietal. It's known for its sweet, unique flavor, which is the reason behind its name. The variety is now on Slow Food USA's Ark of Taste, where they have recognized this heritage vegetable due to its sustainable production, unique taste, and distinct impact on culture in the region. Candy roasters are a favorite in pies, soups, breads, and more. When baked or stewed its flesh can be compared to a sweet potato, only better!

Kohlrabi and Celery Salad
WITH WHITE ANCHOVY AND CITRUS DRESSING

<u>SERVES 4</u>

In the fall I'm always looking for fresh-tasting vegetables to serve with richer dishes and to help lighten up a meal. Kohlrabi really steps in and plays a big role. Sweet, mild, and crunchy, it tastes a little like a mild radish and is delicious raw in salads. I like to add a little funk in everything I cook to help create balance. Here, the addition of savory white anchovies provides some depth along with the punch of orange supremes.

CITRUS DRESSING
- ¼ cup freshly squeezed grapefruit juice
- ¼ cup freshly squeezed orange juice
- ¼ cup freshly squeezed lemon juice
- 1 tablespoon minced shallot
- 2 teaspoons honey
- ¾ cup extra virgin olive oil
- Kosher salt, to taste
- Ground white pepper, to taste

KOHLRABI AND CELERY SALAD
- 2 cups peeled, julienned kohlrabi
- 1 cup thin-bias cut celery
- 1 cup thinly sliced fennel
- ½ cup thinly sliced red onion
- Supremes from 1 orange
- ½ cup toasted, slivered almonds
- 2 tablespoons thinly sliced chives
- 12 white anchovies
- Kosher salt, to taste
- Ground white pepper, to taste

CITRUS DRESSING

1. Place the grapefruit juice, orange juice, and lemon juice into a small saucepan, set over medium-high heat, and reduce to ½ cup. Set aside to cool slightly.

2. Place the juice, shallots, and honey into a blender and puree on high speed. With the motor running, slowly pour in the olive oil to emulsify the dressing. Taste and season with salt and white pepper to taste. Refrigerate until ready to use.

KOHLRABI AND CELERY SALAD

1. Place the kohlrabi, celery, fennel, onion, orange supremes, almonds, chives, and anchovies in a serving bowl. Add ¼ cup of the dressing and gently toss to combine. Add more as desired. Taste and season with salt and white pepper as necessary. Serve immediately.

THOUGHTFUL TIP

Kohlrabi can be cut raw for salads and coleslaws, but it's also great roasted like a turnip to add to a sauté or stir-fry. Try them with the pickled, following the pickling recipes found in this book, and you're in for a treat!

Smoked Turkey Legs

WITH KUMQUAT GLAZE

SERVES 4

Turkey legs are about as caveman as you can get with food. But it's important to let your inner barbarian out from time to time. When smoking food, remember to impart flavor and to keep the meat moist. Here, we use a brown sugar and thyme brine, and we baste our turkey legs with a savory and sweet orange juice mop. The kumquat glaze is delicious with a cheese board, but it finds the perfect home when paired with smoked poultry.

KUMQUAT GLAZE

1 pound kumquats, quartered and seeds removed

2½ cups sugar

1½ cups water

Zest from 1 lemon

½ cup freshly squeezed lemon juice

8 thyme sprigs

2 whole star anise

¼ teaspoon cayenne pepper

TURKEY LEGS

4 turkey legs

1 recipe Standard Brine (page 274)

1 cup orange juice

2 tablespoons Worcestershire sauce

1 teaspoon minced garlic

1 teaspoon kosher salt

½ teaspoon freshly ground black pepper

KUMQUAT GLAZE

1. Place the kumquats in the bowl of a food processor and pulse four or five times, until coarsely chopped. Transfer the kumquats to a medium heavy-bottom sauce-pot. Add the sugar, water, lemon zest, lemon juice, thyme, star anise, and cayenne pepper and stir to combine. Cover the pot and allow the fruit to macerate at room temperature for 2 hours.

2. Remove the lid and place the pot over medium-high heat. Bring the mixture to a simmer, stirring occasionally, about 10 minutes. Reduce the heat to medium and cook, stirring frequently, until the temperature reaches 215°F, 40 to 50 minutes. Remove the thyme and star anise after 20 minutes of cooking.

3. Spoon the glaze into a sanitized glass container or jar and cool to room temperature before covering and refrigerating for up to 6 months, or process by canning in a hot water bath.

TURKEY LEGS

1. Place the turkey legs in a large container and cover with the brine. Refrigerate for 6 to 8 hours.

2. Remove the turkey from the brine, rinse under cold water, and pat dry. Return the legs to the refrigerator to dry for 3 hours.

CONTINUES →

3. Preheat a smoker to 225°F. Combine the orange juice, Worcestershire, and garlic in a small bowl and use as a mop for basting the turkey.

4. Season the turkey legs with salt and pepper and place on the smoker until the turkey reaches an internal temperature of 155°F, 1½ to 2 hours. Baste the turkey legs with the mop every 15 minutes.

5. Remove the turkey legs from the smoker and baste with the kumquat glaze. Place back on the smoker and cook until the glaze sets and the turkey reaches 160°F, 10 to 15 minutes.

6. Remove the turkey legs from the smoker and baste with more of the kumquat glaze. Rest 10 to 15 minutes before serving.

THOUGHTFUL TIP

In Chef Edward Lee's cookbook, *Smoke & Pickles*, Chef Lee says that the appeal for smoked food spans across the globe. But he goes further. "Some say umami is the fifth [taste], in addition to salty, sweet, sour, and bitter. I say smoke is the sixth." Chase your inspiration for smoked meats and vegetables, and experiment with smoking your favorite proteins or veggies.

Pan-Roasted Half Chicken

WITH SWISS CHARD AND FRESH FIGS

SERVES 2

At the beginning of fall, we find ourselves at the crossroads of the seasons, and cool weather greens and fresh figs find themselves at the farmers' markets. This chicken dish is an easy one-pan dinner that's packed full of flavor. The fresh figs add a brightness alongside the savory chicken pan sauce, and the greens provide a bitter counterpoint.

½ bone-in chicken (breast, leg, and thigh)

2 quarts Standard Brine (page 274)

½ teaspoon kosher salt, plus extra to taste

¼ teaspoon freshly ground black pepper, plus extra to taste

2 tablespoons extra virgin olive oil

3 tablespoons unsalted butter

2 shallots, peeled and quartered

2 garlic cloves, peeled

1 bunch Swiss chard, leaves cut into large chiffonade and stems diced

¼ cup aged sherry vinegar

3 thyme sprigs

½ teaspoon lemon zest

2 cups Chicken Stock (page 274)

5 fresh figs, quartered

1. In a clean container, cover the chicken with the brine and refrigerate for 4 hours.

2. Remove the chicken from the brine, rinse under cold water, and lay on a sheet tray lined with a rack. Refrigerate to dry, for at least 2 hours and up to overnight.

3. Preheat the oven to 450°F.

4. Season the chicken with salt and pepper. Place the olive oil and 1 tablespoon of the butter in a large, oven-safe sauté pan over medium-high heat. Add the chicken, skin side down, and cook until golden, 6 to 8 minutes. Cook for 30 to 35 minutes, until the internal temperature is 160°F. Remove from the oven and transfer to a platter.

5. Set the sauté pan over medium-high heat and add the shallots and garlic. Cook, stirring frequently, until the shallots are translucent, about 5 minutes.

6. Add the Swiss chard and cook until the leaves are wilted and the stems are becoming tender, 5 to 6 minutes. Taste and season with salt and pepper as necessary. Transfer the chard to the platter with the chicken.

7. Add the vinegar, thyme, and lemon zest to the pan, and cook until the vinegar reduces to a glaze, 2 to 3 minutes. Add the stock and reduce to about ½ cup, 8 to 10 minutes. Add the remaining 2 tablespoons of butter and stir to combine. Spoon the sauce over the chicken, garnish with the fresh figs, and serve immediately.

THOUGHTFUL TIP

When pan roasting, make sure you use a heavy-duty stainless steel pan or cast-iron pan. Always remove the pan from the oven with a dry kitchen towel. A wet towel conducts heat, and you can get burned more easily with a wet towel than with a dry towel.

Roasted Wild Salmon
WITH SUNCHOKE CHIPS AND PARSLEY SALSA VERDE

SERVES 8 TO 10

I love baked fish! It's a simple, easy, and tasty way to make dinner for the whole family without much mess to clean up afterward. Here, I've made a slow-roasted king salmon fillet rubbed down with a flavorful mustard sauce and topped off with an herbal, tangy French-style salsa verde. The earthiness of crispy sunchoke chips sprinkled over the roasted salmon adds just the right amount of crunch. This is a winner for dinner parties, holidays, or just to celebrate the day!

PARSLEY SALSA VERDE

1 cup chopped flat-leaf parsley

½ cup chopped chervil

½ cup thinly sliced chives

1 shallot, chopped

2 garlic cloves, chopped

1 teaspoon minced white anchovy

¼ cup capers, rinsed

1 tablespoon freshly squeezed lemon juice

1 cup extra virgin olive oil

1 tablespoon finely diced red bell pepper

Kosher salt, to taste

Freshly ground black pepper, to taste

SALMON AND SUNCHOKES

¼ cup Dijon mustard

2 tablespoons extra virgin olive oil1 tablespoon wildflower honey

1 tablespoon minced garlic

1 teaspoon lemon zest

2 tablespoons freshly squeezed lemon juice

1 teaspoon ground Aleppo pepper

1 teaspoon chopped parsley

1 teaspoon thinly sliced chives

½ teaspoon kosher salt, plus extra to taste

Freshly ground black pepper, to taste

One 4-pound king salmon fillet, skin on, pin bones removed

8 ounces sunchokes, cleaned and thinly sliced

Canola oil, for frying

PARSLEY SALSA VERDE

1. Place the parsley, chervil, chives, shallot, garlic, anchovy, capers, and lemon juice in a food processor. Process to a rustic puree. With the motor running, slowly add the olive oil until thoroughly combined and the salsa is a spoonable consistency. Add the red bell pepper and stir to combine. Taste and season with salt and pepper as necessary. Cover and refrigerate until ready to serve.

SALMON AND SUNCHOKES

1. Preheat the oven to 400°F. Line a baking sheet with parchment and set aside.

2. Place the Dijon, olive oil, honey, garlic, lemon zest, lemon juice, Aleppo pepper, parsley, chives, and salt in a small bowl and whisk to combine. Taste and adjust the seasoning with salt and pepper as necessary.

3. Place the salmon, skin side down, onto the prepared sheet tray, thoroughly rub with the mustard mixture, and season lightly with additional salt.

4. Place in the oven and bake until the internal temperature reaches 130°F to 135°F, 15 to 18 minutes. Remove from the oven and rest 5 minutes before serving.

5. While the salmon is baking, prepare the sunchokes.

6. Set a medium saucepan or pot over high heat, add 1 inch of canola oil to the pot, and bring to 350°F. Working in batches, gently slide the sunchokes into the oil and cook until lightly golden in color, 2 to 3 minutes.

7. Remove the sunchokes to a paper towel–lined tray, using a slotted spoon. Season with salt. Repeat until all the sunchokes are cooked. Reserve until ready to serve.

8. Transfer the salmon to a platter using two large spatulas. Spoon the parsley salsa verde over the salmon and sprinkle with the sunchokes. Serve immediately.

THOUGHTFUL TIP

Years ago, I had the chance to explore the wild salmon fishery in Alaska, and I was amazed to discover just how interconnected this whole region is. The entire ecosystem seems to live off of wild salmon. So much so that the indigenous Alaskans say that the salmon is in everything, even the ground that nourishes the trees. Wild salmon season goes from mid-April through mid-October each year on the Pacific coast. The Alaskan salmon fishery in Bristol Bay is considered one of the most sustainable fisheries on the planet and produces an abundance of wild sockeye, king, and coho salmon.

Roasted Wild Salmon with Sunchoke
Chips and Parsley Salsa Verde

Cider-Braised Pork Shank with Farro,
Collard Greens, Honey Nut Squash,
Pickled Red Onions, and Gremolata

Cider-Braised Pork Shank

WITH FARRO, COLLARD GREENS, HONEY NUT SQUASH, PICKLED RED ONIONS, AND GREMOLATA

SERVES 4

Thinking of this meal makes me feel, well, cozy. There's something about the smell of a slow braise cooking in the oven on a lazy day. While most people tend to braise pork shoulder, I love to use pork shanks. They get just as tender, but you get so much flavor from the bone. Serving this alongside a nutty, creamy farro with braised collard greens and a tangy and herbal gremolata rounds out the meal. You're sure to feel those hygge vibes hanging out in your kitchen. A perfect day!

PORK SHANK

Three 2-pound pork hind shanks

2 quarts Standard Brine (page 274)

3 tablespoons canola oil

1 tablespoon kosher salt, plus extra to taste

½ teaspoon freshly ground black pepper, plus extra to taste

2 cups large-dice yellow onion

1 cup large-dice, peeled carrots

1 cup large-dice celery

2 tablespoons tomato paste

4 garlic cloves, smashed

1 cup Calvados or bourbon

3 cups apple cider

3 cups Chicken Stock (page 274)

½ cup apple cider vinegar

6 thyme sprigs

2 bay leaves

1 teaspoon whole black peppercorns

2 tablespoons unsalted butter

SQUASH

Two 1-pound honey nut squash (may substitute butternut)

2 tablespoons canola oil

1 teaspoon kosher salt

½ teaspoon freshly ground black pepper

1 cup water

FARRO

2 tablespoons canola oil

1 cup medium-dice shallot

1 tablespoon minced garlic

¼ teaspoon red pepper flakes

2 cups farro piccolo

1 cup white wine

8 cups water

1 bay leaf

2 tablespoons unsalted butter

½ cup shredded Parmesan

1½ cups Collard Greens (page 170)

2 tablespoons freshly squeezed lemon juice

Kosher salt, to taste

Freshly ground black pepper, to taste

COLLARD GREENS

2 tablespoons blended oil

1 yellow onion, small dice

2 garlic cloves, thinly sliced

½ teaspoon red pepper flakes

3 bunches (about 1 pound) collard greens, de-stemmed and cut into large chiffonade

1 quart water

¼ cup apple cider vinegar

¼ cup soy sauce

2 tablespoons sorghum

2 tablespoons Frank's RedHot

1 tablespoon Worcestershire sauce

1 teaspoon kosher salt, plus extra to taste

¼ teaspoon freshly ground black pepper, plus extra to taste

TO SERVE

½ cup Gremolata (page 273)

½ cup Pickled Red Onions (page 267)

PORK SHANK

1. Place the pork shanks into a clean container, cover with the brine, and refrigerate 24 hours. Remove from the brine, rinse under cold water, and pat dry.

2. Preheat the oven to 325°F.

3. Place the oil into a large, heavy-bottomed pot or Dutch oven and set over medium-high heat. Sprinkle the pork shanks with salt and pepper. Add the shanks to the pot, a few at a time to prevent overcrowding, and cook until browned on all sides, 3 to 4 minutes per side. Remove the shanks to a large plate.

4. Add the onions, carrots, and celery to the pot and cook until the onions are translucent, about 5 minutes. Add the tomato paste and garlic and cook until aromatic, 1 to 2 minutes.

5. Deglaze the pot with the Calvados and reduce by half, scraping the bottom of the pot to release the fond, 2 to 3 minutes. Add the apple cider, chicken stock, vinegar, thyme, bay leaves, and peppercorns and bring to a simmer.

6. Return the pork shanks to the pot, cover with a tight-fitting lid and place into the oven to braise for 3 to 3½ hours, until the shanks are tender and the meat is falling away from the bone.

7. At this point you can store the pork shanks in the braising liquid under refrigeration for up to 5 days or proceed with the recipe

8. Remove the pork shanks from the pot and place on a plate to rest. Remove the thyme, bay leaves, and peppercorns.

9. Put the pot back on a burner over medium-high heat and reduce the liquid by three-fourths.

10. Add the butter and whisk to combine. Taste and adjust the seasoning as necessary with salt and pepper. Reserve the sauce until ready to serve.

SQUASH

1. Preheat the oven to 400°F.

2. Cut one of the squashes in half lengthwise, scoop out the seeds, and rub with 1 tablespoon of the oil and season with half of the salt and pepper. Place cut side down on a sheet tray.

3. Peel the skin from the second squash, cut in half, and remove the seeds. Cut into a large dice, toss with the remaining 1 tablespoon of oil, season with the remaining salt and pepper, and spread on the sheet pan with the other squash. Roast until the squash is tender and golden, about 30 minutes.

4. Scoop the flesh out of the halved squash, transfer to a blender, add 1 cup of water, and carefully puree until smooth. Transfer the puree to a bowl and reserve. Reserve the diced squash.

CONTINUES →

FARRO

1. Place the canola oil in a medium, heavy-bottom pot or Dutch oven and set over medium-high heat. Add the shallots and cook, stirring occasionally, until they caramelize, 4 to 5 minutes. Add the garlic and red pepper flakes and cook, stirring frequently until the garlic is aromatic, 1 to 2 minutes.

2. Add the farro and stir for another minute.

3. Add the white wine and deglaze the pan, scraping up any fond on the bottom of the pot.

4. Add the water and bay leaf and bring to a simmer. Cook the farro, uncovered and stirring occasionally, until tender, 40 to 45 minutes.

5. When the farro is cooked, remove the bay leaf, add the pureed squash, butter, and Parmesan, and stir until the cheese is melted. Add the collard greens, lemon juice, and diced squash and gently stir to combine. Taste and adjust the seasoning with salt and pepper.

COLLARD GREENS

1. Place the oil in a large saucepan or pot and set over medium-high heat. Add the onions and cook, stirring frequently, until they are just beginning to turn golden, about 10 minutes.

2. Add the garlic and red pepper flakes, and cook until aromatic, about 2 minutes.

3. Add the collard greens, water, vinegar, soy sauce, sorghum, hot sauce, Worcestershire, salt, and pepper and stir to combine.

4. Cover the pot, reduce the heat to medium-low and cook, stirring occasionally, until the collards are tender, about 1 hour. Taste and adjust seasoning as necessary.

5. Serve immediately or refrigerate in an airtight container for up to 5 days.

TO SERVE

1. Spoon the warm cider-stock sauce over the warm pork and top with the gremolata. Garnish the pork with the pickled red onions and serve with the farro.

THOUGHTFUL TIP

This is a wonderful meal to plan ahead for. The pork shanks, farro, gremolata, squash, and pickled red onions can all be made days in advance of serving. Get your mise en place together and prepare a different step of this recipe throughout the week. When the weekend comes and you're ready to impress your friends and family you can warm everything up at once. Enjoy serving this five-star meal!

Pumpkin Grits

WITH ROASTED MAITAKE MUSHROOMS

SERVES 4 TO 6

Years ago I was on a trip to Italy and tasted the most memorable polenta with roasted mushrooms, pumpkin, and sage. It was one of those simple dishes that haunted me as a chef, and when I returned home I worked hard to re-create it. Using the ingredients around me, I started experimenting with stone-ground grits and wild mushrooms that grow in the forests near my home. This dish uses a pumpkin puree to create a savory fall version of slow-cooked grits. Finishing it with pan-roasted maitake mushrooms (aka hen of the woods) with garlicky butter and fried sage makes for a memorable side dish. And you don't even need to buy a ticket to Italy.

PUMPKIN GRITS

1 tablespoon canola oil

1 cup small-dice yellow onion

1 tablespoon minced garlic

4 cups water

1 cup stone-ground grits

1 cup roasted pumpkin puree

½ cup heavy cream

½ cup shredded Parmesan cheese

2 tablespoons unsalted butter

1 tablespoon Frank's RedHot

1 teaspoon kosher salt, plus extra to taste

½ teaspoon freshly ground black pepper, plus extra to taste

MUSHROOMS

1 pound maitake mushrooms

3 tablespoons canola oil

8 sage leaves

½ teaspoon kosher salt, plus extra to taste

2 cloves garlic, sliced

2 tablespoons unsalted butter

2 tablespoons freshly squeezed lemon juice

Pinch red pepper flakes

1 tablespoon rough chopped parsley

Freshly ground black pepper, to taste

PUMPKIN GRITS

1. Place the oil in a medium saucepan and set over medium-high heat. Once the oil shimmers, add the onions and cook until translucent, 2 to 3 minutes. Add the garlic and cook until aromatic, 1 minute. Add the water, increase the heat to high and bring to a boil. Add the grits in a slow, steady stream while whisking continually. Bring to a simmer, stirring constantly. Once simmering, decrease the heat to low and cook, stirring frequently, for about 1 hour.

2. Add the pumpkin, cream, Parmesan, butter, hot sauce, salt, and pepper and stir to combine. Taste and adjust seasoning as necessary. Cover and keep warm until ready to serve.

MUSHROOMS

1. Cut the mushrooms into golf ball–size pieces.

2. Place the oil in a large sauté pan and set over medium-high heat. Once the oil shimmers, add the sage and fry until aromatic and crisp, 15 to 20 seconds. Remove the sage to a paper towel–lined plate to drain. Lightly sprinkle with salt.

3. Add the mushrooms to the pan and cook until golden, 2 to 3 minutes. Flip and continue to cook on the other side for 2 to 3 minutes. Add the garlic and cook until lightly golden, about 1 minute.

4. Add the butter, lemon juice, and red pepper flakes and cook until bubbling, about 1 minute. Turn off the heat, add the parsley and ½ teaspoon salt, and stir to combine. Taste and adjust seasoning as necessary.

5. Place the grits into a large serving bowl, spoon the mushrooms around the edge, and garnish with the fried sage. Serve immediately.

THOUGHTFUL TIP

Grits and polenta are very similar. It's all about the texture of the grind when the miller is grinding the dried corn. In Italy they love the finely milled corn in polenta, and here in the States we seem to prefer the more coarse-ground grits. I work with Dave Bauer from the mill Farm & Sparrow in Asheville, North Carolina, and he has collaborated with us to find a unique blend of Tuxpeño White Landrace Corn and Cateto Italian Orange Flint Corn. Experiment for yourself with your favorite variety of corn.

Maitake
Mushroom

Pumpkin Grits with Roasted
Maitake Mushrooms

Pork Porterhouse with Sweet
Potato and Sorghum Fondue

Pork Porterhouse

WITH SWEET POTATO AND SORGHUM FONDUE

SERVES 4

A porterhouse cut isn't just for beef steaks. The bone separates the loin, and the tenderloin and makes for a juicy, flavorful roast. Here, I've pan roasted the pork and finished it with a garlic- and thyme-infused butter baste, or as the French would say, *arroser,* or "to baste." To cut through the richness of the meat, I've topped the pork with an herbal and tangy gremolata and fresh, sweet, and acidic blood oranges. The toppings make the perfect complement to this dish and really brighten up the flavors. The sweet potato fondue is rich and creamy, and the earthy sweet sorghum makes you come back for seconds.

SWEET POTATO AND SORGHUM FONDUE

2 large sweet potatoes, about 4 cups peeled and large dice

4 cups heavy cream

2 tablespoons unsalted butter, room temperature

2 tablespoons Confit Garlic (page 272)

Kosher salt, to taste

Freshly ground black pepper, to taste

2 tablespoons sorghum

PORK

Two 24-ounce bone-in pork porterhouse steaks

2 quarts Standard Brine (page 274)

½ teaspoon kosher salt, plus extra to taste

¼ teaspoon freshly ground black pepper, plus extra to taste

2 tablespoons canola oil

3 tablespoons unsalted butter

3 garlic cloves

4 thyme sprigs

1 cup Gremolata (page 273)

Supremes from 1 blood orange

SWEET POTATO AND SORGHUM FONDUE

1. Place the sweet potatoes and heavy cream into a medium saucepan. Set over medium-high heat and bring to a simmer. Decrease the heat to maintain a simmer and cook until the potatoes are very tender, 30 to 35 minutes. Strain the potatoes and reserve the cream.

2. Transfer the sweet potatoes to a blender and add 1 cup of the cream, butter, and confit garlic. Puree until smooth, adding more cream if needed. Taste and season with salt and pepper. Transfer the sweet potatoes to a serving bowl, drizzle with sorghum, and keep warm.

PORK

1. Place the pork into a clean container, cover with the brine, and refrigerate 12 to 18 hours.

2. Remove the pork from the brine, rinse under cold water, and pat dry.

3. Preheat the oven to 450°F.

4. Season the pork on all sides with salt and pepper.

5. Heat a large cast-iron skillet or oven-safe sauté pan over medium-high heat and add the oil.

6. Add the pork and cook until golden brown on both sides, about 4 minutes per side.

7. Transfer the skillet to the oven and roast 20 to 25 minutes, until the pork reaches an internal temperature of 145°F.

8. Remove the skillet from the oven and place back over medium-high heat. Add the butter, garlic cloves, and thyme. When the butter begins to foam, tilt the pan slightly and using a large spoon, baste the pork 10 to 12 times. The pork should reach 150°F to 155°F for medium temperature.

9. Remove the pork from the pan and place on a sheet tray with a rack to rest for 10 minutes before slicing.

10. Cut the pork off the bone, slice, and place the slices on the platter with the bone. Spoon the pan sauce and the gremolata over the pork and top with the blood oranges. Serve immediately with the sweet potatoes.

THOUGHTFUL TIP

When I was growing up, my mom would make pork chops with baked apples for a special family dinner. They were always delicious, and it was a celebration to have this lean cut of meat. With a thicker-cut pork chop, or porterhouse, it's important to keep it tender and juicy. I'm all about the brine! Experiment with different spices and length of time while brining, but don't be shy when it comes to giving your meat a salt bath. It's an easy way to keep your meat from drying out while adding tenderness and a lot of flavor.

Braised Duck Legs

WITH CHARRED BRUSSELS SPROUTS AND PARSNIPS AND ROSEMARY APPLESAUCE

SERVES 4

Even after I found my confidence in the kitchen, the idea of braising still intimidated me. As crazy as it sounds, you can dry out a piece of meat that's braised in liquid and overcook it. Once I started to experiment with braises, I found that they weren't as scary as I thought. In fact, braising is a way to cook a flavorful meal using tougher cuts of meat. Here, this version of braised duck legs gets a flavor bomb when cured in a salt and sugar mixture before braising in red wine and aromatics. Duck and apples work really well together, the pomegranates add a sweet and bright punch, and the smoky, seared Brussels sprouts with bacon are the perfect accompaniment to this fall dinner.

DUCK

4 duck hindquarters
  (2- to 2½- pounds total)

½ cup kosher salt

5 tablespoons light brown sugar

2 tablespoons freshly
  ground black pepper

½ bunch thyme

10 bay leaves, crumbled

1 teaspoon orange zest

½ teaspoon red pepper flakes

¼ teaspoon ground clove

¼ teaspoon minced garlic

1 tablespoon blended oil

1 yellow onion, large dice

2 celery stalks, large dice

1 carrot, peeled and large dice

1 tablespoon tomato paste

3 garlic cloves, smashed

2 cups dry red wine

2 cups Chicken Stock
  (page 274)

½ bunch thyme

½ teaspoon whole black
  peppercorns

BRUSSELS SPROUTS AND PARSNIPS

Salt for pot of water

8 ounces (about 2 cups)
  Brussels sprouts

2 cups peeled, large dice parsnips

1 cup bacon lardons

1 tablespoon minced garlic

1 tablespoon unsalted butter

1 tablespoon freshly
  squeezed lemon juice

1 teaspoon chopped rosemary

Kosher salt, to taste

Freshly ground black
  pepper, to taste

3 cups Rosemary Applesauce
  (page 275)

½ cup pomegranate seeds

DUCK

1. Place the duck into a gallon zip-top bag and add the salt, brown sugar, black pepper, thyme, bay leaves, orange zest, red pepper flakes, clove, and minced garlic. Seal the bag and toss to ensure the cure is evenly distributed. Refrigerate for 6 to 8 hours.

2. Preheat the oven to 300°F. Remove the duck from the cure, rinse under cold water, and pat dry.

3. Place the oil in a large, steep-sided sauté pan over medium heat. Once shimmering, add the duck, skin side down, to render the fat and brown the duck, 6 to 8 minutes. Flip and cook for another 1 to 2 minutes. Pour off half of the oil.

CONTINUES →

4. Return the pan to the heat, add the onions, celery, and carrots and sauté until golden, about 5 minutes. Add the tomato paste and garlic cloves, stir to combine, and cook until aromatic, about 1 minute.

5. Deglaze the pan with the red wine, stirring to scrape any fond off the bottom of the pan, and add the chicken stock, thyme, and black peppercorns and bring to a simmer. Place the duck, skin side up, into the braising liquid. About two-thirds of the duck should be covered by the liquid.

6. Cover with a tight-fitting lid and place into the oven. Braise the duck for 1 to 1½ hours, until the duck is fork-tender. Remove from the oven, remove the lid, and allow to cool to room temperature.

7. Remove the duck from the pan and place onto a platter. Reheat if necessary.

8. Strain the braising liquid through a fine mesh strainer and return the liquid to the pan. Place over medium-high heat and reduce by three-fourths. Keep warm.

BRUSSELS SPROUTS AND PARSNIPS

1. Bring a pot of water to a boil. Season with enough salt to taste like the ocean. Blanch the Brussels sprouts until tender, 4 to 5 minutes. Use a slotted spoon to transfer the Brussels sprouts to a bowl of ice water. Remove from the ice, cut in half, and drain completely on paper towels. Repeat with the parsnips.

2. Heat a large sauté pan over medium heat and add the bacon lardons. Cook until crisp and tender, about 5 minutes. Remove the bacon from the pan and place on a paper towel–lined plate. Reserve.

3. Pour off half of the fat from the pan and increase the heat to medium-high. Add the Brussels sprouts and parsnips and cook until tender and golden, 5 to 6 minutes. Add the garlic and butter and cook for another 1 to 2 minutes. Add the lemon juice and rosemary, and season to taste with salt and pepper.

TO SERVE

1. Place the vegetables in a serving bowl and garnish with the bacon lardons.

2. Place 3 cups of the warm rosemary applesauce across the bottom of a large platter. Place the warm duck hindquarters on top of the applesauce and spoon the reduced braising liquid over the duck. Sprinkle with the pomegranate seeds and serve immediately with the roasted Brussels sprouts and parsnips.

THOUGHTFUL TIP

Always let your braises cool down in the liquid you cooked them in. This allows for them to keep gaining flavor from the braise. When the meat has cooled, don't discard the braising liquid! Reduce it down for an amazing sauce to use when reheating your braised meats.

Grilled Hanger Steak

WITH FLOWERING CAULIFLOWER AND MUSHROOM BUTTER

SERVES 4

I work with a mushroom forager in Asheville named Brad. He finds some of the most amazing mushrooms in our region and is connected to the earth more than anyone I've ever met. His keen eye for fresh fungus has kept me stocked up with an array of wild mushrooms that are second to none. At our restaurants, we buy *a lot* of mushrooms and always have a lot of trim that comes from processing them. Rather than wasting this trim, I use it to make many different recipes, such as the mushroom butter that adorns the top of this grilled hanger steak. The mushroom butter really adds depth to the robust beef flavor of the steak.

MUSHROOM BUTTER

2 tablespoons extra virgin olive oil

½ cup finely chopped mixed mushrooms

2 tablespoons minced shallots

1 teaspoon minced garlic

Pinch red pepper flakes

1 cup dry red wine

½ cup unsalted butter, room temperature

1 teaspoon finely chopped thyme

½ teaspoon kosher salt

½ teaspoon freshly ground black pepper

HANGER STEAK AND CAULIFLOWER

Four 8-ounce hanger steaks, trimmed

6 tablespoons extra virgin olive oil

½ teaspoon kosher salt, plus extra to taste

1 tablespoon minced garlic

1 teaspoon freshly ground black pepper

1 tablespoon chopped basil

1½ pounds flowering cauliflower, trimmed

1 cup water

1 tablespoon freshly squeezed lemon juice

1 tablespoon unsalted butter

MUSHROOM BUTTER

1. Place a medium sauté pan over medium-high heat and add the oil. When the oil shimmers, add the mushrooms and cook until they begin to give up some of their juices, 3 to 4 minutes. Add the shallots, garlic, and red pepper flakes and cook until aromatic, about 1 minute.

2. Deglaze the pan with the red wine, scraping the fond from the bottom of the pan, and reduce the heat to medium. Cook, stirring from time to time, until the wine has reduced to a loose glaze, 7 to 8 minutes.

3. Transfer the mixture to a bowl and refrigerate until completely cool, about 30 minutes.

4. Once cool, transfer the mushrooms to the bowl of a stand mixer, add the butter, thyme, salt, and pepper and using the paddle attachment, combine on medium-low speed until fully incorporated, 3 to 4 minutes. Taste and adjust seasoning as necessary.

CONTINUES →

5. Lay out a sheet of plastic wrap on a counter and place the butter on top. Wrap the butter and roll into a 1-inch-wide log. Refrigerate until firm. Will keep for up to 10 days.

HANGER STEAK AND CAULIFLOWER

1. Preheat a grill to medium-high heat.

2. To marinate the steaks, mix together 2 tablespoons of the olive oil, minced garlic, black pepper, and basil in a large bowl. Add the steaks and allow to marinate for at least 20 minutes. Remove from the marinade and season the steaks with salt.

3. Grill the steaks on one side until partially cooked through and grill marks appear, about 5 minutes. Flip the steaks and cook until the internal temperature reaches 135°F, 1 to 2 minutes.

4. Remove the meat from the grill and place on a sheet pan with a cooling rack. Set aside to rest for 5 minutes.

5. While the meat is resting, place a large sauté pan over medium-high heat and add the remaining 4 tablespoons of oil. Add the cauliflower and cook until golden on one side, about 5 minutes. Flip the cauliflower and remove the pan from the heat. Add the water and return the pan to the heat. Cook until the water has evaporated and the cauliflower is tender, 2 to 3 minutes. Stir in the lemon juice and butter and season to taste with salt and pepper.

6. Place a slice of the mushroom butter on top of each steak and serve with the cauliflower.

THOUGHTFUL TIP

Cauliflower comes in a lot of different shapes and sizes. One of my favorites is the flowering version. Also known as Fioretto, which means "little flower" in Italian, this cruciferous vegetable looks like white broccoli or even baby's breath flowers. It's very tender and can be eaten raw, but it is also wonderful for sautés, stir-fries, tempura-fried, or even pickled.

Corn Bread, Olive Oil, Country Ham Cracklins', Espelette Pepper Jelly

Where I'm from, people always argue about whether or not you should add sugar to your corn bread. I'm here to tell you that yes, you should add a little sugar. For me the argument isn't about who is right or wrong, but whether or not your corn bread is dry or moist. And here's where things really deviate. In my recipe, I've come up with a foolproof plan to keep corn bread moist and delicious by replacing the butter with fruity, savory olive oil. The diehard bakers will think I'm crazy, but give this recipe a try and you'll be a believer. Don't forget to add the pepper jelly and country ham cracklins' to take this recipe over the top.

CORN BREAD

- 1 tablespoon unsalted butter, melted
- 1 cup fine-ground yellow cornmeal
- 1 cup all-purpose flour
- 3 tablespoons sugar
- 1 teaspoon baking soda
- 1 teaspoon kosher salt
- 2 large eggs, room temperature
- 1¾ cups buttermilk, room temperature
- 2 tablespoons olive oil

HAM CRACKLINS' (OPTIONAL)

- 2 cups medium dice country ham
- 2 cups canola oil

TO SERVE

Espelette Pepper Jelly (page 270; optional)

CORN BREAD

1. Preheat the oven to 425°F. Brush a 10-inch cast-iron skillet with the butter and set aside.

2. Place the cornmeal, flour, sugar, baking soda, and salt into a mixing bowl and whisk to combine.

3. Place the eggs, buttermilk, and olive oil in a separate bowl and whisk to combine.

4. Add the dry ingredients to the wet mixture and stir just until combined. Do not overmix.

5. Pour the batter into the prepared skillet and bake until golden brown and cooked through, about 25 minutes.

6. Remove from the oven, turn out onto a platter and cool 10 minutes before slicing.

HAM CRACKLINS'

1. Place the country ham into a small saucepan and cover with the canola oil. Set over medium heat and bring to a simmer, about 5 minutes. Cook until the bubbles are starting to slow down, and the ham is beginning to crisp, 15 to 20 minutes.

CONTINUES →

2. Use a slotted spoon to transfer the ham to a paper towel–lined plate to cool completely.

3. Place the cooled ham in a food processor and pulse until it is finely chopped.

TO SERVE

1. Serve the corn bread with the ham cracklins' and espelette pepper jelly, if desired.

THOUGHTFUL TIP

In this simple recipe, a good extra virgin olive oil that's fruity, savory, and peppery will make an outstanding corn bread. In the pepper jelly, piment d'Espelette is a revered pepper hailing from the Basque region of France. It is named after the village of Espelette in the Nive Valley and has a flavor with hints of peach, the ocean, as well as a nuanced and subtle heat.

Dark Chocolate and Dulce de Leche Brownies

WITH BURNT MARSHMALLOW FLUFF

SERVES 8 TO 10

I first made these brownies about 10 years ago when I was working on a new dessert for my restaurant. I wanted to create something approachable but also fun and full of flavor. My mind started to wander and I came up with this whimsical brownie that is stuffed full of dulce de leche caramel and topped with a cloud of burnt marshmallow fluff. It's a campfire marshmallow on top of a warm, gooey chocolate caramel brownie! It's been part of my dessert arsenal ever since.

DULCE DE LECHE
2 cans sweetened condensed milk

BROWNIES
1 cup unsalted butter, cut into cubes

12 ounces bittersweet chocolate, finely chopped

½ cup unsweetened cocoa powder, sifted

6 large eggs

2 cups granulated sugar

2 teaspoons vanilla extract

2 cups all-purpose flour

MARSHMALLOW FLUFF
6 tablespoons water

¾ cup granulated sugar

¾ cup light corn syrup

3 large egg whites

Pinch cream of tartar

Pinch kosher salt

1½ teaspoons vanilla extract

DULCE DE LECHE

1. Preheat the oven to 425°F. Place the cans of condensed milk in a loaf pan and cover with aluminum foil.

2. Place the loaf pan into a 13-by-9-inch cake pan and pour in hot water until it reaches halfway up the sides of the smaller pan.

3. Place the pans into the oven, and bake for 1 to 1½ hours, checking to see if more water is needed in the larger pan to maintain its level.

4. Remove the cans from the water and set aside to cool completely. Once cool enough to handle, open the can, and set aside until needed or refrigerate for up to 1 week.

BROWNIES

1. Preheat the oven to 350°F. Line a 13-by-9-inch pan with aluminum foil that covers the bottom and reaches up the sides. Grease the bottom and sides of the foil with pan spray.

2. Melt the butter in a large bowl set over a water bath. Add the chocolate pieces and stir constantly until the chocolate is melted. Remove the bowl from the water bath and set on a towel. Add the cocoa powder and whisk until smooth.

3. Add the eggs, one at a time, whisking until incorporated. Add the sugar and vanilla and whisk to combine. Add the flour and stir just until combined.

CONTINUES →

4. Scrape half of the batter into the prepared pan. Pour half of the dulce de leche, evenly spaced, over the brownie batter. Drag a knife through to swirl it slightly.

5. Spread the remaining brownie batter over the top, then spoon the remaining dulce de leche in dollops over the top of the brownie batter. Again, use a knife to swirl the dulce de leche slightly.

6. Place in the oven and bake 45 to 50 minutes, until the center feels slightly firm. Remove the pan to a wire rack and cool completely.

MARSHMALLOW FLUFF

1. Place the water, sugar, and corn syrup in a medium saucepan and set over medium-high heat. Cook until the mixture reaches 240°F on a candy thermometer, stirring from time to time, 8 to 10 minutes.

2. While the sugar is heating, place the egg whites in the bowl of a stand mixer fitted with the whisk attachment and beat on medium speed until foamy and turning white. Increase the speed to high and add the cream of tartar and salt. Continue to mix until soft peaks form.

3. Carefully remove the sugar from the heat and set aside to cool for 20 to 30 seconds.

4. With the mixer running on high, slowly stream the sugar mixture into the egg whites. Continue to mix until the outside of the mixing bowl is barely warm, 8 to 10 minutes. Add the vanilla extract, and whip to medium-stiff peaks. Store in an airtight container under refrigeration for up to 2 weeks.

TO SERVE

1. Heat the oven to 400°F. Cut the brownies into 2- by 3-inch pieces and reheat until the brownies are warmed through, 4 to 5 minutes. Drizzle each brownie piece with any extra dulce de leche.

2. Place the marshmallow fluff into a piping bag with a star tip and pipe the marshmallow fluff on top of each brownie. Using a culinary torch, brûlée the marshmallow fluff until golden brown. Serve immediately.

THOUGHTFUL TIP

This is the chance you've been waiting for to break out that culinary torch you were gifted for Christmas years ago. When using a torch in the kitchen, make sure you're working on a firm and stable work surface, and don't work directly over a cutting board (you don't want to burn it). When torching the marshmallow fluff, make a few passes back and forth over the fluff until it's torched to your desired doneness. Just like cooking marshmallows over the campfire, we each have our preference: from cooked a little brown to charred and extra crispy.

Apple Tart
WITH CINNAMON BROWN BUTTER ICE CREAM

SERVES 6 TO 8

As soon as the weather cools off, we head to the apple orchard with our family. There are many apple orchards around the region where we live in western North Carolina, and without fail we end up tramping around the orchard with our family, on school trips, and work outings. Invariably we return with overflowing baskets of apples, jugs of apple cider, and a sampling of delicious desserts the fruit stands sell. I love apples in all shapes, sizes, and varieties, but my favorite way to eat apples is in a traditional French apple tart with a filling of sweet almond frangipane. Paired with the cornmeal crust, this apple tart is sweet and slightly savory. It's a wonderful way to finish a meal. And if you're like me, any leftovers go hand in hand with a cup of coffee for breakfast.

FRANGIPANE

3 tablespoons unsalted butter, room temperature

¼ cup sugar

½ cup almond meal

1 large egg

¾ teaspoon vanilla extract

1 tablespoon all-purpose flour

TART

1 recipe Cornmeal Pâte Brisée (page 76)

4 Granny Smith apples, cored and thinly sliced

⅓ cup sugar

1 tablespoon freshly squeezed lemon juice

1 teaspoon vanilla extract

½ teaspoon ground cinnamon

4 tablespoons apricot preserves

Cinnamon Brown Butter Ice Cream (page 277)

FRANGIPANE

1. Place the butter and sugar into a stand mixer fitted with the paddle attachment and cream the mixture on high until it is light yellow in color and fluffy, 2 to 3 minutes, scraping the sides of the bowl as needed.

2. Reduce the speed to medium, add the almond meal and mix until well combined. Add the egg and mix well. Stop to scrape the sides of the bowl at least once. Add the vanilla and mix until combined.

3. Add the flour and mix to thoroughly combine.

4. Cover and refrigerate the frangipane until ready to use. The frangipane may also be refrigerated for up to 5 days, or tightly wrapped and frozen until needed.

TART

1. Preheat the oven to 350°F.

2. Place the cornmeal pâte brisée in a 12-inch tart pan. Place a sheet of parchment paper over the tart shell, cover with pie weights or beans, and blind bake for 12 minutes.

3. Remove the tart shell from the oven, discard the parchment, and remove the weights. Set the shell aside to cool.

4. Place the apples, sugar, lemon juice, vanilla, and cinnamon in a bowl, toss to combine, and set aside to macerate for 10 minutes.

5. Evenly spread the frangipane in the bottom of the tart shell.

6. Stir the apples in the bowl, and then starting in the middle of the pan, overlap the apple slices and shingle them like a rose flower, working in circles from the center to the edge of the pan.

7. Place the tart pan on a sheet tray, set in the oven, and bake 40 to 45 minutes, until the apples are tender and the crust is golden brown.

8. Remove to a cooling rack and set aside. Once the tart has cooled, brush with the apricot preserves.

9. Serve warm with the cinnamon brown butter ice cream.

THOUGHTFUL TIP

If you like pie more than a tart, don't fret. Add another two apples to the recipe and roll the dough out to fit a standard pie tin. Keep the layer of frangipane, and add the extra apples to fill the pie out more. The bake time for a pie will vary by about another 10 to 15 minutes more in the oven.

Apple Tart with Cinnamon
Brown Butter Ice Cream

Benton's Old-Fashioned

Benton's Old-Fashioned

MAKES ONE
750-MILLILITER
BOTTLE BOURBON
AND 2 COCKTAILS

Allan Benton from Madisonville, Tennessee, has been a good friend of mine for years. He is the kindest man you'll ever meet. A true Southern gentleman, he is also the producer of some of the world's best bacon and country hams. If you've ever had the chance for these pork products to grace your palate, then you know why he's so revered among chefs. This recipe is an homage to the cocktail created by PDT Bar in Manhattan and to the King of Pork, Mr. Allan Benton.

BACON-INFUSED BOURBON

One 750-milliliter bottle bourbon

18 ounces rendered and strained bacon fat

OLD-FASHIONED

Ice

4 ounces bacon-infused bourbon (from this recipe)

½ ounce maple syrup

6 dashes Angostura bitters

2 large ice cubes

2 pieces orange peel

BOURBON

1. Pour the bourbon into a nonporous container. (Plastic works best.) Add the bacon fat, cover, and infuse at room temperature for 4 hours or up to 1 day.

2. Place the container in the freezer until the fat solidifies and rises to the top, about 4 hours.

3. Remove the fat from the top using a slotted spoon and strain the mixture through a fine mesh strainer back into the bottle.

4. Keep at room temperature for up to 1 month.

OLD-FASHIONED

1. Fill a mixing glass halfway with ice. Add the bacon-infused bourbon, maple syrup, and bitters and stir until chilled.

2. Strain the mixture into two old-fashioned glasses with one large ice cube each.

3. Twist an orange peel over each drink, rub the glass rim with the peel, and place into the glass. Serve immediately.

THOUGHTFUL TIP

Fat washing is an infusion trick that bartenders use to add flavor to liquors. Various types of fat can be used for the infusion. To fat wash a spirit, you add an oil such as melted butter, bacon fat, sesame oil, or chile oil to the spirit and let it sit at room temperature for a few hours. You then chill the infused spirit in the freezer until the fat rises to the top and solidifies. The fat can then be skimmed off and strained, leaving a spirit that retains the flavor of fat used in the infusion.

Black Walnut Manhattan

MAKES 2
COCKTAILS

Who doesn't love a good Manhattan? This version uses black walnut nocino in place of the sweet vermouth from the traditional recipe, plus a touch of Luxardo cherry liqueur to balance the cocktail. The deep, aromatic, nutty flavor or the nocino helps to bring this Manhattan to new levels.

4 ounces bourbon
2 ounces nocino
1½ ounces Luxardo liqueur
6 dashes Angostura bitters
2 Luxardo or Amarena cherries

1. Fill a mixing glass halfway with ice. Add the bourbon, nocino, Luxardo liqueur, and Angostura bitters and stir until well chilled.

2. Strain into two coupe glasses and garnish with a cherry. Serve immediately.

THOUGHTFUL TIP

This is a great cocktail to batch for parties. You can combine the bourbon (or rye if you like) with the nocino, Luxardo, and Angostura bitters and stir together. Keep this mixture refrigerated until needed. When you're ready to serve it, just stir in ice to chill the drink. Strain it into coupe glasses prepared with cherries, and get ready to impress your crew and be the hit of the party.

EATING LOCAL

When it comes to what we put on our plates, you are what, and where, you eat. My love affair with local food started when I was a child, and as I've learned more about how the world works, I've found myself touting locally sourced food. In the constant online scroll, we can't help but see the doom and gloom in the news. Our food system is broken, and we seem to be evolving further and further away from being in touch with nature as we become more disconnected from where our food comes from. But there is a light if you choose to see it. I've seen firsthand how fresh ingredients make our food not only taste better, but the benefits it creates for our personal health, the positive effects it has on the economy of our communities, how it brings people together in person and out from behind their screens, and how it helps to protect the environment by lessening our impact on the world around us.

I was fortunate that I could visit my grandparent's farm when I was a child, and that my parents grew a small garden at home in the summertime. We really didn't think much about where our food was coming from, but we honored the opportunity to spend time outdoors and soak in nature. In my family of five, both of my parents worked, and as soon as I was able to ride a bike I was out slinging newspapers, mowing lawns, and washing dishes. As a child of the '90s, I ate my fair share of Happy Meals and TV dinners alongside my mom's home-cooked meals. Now, as a parent myself, I know how hard it can be to slow down and find time to plan and cook a healthy meal, let alone make it to the grocery store or farmers' market. It's no easy feat to feed a family.

For me, cooking seasonally has created a laser-sharp attunement to the seasons. You can almost feel it in the air when the first strawberries and asparagus of the season are ripening, because you know winter is over. You can smell it in the warming air and see it in the green hue of new life as it starts creeping in from all angles and takes over the brown and gray from winter. In the fall, the hearty greens, radishes, and root vegetables are plentiful, and it's like Mother Earth knows we need these vitamins before winter arrives. The humidity begins to leave the air, and the leaves turn all shades of the rainbow. Throughout the year, our world evolves and so do we. Being more aware of the world around me has helped teach me how to cook, and what nutrients our bodies need.

So, what exactly does "eating local" mean, and how can we do it consistently? It's not just eating in season and having some sort of acute awareness as to what's on the stand at the farmers' market. There's an ongoing debate as to what it means to source our ingredients locally. Does it come from down the street, did the farmer grow it from within 100 miles away, or was it grown across the state? For me, I define "local" as products sourced within my "foodshed." Think of a foodshed like a watershed. Water trickles down the mountain into the creeks and rivers and makes its way toward the ocean. A foodshed is quite similar in theory. It's the region that produces the food for that particular population and outlines the flow of feeding those people. Food flows from that area where it's grown, along the route it travels, through the markets and restaurants where it's sold and cooked, and finally to the tables where it's eaten. Typically, this is within a 1- to 300-mile radius within a given region, or even closer to home. Think about drawing this size of a circle around where you live, and make it an opportunity to discover the abundance within that foodshed.

The act of sourcing local is more than eating the fresh ingredients produced by our local farmers. Buying local means supporting the people and businesses that have a hand in bringing food from the farm to the table. While we can all debate and overthink what local means, we can't forget the value that it brings when we support our community and the local economy we share with our neighbors. This creates a deep value system that helps to shape and benefit our personal health, the impact on our carbon footprint, and our relationships with those within our community. It provides a much deeper impact and connection than buying something online that shows up in a brown box on your front porch.

We can all agree that our lives are trending to be busier and we're more engaged in our phones than in our real relationships. Guilty as charged. Our busy lives keep us from cooking day to day, and so we find ourselves eating fast food pumped full of preservatives, which tend to fill us with a quick burst of energy and then slow us down. When thinking about the benefits of eating local, I like to use the analogy of eating a fresh tomato. Would you prefer to eat a tomato in January or in July? Just like vintners making wine, every fruit and vegetable has a brix level, which is a measurement of the natural sugar content indicating the degree of ripeness. A vintner uses a fancy device called a mass spectrometer to calculate the brix so they know when it's time to harvest the grapes and make flavorful, delicious wine. Well, all fruits and vegetables have a brix level. The closer we can eat that tomato from the plant, the riper it will be—and better its flavor, the brighter its color, and the higher its quantity of nutrients.

As *thoughtful eaters* let's be more inquisitive about where our food comes from and take the time to eat what's in season. Ask a farmer about what they're growing or a fisherman about what the fresh catch is today. You'll learn a lot about what's happening in your community and make some new friends along the way.

WINTER

What's in Season?

Beets, Blood Oranges, Fennel, Cabbage, Sunchokes, Kale, Carrots, Kohlrabi, Satsuma Oranges, Lentils, Farro, Hakurei Turnips, Parsnips, Frisée, Potatoes

The energy changes after the winter equinox. The days get shorter, the air gets colder, and we spend our evenings indoors, milling around in the dark. That doesn't mean that we can't bring some sunshine to our kitchen! It's the time of the year for holiday celebrations, bringing family together, and spending time with one another. Add a warming meal that's cooked slow and low on the stove, or in the oven, and you're in a little piece of cold weather heaven.

After working all week in our restaurants, I like to stay close to the home front on weekends. We have a modest home, and I'm always happiest spending time with my family and friends in the kitchen and around the fire. On the frigid nights, there's so much comfort in creating celebration around the house and inviting others to share in the cheer of the season. I dip into my pantry to find some delicious preserved vegetables and sauces. We seriously can't eat kale every day, right? Preservation allows us to open a can of last spring or summer's harvest, shine some much-needed light on our winter meals, and nourish our loved ones. You can see the joy in your friend's and family's faces.

This time of year, we're planning celebrations for the holidays and meanwhile hunkering down for the slower, colder days of winter. If you're like me, you love prepping in the kitchen and cooking satisfying meals to pass the time when the weather's cold. Typically, we're all a lot more open to indulging when it's colder. This is the season to tuck into hearty dishes like red wine–braised beef short ribs, yellow lentil and Carolina Gold Rice kichadi, and shiitake mushroom spoonbread. These can be paired with a vegetable-forward, herbal, and crunchy side, such as a roasted beet salad, roasted sunchokes with satsuma oranges, or charred romaine with miso tahini dressing.

Mix up some cocktails and let the tall tales begin! Bring your friends and family together and create some new traditions around the table. Light a fire and cuddle up for a relaxing winter evening.

Jalapeño Biscuits

When I lived in Charleston, South Carolina, I was introduced to the Southern black pepper biscuit from Chef Donald Barickman of Magnolia's Restaurant. It was traditionally served on holidays such as Christmas and Easter, alongside baked ham and Dijon mustard. While I have always loved this traditional style of biscuit, I began experimenting with the recipe and replaced the black pepper with fresh, diced jalapeños. The heat from the jalapeño combined with the richness of the buttermilk creates a biscuit that explodes with flavor. This is a recipe I haven't looked back on since.

20 ounces self-rising flour, plus extra for rolling
1½ teaspoons kosher salt

3 jalapeños, small dice
8 ounces frozen unsalted butter

2 cups cold, whole milk buttermilk
¼ cup unsalted butter, melted

1. Preheat the oven to 450°F. Line a sheet tray with parchment paper and set aside

2. Place the flour and ¾ teaspoon of the salt into a large bowl and whisk to combine. Add the jalapeños and stir to combine. Grate the frozen butter, using the large hole on a box grater, into the flour. Work the butter into the flour by rubbing between your fingers, until it looks like small BBs.

3. Add the buttermilk to the flour mixture and mix into a shaggy wet mass. Turn the mixture out onto a floured work surface.

4. Using a rolling pin, roll the dough to 1¼ inches thick, and then cut the biscuits using a 3-inch round cutter, making sure to press straight down and not twist the cutter. Gather the scraps, pat out, and cut out biscuits as above. Place the biscuits on the prepared sheet tray and refrigerate for 30 minutes. Discard any remaining scraps.

5. Place on the middle rack of the oven and bake 20 to 25 minutes, until golden brown and cooked through.

6. Remove the biscuits from the oven, brush with the melted butter, and sprinkle with the remaining ¾ teaspoon of kosher salt. Serve immediately.

THOUGHTFUL TIP

If you can't find buttermilk at the grocery store or market, you can replace the same amount of buttermilk with heavy cream. You'll get a similar consistency with the recipe minus the tang of the buttermilk.

Banana Bread French Toast

WITH MASCARPONE, RASPBERRY PRESERVES, AND MAPLE SYRUP

SERVES 4

Isn't breakfast the most important meal of the day? It's a lot more important when you head to bed at night already craving what's on the menu the next morning. Banana bread is a great snack to accompany a cup of coffee or tea, but let's take it up a notch and make the most decadent breakfast ever! My kids love this recipe and ask for it every weekend, but we save it for fun celebrations and occasions. But, then again, sometimes you need to celebrate that you made it to the middle of this week. Treat yourself!

BANANA BREAD

½ cup plus 1 tablespoon unsalted butter, room temperature

1 cup sugar

2 large whole eggs, room temperature

3 ripe bananas

1 tablespoon whole milk

1 teaspoon vanilla extract

¾ teaspoon ground cinnamon

2 cups all-purpose flour

1 teaspoon baking powder

1 teaspoon baking soda

1 teaspoon kosher salt

FRENCH TOAST

4 large whole eggs

½ cup buttermilk

1 tablespoon sorghum

1 teaspoon vanilla paste

1 teaspoon ground cinnamon

Pinch kosher salt

2 tablespoons canola oil

½ cup whipped mascarpone cheese

½ cup Raspberry Preserves (see 269)

Fresh fruit for serving

Maple Syrup for serving

BANANA BREAD

1. Preheat the oven to 325°F. Butter a 9-by-5-by-3-inch loaf pan with 1 tablespoon of the butter.

2. Place the sugar and remaining butter into the bowl of a stand mixer fitted with the paddle attachment and beat on medium speed until lightened in color and fluffy, 2 to 3 minutes. Add the eggs, one at a time, beating after each addition, stopping to scrape down the sides of the bowl at least once.

3. Place the bananas in a small bowl and mash with a fork. Add the milk, vanilla extract, and cinnamon and stir to combine. Place the flour, baking powder, baking soda, and salt into a separate bowl and whisk to combine.

4. Add the banana mixture to the creamed butter mixture and mix on low speed for 1 minute. Add the dry ingredients and mix on low speed just until incorporated.

5. Pour the batter in the prepared pan and bake 55 to 60 minutes, until a toothpick inserted into the center comes out clean.

6. Set aside to cool on a rack for 15 minutes. Remove the bread from the pan, invert onto a rack, and cool completely before slicing.

FRENCH TOAST

1. Place the eggs, buttermilk, sorghum, vanilla paste, cinnamon, and salt into a blender. Blend on high to completely incorporate all the ingredients. Pour the egg mixture into a shallow, flat pan.

2. Cut the banana bread into eight equal slices.

3. Preheat a pan or griddle to medium heat and brush with the canola oil. Working in batches, dredge the banana bread slices into the egg mixture and place directly onto the preheated pan. Cook until golden brown, about 4 minutes. Flip and cook until golden brown on the other side, another 2 to 3 minutes. Remove the banana bread French toast from the pan and reserve warm.

4. Divide the mascarpone between four plates and smear across each plate.

5. Place two slices of the French toast on each plate and garnish with 2 tablespoons of the raspberry preserves over the French toast on each plate. Serve with fresh fruit of your choosing and the maple syrup on the side. Serve immediately.

Flat Iron Steak Sandwiches

WITH RED WINE CABBAGE, ARUGULA, AND BLUE CHEESE DRESSING

SERVES 4

I'm a carnivore and butcher at heart, although I definitely eat less meat these days. In the winter months, I tend to crave more iron, and this flat iron steak sandwich is a great way to power up your day. Here I pair the marinated and grilled flat iron steak with slowly braised red cabbage for a punch of flavor. And I top it off with a creamy blue cheese dressing to offer some richness to the sandwich.

STEAK

¼ cup extra virgin olive oil

1 teaspoon minced garlic

1 teaspoon freshly ground black pepper, plus extra to taste

1 teaspoon lemon zest

1 teaspoon finely chopped basil

1½ pounds flat iron steak, trimmed

1 teaspoon kosher salt, plus extra to taste

CABBAGE

2 tablespoons unsalted butter

¾ cup julienned red onion

1 tablespoon minced garlic

½ small head red cabbage, cored and julienned

⅓ cup red wine

5 tablespoons light brown sugar

5 tablespoons red wine vinegar

½ teaspoon kosher salt, plus extra to taste

Pinch freshly ground black pepper, plus extra to taste

Pinch red pepper flakes, plus extra to taste

BLUE CHEESE DRESSING

½ cup mayonnaise

2 tablespoons sour cream

2 tablespoons buttermilk, more if needed

3 ounces crumbled blue cheese

1 tablespoon freshly squeezed lemon juice

1 tablespoon apple cider vinegar

½ teaspoon Frank's RedHot

½ teaspoon Worcestershire sauce

2 teaspoons thinly sliced chives

¼ teaspoon kosher salt, plus extra to taste

Pinch freshly ground black pepper, plus extra to taste

8 slices thick-cut sourdough bread, toasted

½ cup thinly sliced red onion

2 cups arugula

STEAK

1. Place the olive oil, garlic, black pepper, lemon zest, and basil in a small bowl and stir to combine. Rub the steaks with the marinade, cover, and refrigerate for 2 hours. Remove from the refrigerator for at least 1 hour before cooking.

2. Preheat a grill to medium-high heat.

3. Remove the steaks from the marinade and season with salt.

4. Sear the steaks until browned on one side, 5 to 6 minutes. Flip and cook until the steaks reach an internal temperature of 135°F, 2 to 3 minutes. Remove to a cutting board and rest 5 minutes before slicing. Keep warm.

CABBAGE

1. Place a large, straight-sided pan or braising pan over medium-high heat and add the butter. Add the onions and garlic and cook until aromatic, 2 to 3 minutes.

2. Add the cabbage, stir to combine, and cook just until the cabbage begins to wilt, 2 to 3 minutes. Add the red wine, brown sugar, vinegar, salt, pepper, and red pepper flakes and stir to combine. Bring to a simmer. Decrease the heat to low, cover, and cook, stirring occasionally, until the cabbage is tender, about 1 hour.

3. Taste and adjust the seasoning. Keep warm until ready to use or cool and refrigerate for up to 2 days.

BLUE CHEESE DRESSING

1. Place the mayonnaise, sour cream, buttermilk, blue cheese, lemon juice, vinegar, hot sauce, Worcestershire sauce, chives, salt, and pepper in a mixing bowl and stir to combine. Taste and adjust seasoning as necessary. Add more buttermilk if dressing is too thick. Refrigerate for up to 1 week.

TO SERVE

1. Evenly divide the steak across four pieces of toast and top each with 4 tablespoons of red cabbage. Sprinkle the red onions over the cabbage. Place the arugula on top and spoon the blue cheese dressing on top. Cover with the remaining toast pieces and serve immediately.

THOUGHTFUL TIP

The flat iron is a tender and beefy cut that cooks quickly on the grill. I love to quickly marinate flat iron steaks and cook them to a tender medium-rare temperature over high heat on a grill for a delicious char.

Heirloom Corn Grits

WITH MUSHROOM RAGOUT AND POACHED EGGS

SERVES 4

These creamy, stone-ground grits with the shiitake mushroom ragout are a crowd-pleaser. And when you put a soft-poached egg on top, it's out of this world. The savory bowl of grits can be a nice appetizer or side dish, but it can also be a meal to itself. Get creative and try different varieties of mushrooms in your ragout, and try red wine instead of white for a fruitier flavor.

GRITS

2 tablespoons canola oil

1 cup small-dice yellow onion

1 tablespoon minced garlic

4 cups water

1 cup stone-ground grits

½ cup heavy cream

4 tablespoons unsalted butter

2 ounces Parmesan cheese, shredded

3 teaspoons Frank's RedHot

1 teaspoon kosher salt, plus extra to taste

Pinch freshly ground black pepper, plus extra to taste

MUSHROOM RAGOUT

2 tablespoons extra virgin olive oil

1 pound shiitake mushrooms, stems removed and sliced

1 cup julienned shallot

1 tablespoon minced garlic

¼ teaspoon red pepper flakes

1 cup dry white wine

2 tablespoons unsalted butter

2 tablespoons chopped parsley

½ teaspoon kosher salt, plus extra to taste

Pinch freshly ground black pepper, plus extra to taste

POACHED EGGS

2 quarts water

4 teaspoons distilled vinegar

4 large eggs

Kosher salt, to taste

Freshly ground black pepper, to taste

1 ounce Parmesan cheese, shredded

GRITS

1. Place the oil in a medium saucepan, set over medium heat, and add the onions. Cook, stirring occasionally, until the onions are translucent, about 5 minutes. Add the garlic, stir to combine, and cook until aromatic, about 1 minute.

2. Increase the heat to high, add the water, whisk to combine, and bring to a boil.

3. Add the grits in a slow steady stream while whisking continually. Bring to a simmer, stirring constantly. Once simmering, decrease the heat to low and cook, stirring frequently, until the grits are just tender, about 1 hour.

4. Bring the grits back to a simmer, add the cream, butter, Parmesan, hot sauce, salt, and pepper and whisk to combine. Keep warm.

MUSHROOM RAGOUT

1. Place a large sauté pan over medium-high heat and add the olive oil. Add the mushrooms, stir to combine, and cook until the mushrooms begin to give up some of their liquid, 6 to 7 minutes.

2. Add the shallots, garlic, and red pepper flakes and stir to combine. Cook until the shallots are translucent, 4 to 5 minutes.

3. Add the wine and deglaze the pan, scraping any fond from the bottom of the pan. Cook, stirring frequently, until the wine reduces to $\frac{1}{4}$ cup, about 5 minutes. Add the butter, parsley, salt, and pepper. Taste and adjust seasoning as necessary. Reserve warm.

POACHED EGGS

1. Place the water and vinegar in a medium saucepan, set over medium heat, and bring to a simmer.

2. Crack the eggs and place them into four small ramekins. Gently slide the eggs, one at a time, into the simmering water and cook for about 3 minutes for a soft yolk.

TO SERVE

1. Divide the grits among four bowls and then equally divide the mushroom ragout over top of each bowl of grits. Place a small divot in the grits and mushrooms with the back of a spoon. Remove the eggs from the pot with a slotted spoon and place a poached egg into the divot in each bowl of grits. Season with salt and pepper, sprinkle on the Parmesan, and serve immediately.

THOUGHTFUL TIP

When poaching eggs, I add white vinegar to the poaching water. The inherent acidity of the vinegar helps the egg whites coagulate faster and helps make the egg whites more tender. I recommend using 2 teaspoons of vinegar for every quart of water when poaching eggs.

Charred Romaine
WITH MISO TAHINI DRESSING, FRIED CROUTONS, AND MINT

SERVES 4

Caesar salad is a staple around our home. Our son, Cole, will always eat his salad when it's a Caesar. This rendition strays from the norm but is is equally flavorful with the use of tahini paste and miso in the dressing. The fried croutons provide just the right amount of crunch to enhance one of my favorite versions of this classic.

MISO TAHINI DRESSING

5 tablespoons tahini

2 tablespoons white or yellow miso

2 tablespoons freshly squeezed lemon juice

1 tablespoon minced garlic

1 teaspoon honey

¼ cup water, plus extra as needed

¼ teaspoon kosher salt, plus extra to taste

Pinch freshly ground black pepper

CROUTONS AND ROMAINE

8 tablespoons extra virgin olive oil

2 cups large-dice Pullman bread

Kosher salt, to taste

Freshly ground black pepper, to taste

4 romaine hearts, cut in half lengthwise

4 ounces Parmesan cheese, grated

1 small bunch mint, torn

2 tablespoons lemon zest

MISO TAHINI DRESSING

1. Place the tahini, miso, lemon juice, garlic, honey, water, salt, and pepper into a small bowl and whisk to combine. Add more water if the dressing is too thick to drizzle.

CROUTONS AND ROMAINE

1. Place 4 tablespoons of the oil in a medium sauté pan and over medium-high heat. Add the diced bread and fry, stirring occasionally, until golden brown, 4 to 5 minutes. Transfer to a paper towel–lined plate and sprinkle with salt and pepper.

2. Preheat a grill or grill pan to high.

3. Brush the cut sides of the romaine with the remaining 4 tablespoons of oil and sprinkle with salt and pepper. Place the romaine, cut side down, onto the grill and char for about 3 minutes, or until there are grill marks. Remove from the grill.

4. Drizzle the romaine with the dressing and garnish with the croutons, Parmesan, mint, and lemon zest.

THOUGHTFUL TIP

The legend has it that a man named Caesar Cardini invented it while working at his restaurant, Caesar's, in 1924. It's a salad recipe that has remained immensely popular for a century. While there has been a lot of myth around the origin, what is certain is that the original salad did not contain grilled romaine. My modern take adds a touch of smoky, grilled flavor that pairs wonderfully with the umami-laced miso tahini dressing.

Roasted Beet Salad

WITH BLOOD ORANGE, FARMER'S CHEESE, AND RED WINE VINAIGRETTE

SERVES 4

Roasted beets are a staple all winter long on my menus. The process of slow roasting concentrates the natural sugars and flavor of beets. Give this recipe a try, and those canned beets you dreaded as a kid will become mere thoughts from the past. Serve them as an accompaniment to roasted poultry or pork, or make them the star of the show in a salad. Here, I pair them with blood oranges, cashews, homemade farmer's cheese, and peppery mizuna. The red wine vinaigrette balances the relationship between the sweet, savory beets and the bitter mizuna.

½ cup red wine vinegar

1 teaspoon Dijon mustard

1 teaspoon minced shallots, minced

½ teaspoon minced garlic

1¼ cups plus 1 tablespoon extra virgin olive oil

1 tablespoon chopped parsley

2 teaspoons honey

1 teaspoon kosher salt, plus extra to taste

¼ teaspoon ground white pepper

1½ pounds medium yellow beets, cleaned

4 blood oranges, cut into supremes

1 cup Farmer's Cheese (page 275)

2 cups mizuna

1 cup roasted, salted cashews

Freshly ground black pepper, to taste

1. Place the vinegar, mustard, and shallots in a blender and blend until combined. With the blender running, gradually add the 1¼ cups of oil until the mixture is emulsified. Add the parsley, honey, salt, and white pepper and blend to combine. Taste and adjust seasoning as necessary.

2. Preheat the oven to 400°F.

3. Toss the beets with the 1 tablespoon of olive oil, place into a large ovenproof pan, cover tightly, and place in the oven. Roast until tender when pierced with a knife, 35 to 40 minutes.

4. Remove the pan from the oven and keep covered for 10 minutes to steam. Uncover, and using a paper towel or cloth, wipe the skins off the beets. Cut the beets into a large dice and set aside. You may refrigerate for up to 5 days.

5. Place the beets, blood oranges, farmer's cheese, mizuna, and cashews into a large bowl, add ½ cup of the red wine vinaigrette, and toss to combine. Taste and season with salt and pepper as necessary. Serve immediately.

THOUGHTFUL TIP

When roasting beets, try different varieties like 'Bull's Blood,' Chioggia, and golden beets. Make sure to roast them separately so the colors don't bleed into one another. The aim is to keep the colors vibrant across the varieties.

Rainbow Root Vegetable Gratin

SERVES 8

Taste the rainbow! It's winter and we need some bold colors in our lives. My rainbow root vegetable gratin will brighten up your dinner table and put a smile on your guests' faces. This is a riff on a traditional French potato gratin and is rich and creamy. It's a favorite side dish for children and adults alike. I love making this dish, as I enjoy the methodic slicing and then shingling up the vegetables like soldiers about to march to the oven for dinner service.

1 tablespoon extra virgin olive oil

2 tablespoons minced garlic

2 tablespoons unsalted butter, cut into 8 small pieces

1 pound Yukon Gold potatoes, peeled

1 pound sweet potatoes, peeled

1 pound celery root, peeled

1 pound red beets, peeled

3 cups heavy cream

4 large eggs

¼ teaspoon ground nutmeg

12 ounces Parmesan cheese, shredded

2 teaspoons kosher salt, plus extra as necessary

1½ teaspoons freshly ground black pepper, plus extra as necessary

Nonstick cooking spray

1. Preheat the oven to 400°F. Rub a 13-by-9-inch baking dish or roasting pan with the olive oil.

2. Sprinkle the minced garlic across the bottom of the pan and evenly dot with the butter.

3. Slice the potatoes, sweet potatoes, celery root, and beets ⅛ inch thick on a mandoline and set aside separately.

4. Place the heavy cream, eggs, nutmeg, ½ cup of the Parmesan, 1 teaspoon salt, and ½ teaspoon pepper in a mixing bowl and whisk together. Transfer one-quarter of the mixture to a separate bowl, add the beets, and toss to coat.

5. Shingle the beets from left to right across the bottom of the baking pan. Season with ¼ teaspoon each of salt and pepper, and sprinkle with ½ cup of the Parmesan.

6. Toss the celery root in the heavy cream mixture and layer as above. Repeat with the sweet potatoes and finish with the Yukon Gold potatoes.

7. Pour any remaining custard over the vegetables, pushing down to fully incorporate. You may not use all the custard. Sprinkle any remaining Parmesan on top of the potatoes.

8. Spray the bottom side of a piece of aluminum foil with cooking spray and place this side down over the baking dish.

9. Place the baking dish into a large roasting pan and place in the oven. Pour hot water in the roasting pan until it comes three-quarters of the way up the side of the baking dish.

10. Bake about 1½ hours, until the vegetables are tender when pierced with a knife.

11. Remove the foil and continue to bake until golden brown, about 20 minutes.

12. Remove from the oven and set aside to rest for 15 minutes.

13. Serve immediately or cool to room temperature. You may also place the vegetable gratin in the refrigerator for 6 hours to overnight to set. The next day cut into equal portions and reheat in a 400°F oven before serving.

THOUGHTFUL TIP

When making this gratin, always make sure to put the red beets on the bottom, and use a separate bowl to toss the beets in the custard before layering. I've made layering and mixing mistakes a few times, and instead of creating a beautiful rainbow, I've been left with a pink-colored gratin. If you want the vegetable gratin to be more even and restaurant-style, gently press the gratin while it's cooling in the refrigerator. Simply cover a piece of cardboard with aluminum foil, put it on the gratin, and place a few cans of soup on top.

Shiitake Mushroom Spoonbread

Over the holidays, I always look forward to stuffing. Yet, it always seems to be dry. Awhile back, I started making a bread pudding for dessert, and I thought it would be a great idea to make a savory bread pudding or spoonbread, and soon enough my shiitake mushroom spoonbread was born. Savory, Parmesan-filled custard helps to keep this stuffing-like dish moist and full of flavor. I like to serve it alongside a perfectly roasted piece of chicken with pan jus, and then settle into dinnertime bliss.

1 gallon large-dice Pullman bread

1 tablespoon unsalted butter

3 tablespoons extra virgin olive oil

2 cups julienned yellow onion

2 quarts stemmed and julienned shiitake mushrooms

2 tablespoons minced garlic

½ teaspoon red pepper flakes

½ teaspoon kosher salt

¼ teaspoon freshly ground black pepper

1 cup dry white wine

1 quart heavy cream

7 large eggs

8 ounces Parmesan cheese, grated

¼ cup chopped thyme

Nonstick cooking spray

1. Spread the bread on a sheet tray and leave out overnight to dry.

2. Preheat the oven to 350°F.

3. Grease a 13-by-9-inch baking dish or pan with the butter and set aside.

4. Place the olive oil in a large sauté pan and set over medium-high heat.

5. Add the onions and cook, stirring occasionally, until translucent, 3 to 4 minutes. Add the mushrooms, garlic, red pepper flakes, salt, and pepper and cook until the mushrooms have given up some of their liquid and are beginning to brown slightly, 7 to 8 minutes.

6. Add the wine and deglaze the pan, scraping any fond from the bottom of the pan. Cook, stirring continually until the wine reduces to a glaze, 5 to 6 minutes. Remove from the heat and cool to room temperature before proceeding.

7. Place the heavy cream, eggs, Parmesan, and thyme in a large bowl and whisk to combine. Add the cooled mushroom mixture and bread and stir to combine. Set aside for 5 minutes so the bread can absorb some of the liquid.

8. Scoop the mixture into the prepared baking pan and gently press down.

9. Spray the bottom side of a piece of aluminum foil with cooking spray and place this side down over the baking pan (this will keep the spoonbread from sticking to the foil).

CONTINUES →

10. Place the baking pan in a large roasting pan and set in the oven. Pour hot water in the roasting pan until it comes three-quarters up the sides of the baking pan.

11. Bake for 1 hour, remove the foil, and continue to cook until lightly browned on top, about 20 minutes.

12. Remove from the oven and serve immediately or cool to room temperature. You may also place the spoonbread in the refrigerator for up to 5 days. Cut into equal portions and reheat in a 400°F oven before serving.

THOUGHTFUL TIP

For your savory spoonbread, get creative and try adding sautéed greens or roasted winter squash, and add dollops of blue cheese or chèvre for even more flavor. This dish can become one for your repertoire.

Gnocchi

WITH BRAISED GREENS, PARSNIPS, ROASTED MUSHROOMS, AND BENNE TAHINI

SERVES 6

The word *gnocchi* can be difficult to spell—and sometimes tougher to pronounce—and gnocchi is definitely more persnickety than other Italian dishes like pasta or risotto, but these little dumplings are a favorite no matter how you spell it. My recipe puts a twist on the classic potato gnocchi with the addition of a tangy benne seed tahini, braised kale, and roasted parsnips. Gnocchi are perhaps the underdogs of Italian cuisine, falling behind pasta, but they are a wonderful dumpling to add to your kitchen menu.

BENNE TAHINI

- ½ cup benne seeds
- ¼ cup extra virgin olive oil
- 2 tablespoons freshly squeezed lemon juice
- ½ teaspoon kosher salt, plus extra to taste
- Water, as necessary

PARSNIPS

- 2 cups peeled, large-dice parsnips
- 1 tablespoon canola oil
- ½ teaspoon kosher salt

GNOCCHI

- 2½ pounds Yukon Gold potatoes
- 2 cups 00 flour, plus extra for kneading and shaping
- 1 teaspoon kosher salt, plus extra as necessary
- 2 large eggs
- 3 egg yolks
- 3 tablespoons extra virgin olive oil
- 4 tablespoons unsalted butter
- Freshly ground black pepper, to taste

- 2 cups quartered button mushrooms
- 2 tablespoons julienned shallot
- 1 teaspoon minced garlic
- ¼ teaspoon red pepper flakes
- 4 cups large chiffonade kale
- 2 cups Vegetable Stock (page 273)
- 4 tablespoons freshly squeezed lemon juice

BENNE SEED TAHINI

1. Place the benne seeds into a blender and process on medium-low speed until ground to a paste.

2. With the blender running, add the olive oil in a slow steady stream until well combined and a smooth paste is formed. Add the lemon juice and salt and continue to process to make a smooth, spoonable sauce. Adjust the consistency with water if necessary.

PARSNIPS

1. Preheat the oven to 400°F. Toss the parsnips in the oil and sprinkle with salt. Evenly spread the parsnips on a sheet tray and roast for 15 to 20 minutes or until tender. Remove from the oven and set aside.

CONTINUES →

1. Place the potatoes in a large pot, cover with water 2 inches above the potatoes, and add a heavy pinch of salt. Set over medium-high heat and bring to a simmer. Cook until the potatoes are fork-tender, about 30 minutes.

2. Line two sheet trays with parchment paper and lightly dust one with flour. Set aside.

3. Peel the potatoes and pass them through a food mill or potato ricer into a large bowl.

4. Add 1 cup of the flour and 1 teaspoon of salt and stir to combine.

5. Add the eggs and egg yolks and stir to combine. Add the remaining cup of flour and stir until fully combined and a dough begins to form.

6. Knead the dough in the bowl until it is smooth and soft to the touch without being sticky, 2 to 3 minutes. Be careful not to overwork the dough or it will become tough. Add extra flour to the dough a little at a time until it is no longer sticky.

7. Lightly dust a work surface with flour and turn out the dough.

8. Cut the dough into four equal pieces. Working with one piece of the dough at a time, roll the dough back and forth to create a 1-inch-thick "rope." Using a knife or bench scraper, cut the dough into 1-inch pieces.

9. Use a gnocchi board or the tines of a fork and roll the dough away from you while pressing with your thumb to shape the gnocchi and give it "ridges." Place the gnocchi on the prepared sheet tray. Repeat with all the dough.

10. Bring a large pot of water to a boil and generously salt. Line two sheet trays with parchment and set aside.

11. Add the gnocchi to the water, cook until they float to the surface, and then cook for another 30 to 45 seconds or until cooked through. Remove from the water with a slotted spoon and place onto the prepared sheet tray to dry.

12. Place 2 tablespoons of the olive oil in a large sauté pan and set over medium-high heat. Add the gnocchi, in batches if necessary to not overcrowd the pan, and sear until golden, 3 to 4 minutes. Flip and add 1½ tablespoons of the butter and continue to cook until tender and golden, 5 to 6 minutes. Season to taste with salt and pepper. Transfer to a bowl and keep warm. Repeat with the remaining gnocchi and butter.

13. Place the remaining tablespoon of olive oil in the sauté pan. Add the mushrooms and cook, stirring frequently, until golden, 3 to 4 minutes.

14. Add the shallots, garlic, and red pepper flakes and cook until aromatic, about 2 minutes.

15. Add the kale and cook for another minute. Add the vegetable stock, stir to combine, and cook until the liquid reduces to ½ cup.

16. Add the parsnips, 2 tablespoons of the lemon juice, and remaining 1 tablespoon of butter and stir to combine. Taste and adjust seasoning as necessary.

17. Divide the gnocchi and kale mixture evenly among six plates and drizzle with the benne tahini and the remaining 2 tablespoons of lemon juice. Serve immediately.

THOUGHTFUL TIP

There are three types of gnocchi: potato, ricotta, and Parisienne. Technically, gnocchi are not pasta, but rather dumplings. Potato gnocchi is the most common, made with flour, eggs, and boiled potatoes. The second most common is ricotta gnocchi, which is similar to potato gnocchi but has a lighter and more tender texture. Parisienne gnocchi is made from pate a choux, the same dough used to make classic French pastries such as cream puffs, éclairs, or profiteroles, and makes for a sturdy dumpling that stands up to any sauce.

Cioppino

WITH TOMATO AND FENNEL BROTH AND SOURDOUGH TOAST
WITH SAFFRON AIOLI

SERVES 6

As the holidays approach, I start thinking about menu planning for our family gathering, and I head straight for dishes that are easy to make, full of flavor, and can feed a crowd. My cioppino perfectly meets those requirements. I grew up around many Italian families, and they celebrated with the Feast of the Seven Fishes near Christmastime. This dish draws its inspiration from the Italian fishermen from the wharf in San Francisco. Let the seafood from your region help guide what varieties of fish and shellfish you choose for this recipe.

SAFFRON AIOLI

- 1 teaspoon saffron
- 1 cup water
- 1 cup mayonnaise
- 1 tablespoon Confit Garlic (page 272)
- 1 tablespoon freshly squeezed lemon juice
- ½ teaspoon kosher salt, plus extra to taste
- ¼ teaspoon ground white pepper, plus extra to taste

CIOPPINO

- 4 tablespoons extra virgin olive oil
- 1½ cups small-dice yellow onion
- 1 cup small-dice fennel bulb
- ½ cup small-dice celery
- 2 tablespoons minced garlic
- ½ teaspoon red pepper flakes
- 1 cup dry white wine
- ½ cup Pernod
- One 28-ounce can San Marzano tomatoes
- 4 cups fish stock
- Kosher salt, to taste

- Freshly ground black pepper, to taste
- 2 dozen littleneck clams, cleaned and steamed
- 1 pound mussels, cleaned and beards removed
- 1 pound snapper, large dice
- 1 pound 21/25 count shrimp, peeled and deveined
- 4 tablespoons chopped basil
- 4 tablespoons chopped parsley
- 6 thick slices sourdough bread, toasted

SAFFRON AIOLI

1. Place the saffron and water into a small saucepan, set over medium-high heat, and simmer until there is only 1 tablespoon of liquid left, about 10 minutes. Remove from the heat and set aside to cool completely.

2. Place the saffron mixture, mayonnaise, confit garlic, lemon juice, salt, and white pepper into a small bowl and whisk to combine. Set aside or refrigerate until ready to use.

3. Refrigerate for up to 1 week.

CIOPPINO

1. Place 3 tablespoons of the olive oil in a large heavy-bottom pot or Dutch oven and set over medium-high heat. Add the onions, fennel, and celery and stir to combine. Cook until the vegetables are translucent and tender, 5 to 6 minutes.

2. Add the garlic and red pepper flakes, and cook until aromatic, about 2 minutes.

3. Add the white wine and Pernod and stir to combine. Cook until the liquid reduces by half, 5 to 6 minutes.

4. Add the tomatoes and fish stock and stir to combine. Bring to a simmer and cook uncovered, stirring occasionally, until the tomatoes are tender, 25 to 30 minutes. Remove from the heat and use an immersion blender to puree to a rustic consistency. Taste and adjust seasoning with salt and pepper to taste.

5. Return to medium heat, add the clams, mussels, snapper, and shrimp, and stir to combine. Cover and cook until the mussels have opened, and the seafood is cooked through, about 5 minutes.

6. Ladle the cioppino into large, shallow bowls and drizzle with the remaining tablespoon of olive oil and garnish with the basil and parsley. Serve with toasted sourdough smeared with the saffron aioli.

THOUGHTFUL TIP

During the summer months, I can as many tomatoes as possible so that I can enjoy them over the winter months. Here's five quick steps to can your own fresh tomatoes:

1. Wash and peel the tomatoes.
2. Fill the canning jars with the tomatoes, pressing them down as you add more.
3. Add lemon juice and salt—2 tablespoons of lemon juice and 1 teaspoon of salt for quart canning jars. Leave ½ inch of head space.
4. In a boiling water canner, process the quarts for 45 minutes.
5. Cool to room temperature and store in a cool, dark place for up to 1 year.

Cioppino with Tomato and Fennel Broth
and Sourdough Toast with Saffron Aioli

One-Pan Roasted Winter Vegetables,
Rosemary, EVOO

One-Pan Roasted Winter Vegetables, Rosemary, EVOO

SERVES 4 TO 6

Looking for a quick way to please a crowd? Take a look in my oven before a party at home and you'll find winter roots roasting away. This is a super easy dish that my kids love, as do the guests in our restaurants. The key is to cut the vegetables into the same size so they roast evenly while cooking. The addition of lemon juice and lemon zest gives the veggies a much-needed zip so that their natural flavors shine. Make sure you don't overcrowd the pan or the vegetables will steam rather than properly brown while cooking.

1 cup peeled and halved cipollini onions

1 cup peeled and oblique cut carrots (see Thoughtful Tip)

1 cup peeled and oblique cut parsnips (see Thoughtful Tip)

1 cup halved radishes

1 cup halved small turnips, or quartered if larger

1 cup cauliflower florets

1 cup large-dice potatoes

1 tablespoon minced garlic

1 tablespoon lemon zest

1 tablespoon freshly squeezed lemon juice

1½ teaspoons Aleppo pepper

2 tablespoons extra virgin olive oil (EVOO)

2 tablespoons chopped rosemary

1 teaspoon kosher salt, plus extra to taste

½ teaspoon freshly ground black pepper, plus extra to taste

2 tablespoons unsalted butter, cubed

1. Preheat the oven to 400°F.

2. Place the onions, carrots, parsnips, radishes, turnips, cauliflower, potatoes, garlic, lemon zest, lemon juice, Aleppo pepper, olive oil, 1 tablespoon of the rosemary, salt, and pepper into a large mixing bowl and toss to combine.

3. Evenly spread the vegetables onto a sheet tray and dot with the cubed butter.

4. Place in the oven and roast for 20 minutes. Turn the vegetables over with a spatula and return to the oven and roast another 20 to 25 minutes, until they are tender and lightly browned.

5. Remove from the oven and transfer to a large serving bowl. Add the remaining rosemary and toss to combine. Taste and adjust the seasoning as necessary. Serve immediately.

You're probably reading the recipe and wondering what an oblique cut is. It's also known as a roll cut. It's used on vegetables to create two angled sides, and it works well on tapered vegetables to fashion pieces that are the same size and will cook evenly. The cut side creates an exposed surface that's ideal for glazing, roasting, or stir-frying. It's also an attractive cut for soups, stews, or raw vegetable platters.

Here's how to do it:

1. Starting at the tapered end of the vegetable, hold your knife at 45 degrees toward the vegetable and make a diagonal cut.

2. Roll the vegetable 90 degrees (about a quarter turn) and cut it again at the same angle.

3. Continue to roll and cut along the length of the vegetable. For very tapered vegetables, position your knife to make the cut angle more acute at the thicker end and more obtuse at the thinner end.

Roasted Sunchokes, Satsuma Orange, Shaved Tomme, and Marcona Almond

SERVES 4

It's wintertime and we can't eat only potatoes. Enter sunchokes! These fun, knobby little nuggets taste amazing when roasted just like their tuber counterpart, and they are even better when paired with sweet satsuma oranges, shaved buttery Tomme, and toasted Marcona almonds. Pair this side dish with a piece of roasted fish or chicken for a well-rounded dinner, or bring it to your next dinner party—your friends will definitely be inviting you back.

2 pounds sunchokes, cleaned and cut into 1-inch pieces

1 tablespoon canola oil

1 tablespoon unsalted butter, melted

½ teaspoon kosher salt, plus extra to taste

Pinch freshly ground black pepper

12 sprigs plus 1 tablespoon chopped thyme

6 garlic cloves, smashed

2 satsuma oranges, pulled into pieces

2 ounces Tomme, shaved

¾ cup Marcona almonds

1. Preheat the oven to 400°F.

2. Place the sunchokes, canola oil, butter, salt, and pepper in a medium bowl and toss to combine.

3. Evenly spread the sunchokes onto a nonstick sheet tray or a tray lined with parchment paper and scatter the thyme sprigs and garlic cloves around the tray.

4. Roast until the sunchokes are golden and tender, 30 to 35 minutes.

5. Remove the thyme sprigs and transfer the sunchokes to a serving bowl. Scatter the satsuma segments, Tomme, and almonds over the sunchokes and sprinkle with chopped thyme. Serve immediately.

THOUGHTFUL TIP

Satsuma mandarin oranges are typically a little smaller and sweeter than your standard oranges, and they have a looser skin that makes them easier to peel. First appearing some 700 years ago and named after their place of origin, the Satsuma region of Japan, these oranges usually have 10 to 12 segments that easily pull apart. This makes them the perfect snack when you're on the go.

Kichadi, Split Yellow Lentils, Carolina Gold Rice, Lime Yogurt, and Almond Chile Crumble

SERVES 4

When I think of comfort food, I reminisce on my youth when I was sick and home from a day at school. My mom would make me tomato soup and grilled cheese, and I would watch *The Price is Right* and *The French Chef* hosted by Julia Child and all seemed to be right in the world. Fast forward to today: I'm married to a wonderful Indian woman who has introduced me to many new flavors, as well as new types of comfort food. For her, comfort food is kichadi, undhiyu, or thepla with ghee and jaggery. Kichadi is a quick and easy dinner that's packed with protein and flavor. We love it when we need a pick-me-up or a healthy dinner on the go.

LIME YOGURT

½ cup Greek yogurt

1 teaspoon lime zest

1 teaspoon freshly
  squeezed lime juice

½ teaspoon ground cumin

½ teaspoon kosher salt,
  plus extra to taste

CHILE CRUMBLE

2 tablespoons extra virgin olive oil

1 teaspoon minced garlic

1 tablespoon minced
  Fresno pepper

½ cup slivered, toasted almonds

¼ cup Panko bread crumbs

1 tablespoon chopped cilantro

½ teaspoon kosher salt,
  plus extra to taste

KICHADI

½ cup split yellow lentils

½ cup Carolina Gold rice

1 tablespoon extra virgin olive oil

1 teaspoon peeled, minced ginger

1 teaspoon minced garlic

½ teaspoon ground cumin

¼ teaspoon brown mustard seeds

¼ teaspoon ground turmeric

¼ teaspoon asafetida

¼ teaspoon ground red
  chili powder

2 whole cloves

½ teaspoon kosher salt,
  plus extra to taste

4 cups water

1 teaspoon freshly
  squeezed lime juice

Pinch freshly ground black pepper

¼ cup unsalted butter

4 curry leaves

½ cup cilantro sprigs

4 lime wedges

LIME YOGURT

1. Place the yogurt, lime zest, lime juice, cumin, and salt into a small bowl and whisk to combine. Taste and adjust seasoning as necessary. Cover and refrigerate for up to 3 days.

CHILE CRUMBLE

1. Place the olive oil in a small sauté pan set over medium heat. Add the garlic and cook until aromatic, about 30 seconds. Add the Fresno peppers, stir to combine, and remove the pan from the heat. Cool to room temperature.

2. Place the almonds and bread crumbs into a food processor and pulse five or six times, until roughly chopped. Add the Fresno pepper and garlic mixture and process to combine. Add the cilantro and salt and process to combine. Taste and adjust seasoning as necessary. Cover and refrigerate for up to 3 days.

KICHADI

1. Place the lentils and rice into a small bowl, cover with water by 1 inch, and set aside to soak for 20 minutes. Strain the mixture through a fine mesh strainer.

2. Place the olive oil in a large heavy-bottom pot or Dutch oven and set over medium heat. Add the ginger and garlic and cook until aromatic, about 1 minute. Add the cumin, mustard seeds, turmeric, asafetida, red chili powder, cloves, and salt and stir to combine. Cook, stirring frequently, to toast the spices, about 30 seconds.

3. Add the lentil and rice mixture and stir for 1 minute. Add the water and stir to combine. Bring the mixture to a boil and cook for 1 minute. Cover with a tight-fitting lid and reduce the heat to low. Cook for 10 minutes and then turn off the heat and leave to steam until the rice and lentils are tender, 7 to 8 minutes.

4. Remove the lid and fluff the kichadi with a fork. Add the lime juice and freshly ground black pepper. Taste and adjust the seasoning as necessary.

5. Place the butter in a small sauté pan set over medium heat. When the butter begins to bubble, add the curry leaves and cook until they are lightly fried and aromatic, 1 to 2 minutes. Remove to a paper towel–lined plate to drain. Reserve the butter and leaves separately.

6. Divide the kichadi among four bowls. Garnish each bowl with a tablespoon of the lime yogurt and almond chile crumble. Equally spoon the reserved butter over each dish and garnish with the cilantro and a curry leaf. Serve with lime wedges.

THOUGHTFUL TIP

A complete protein that packs a big nutritional punch, kichadi is a very beneficial food for gut and digestive health. It helps to cleanse and rejuvenate your system. And on top of that, it packs a powerful boost to energize your body for the day. While there are many renditions of this dish, it's no wonder that every variation is a staple in the diet of so many across the continent of India!

Kichadi, Split Yellow Lentils, Carolina Gold Rice, Lime Yogurt, and Almond Chile Crumble

Raw Oysters on the Half Shell with Fennel, Chile, and Orange Mignonette

Raw Oysters on the Half Shell

WITH FENNEL, CHILE, AND ORANGE MIGNONETTE

SERVES 4

Oysters have been around planet Earth for about 15 million years! They are a delicious and very sustainable bivalve mollusk. Their salty, briny, sweet, and even cucumber-like finish is a craveable delicacy. This simple recipe for mignonette, a typical accompaniment for oysters, is perfect to use with shucked raw oysters. Here, I'm using Mintersweet oysters from Minter Bay, which are a wonderful oyster from the cold waters of Washington State. The fennel, chile, and orange mignonette is an easy way to bring a bright burst of flavor to these freshly shucked oysters without overshadowing their raw beauty. Break out your oyster knife and give it a try!

½ cup champagne vinegar

1 tablespoon orange zest

¼ cup freshly squeezed orange juice

1 teaspoon freshly ground black pepper

1 tablespoon brunoise-cut shallots

2 tablespoons brunoise-cut fennel bulb

1 teaspoon finely chopped fennel fronds

1 tablespoon seeded, brunoise-cut Fresno chile

Pinch kosher salt

2 dozen fresh oysters, scrubbed clean

Crushed ice, for serving

4 lemon wedges, for serving

1. Combine the vinegar, orange zest, orange juice, black pepper, shallots, fennel bulb, fennel fronds, and chile in a small bowl. Taste and adjust the salt as necessary.

2. Lay a folded kitchen towel on a work surface and place a cleaned oyster on the towel. Place another towel in the hand opposite of your shucking hand and place this towel directly onto the oyster to stabilize and secure it.

3. Place the oyster knife tip into the rear hinge of the oyster and twist the knife to pry open the shell. Rotate the blade to separate the top shell from the bottom shell.

4. Wipe the blade clean on the towel, and sever the muscle (the oyster) from the foot to detach it from the shell. Be careful not to puncture the oyster as you are in the process of shucking.

5. Place the oysters on their shells, onto a platter with crushed ice, and serve with the mignonette and lemon wedges.

THOUGHTFUL TIP

One oyster can filter up to 50 gallons of water per day, helping to both clean the water they live in and sequester carbon dioxide and nitrogen from the atmosphere. Oysters also establish reefs that attract many species of fish and shellfish, which in turn create a habitat for even more species in our oceans.

Smoked Rainbow Trout

WITH ROASTED BEETS, PRESERVED LEMON, ENDIVE,
AND GREEN GODDESS DRESSING

SERVES 4

Roll cast, mend, repeat. That's the mindset of a fly fisherman. When I actually have time to get away, I spend time in the water, watching the river run by and searching for elusive brown and rainbow trout. Fly-fishing has become one of my favorite hobbies. There is something therapeutic about being in nature, looking under rocks on the streamside to see what bugs and larvae are hatching, and being on the hunt for wild trout, knee-deep in rushing water. For me, it's a way to reset and recharge before starting any of life's big adventures. Here, I've taken some rainbow trout and gently smoked them to make a salad that goes great for lunchtime, or makes a showstopper first course at dinner.

SMOKED TROUT AND PECANS

Two 8-ounce skin-on trout
  fillets, pin bones removed
1 quart Standard Brine (page 274)
1 cup pecan halves
1 teaspoon canola oil
½ teaspoon light brown sugar
½ teaspoon ancho chili powder
¼ teaspoon kosher salt

TO SERVE

1 pound yellow beets,
  roasted, peeled, and cut
  into bite-size pieces
4 heads Belgian endive, stem
  end removed and quartered
½ cup thinly sliced radishes
¼ cup julienned Preserved
  Lemons (page 269)
¼ cup thinly sliced fennel bulb

⅓ cup White Wine and Herb
  Vinaigrette (page 273)
1 teaspoon kosher salt,
  plus extra to taste
¼ teaspoon freshly ground black
  pepper, plus extra to taste
½ cup Green Goddess
  Dressing (page 273)
¼ cup chives, cut into 1-inch sticks
¼ cup trout roe, for
  serving (optional)

SMOKED TROUT AND PECANS

1. Preheat a smoker to 185°F.

2. Place the trout fillets into the brine for 20 minutes.

3. Remove the trout from the brine, rinse under cold water, and pat dry. Place directly onto the smoker and cook for 45 minutes to 1 hour, until the internal temperature of the trout reaches 145°F, and the trout flakes easily.

4. Remove the trout from the smoker and set aside until ready to use. You may wrap tightly in plastic wrap and refrigerate for up to 5 days.

5. Place the pecans, canola oil, brown sugar, chili powder, and salt in a cast-iron skillet and toss to combine. Place the skillet in the smoker and smoke for 30 minutes, or until the smoke flavor has penetrated the nuts. Allow to cool and keep at room temperature in a tightly sealed container for up to 2 weeks.

CONTINUES →

1. Place the pecans, beets, fennel, endive, radishes, preserved lemons, white wine, and herb vinaigrette, salt, and pepper into a large bowl and toss to combine.

2. Spread 2 tablespoons of the green goddess dressing across each of the four plates. Equally divide the salad among the plates.

3. Break the smoked trout into 16 equal pieces and divide among the plates. Garnish with the chives and trout roe, if using, and serve immediately.

THOUGHTFUL TIP

Trout caviar, aka trout roe, may not be the exotic and expensive delicacy that we get from sturgeon caviar, but it is an exceptional product. Trout are the quintessential North American fish that run across the United States and Canada. Found in the same family as salmon and char, they live in cold fresh water, typically in mountain streams and lakes. Their roe, or caviar, have a deep orange hue and deliver a sensational "pop" when eaten. The delicate, sweet, salty roe are the perfect garnish for salads, soups, custards, and other light fare.

Wild Striped Bass

WITH ROASTED CARROTS, BRAISED CIPOLLINI ONIONS, AND HAM HOCK JUS

SERVES 4

Years ago, I had the chance to eat at the famed Highlands Bar & Grill in Birmingham, Alabama. Chef Frank Stitt had the most amazing snapper dish on his menu, which was served with a rich jus scented with red wine and smoked ham hocks. The dish haunted and enticed me for years as I tried to re-create his recipe. It's amazing how food memories can imprint on our mind and flavors can stay with you and remind you of past times. But while I'll never be able to replicate that particular experience, I have created my rendition of his recipe. I use wild striped bass and its skin gets super crispy when pan roasted. Try other firm but tender white fish such as snapper, sea bass, branzino, or flounder in this recipe. My ham hock jus uses apple cider in a few different forms to create a sweet acidity that helps balance the rich smokiness of the ham hocks.

HAM HOCK JUS

4 quarts Chicken Stock (page 274)

1 ham hock

One 12-ounce bottle hard apple cider

1 quart fresh apple cider

½ cup apple cider vinegar

ROASTED CARROTS

1 pound petite carrots, ends removed and peeled

1 tablespoon extra virgin olive oil

½ teaspoon kosher salt, plus extra to taste

¼ teaspoon freshly ground black pepper, plus extra to taste

1 tablespoon unsalted butter

BRAISED CIPOLLINI ONIONS

1 tablespoon extra virgin olive oil

1 pound cipollini onions, peeled

½ teaspoon kosher salt, plus extra to taste

¼ teaspoon freshly ground black pepper

3 garlic cloves, smashed

6 thyme sprigs

1 cup white wine

1 tablespoon unsalted butter

STRIPED BASS

Four 6- to 8-ounce skin-on wild striped bass fillets, pin bones removed

½ teaspoon kosher salt, plus extra to taste

½ teaspoon ground white pepper, plus extra to taste

2 tablespoons extra virgin olive oil

3 garlic cloves, smashed

6 thyme sprigs

2 tablespoons unsalted butter

HAM HOCK JUS

1. Place the chicken stock and ham hock into a large, heavy-bottom pot or Dutch oven, set over medium-high heat, and reduce to 4 cups, about 1 hour.

2. Place the hard apple cider, fresh apple cider, and apple cider vinegar into a medium, heavy-bottom pot, set over high heat, and reduce to 1½ cups.

3. Add the reduced cider mixture to the pot with the ham hock, set over high heat, and reduce the liquid to about 2½ cups, 15 to 20 minutes.

4. Remove the ham hock and set aside to cool. Once cool enough to handle, remove the skin from the ham hock and dice the meat. Return the meat to the sauce.

5. Allow the sauce to cool and refrigerate for up to 1 week or freeze for later use.

CONTINUES →

ROASTED CARROTS

1. Preheat the oven to 425°F.

2. Place the carrots in a large bowl and toss with the olive oil, salt, and pepper.

3. Arrange the carrots in a single layer on a sheet tray and dot with the butter. Place in the oven and roast 20 to 25 minutes, until the carrots are golden and tender when pierced with a knife. Remove from the oven and reserve warm.

CIPOLLINI ONIONS

1. Heat the olive oil in a large sauté pan over medium-high heat. Add the onions to the pan, stem side down, sprinkle with salt and pepper and cook until the onions are golden brown, 5 to 6 minutes.

2. Flip the onions and cook for another 2 minutes. Add the garlic and thyme and deglaze the pan with the white wine, scraping any fond from the bottom of the pan.

3. Reduce the heat to medium-low and cover the pan with a tight-fitting lid. Braise the onions for 5 minutes. Remove the lid and increase the heat to medium, cooking until the sauce has reduced by half, about 3 minutes. Add the butter and stir to combine. Remove from the heat and keep warm.

STRIPED BASS

1. Score the skin to keep it from curling while cooking and dry the skin with a paper towel. Season the fish with salt and white pepper.

2. Heat the olive oil in a large oven-safe sauté pan, set over medium-high heat and once the oil shimmers, place the fish skin side down into the pan. Make sure to lay the fish down away from you so you don't splash oil. Cook until the skin is golden and crispy, 3 to 4 minutes. Place the pan into the oven without disturbing the fish and roast for another 4 to 5 minutes, until a meat thermometer registers 140°F. Remove the fish from the oven and place back on a burner over medium-high heat. Add the garlic, thyme, and butter. As the butter melts, baste the fish three to four times. Remove the fish from the pan and keep warm.

3. Divide the vegetables among four shallow bowls and ladle the ham hock jus around the vegetables, making sure to spoon some of the meat around the bowl. Place a portion of fish over the vegetables and serve immediately.

THOUGHTFUL TIP

If you are strapped for time, you can cook the dish more quickly by pan roasting the onions and carrots and then adding the ham hock directly to that pan and slowly simmering the vegetables in the ham hock jus until they are tender.

Crispy Pork Belly

WITH PINK LADY APPLE AND FRISÉE SALAD
WITH BOURBON CIDER DRESSING

SERVES 6

There's nothing as delicious as a slow-roasted piece of pork belly. It takes a day or two to prepare, but everyone in your household will thank you when the scent of slow-roasting pork emanates from the kitchen. I love to top my crispy, slow-roasted pork belly with a sweet sauce to offset the richness of the pork. Earthy and sweet sorghum provide a wonderful contrast, and the crunchy roasted peanuts give it the perfect bite. To lend a vibrant and refreshing bite to accompany the pork, round out the meal with a bitter and sweet frisée and apple salad, tossed in my bourbon cider dressing.

PORK BELLY

½ cup kosher salt

½ cup minced garlic

5 tablespoons brown sugar

2 tablespoons freshly ground black pepper

2 tablespoons orange zest

1 bunch thyme sprigs

10 bay leaves, crumbled

3-pound slab, skin-off pork belly

APPLE AND FRISÉE SALAD

¼ cup apple cider vinegar

½ cup apple cider

2½ tablespoons sorghum

1 tablespoon minced shallot

1 tablespoon bourbon

½ tablespoon Dijon mustard

1 teaspoon minced garlic

½ teaspoon kosher salt, plus extra to taste

¼ teaspoon freshly ground black pepper

½ cup extra virgin olive oil

4 cups frisée

1 large thinly sliced Pink Lady apple

½ cup julienned red onion

2 tablespoons sliced chives

6 tablespoons sorghum

1 cup roasted, salted, and crushed peanuts

PORK BELLY

1. Place the salt, garlic, brown sugar, black pepper, orange zest, thyme, and bay leaves in a medium bowl and stir to combine. Place the pork belly into a container where it can lay flat and rub with the cure, making sure to pack the cure around the belly. Refrigerate for 6 to 8 hours to cure.

2. Remove from the refrigerator, rinse off the cure under cold water, and pat dry.

3. Preheat the oven to 450°F.

4. Place the pork belly fat side up in a roasting pan, set in the oven, and cook for 1 hour, basting once or twice, until the pork begins to brown.

5. Decrease the heat to 250°F and cook for another 1½ hours, or until the pork is tender when pierced with a knife.

6. Remove the pork from the oven and set aside in the pan to cool to room temperature.

CONTINUES →

7. Drain the fat from the roasting pan. Place another pan on top of the belly and weigh down with canned vegetables to press the pork. Place in the refrigerator for at least 2 hours to completely cool, or overnight.

8. Remove the pork from the refrigerator and cut into six equal, square portions.

9. Place the pork, fat side down, into a large sauté pan and set over medium-low heat. Cook until the pork is crisp and brown, 4 to 5 minutes.

10. Flip the pork over and cook for an additional 4 to 5 minutes, until the pork is crispy and heated through. Set aside and keep warm.

APPLE AND FRISÉE SALAD

1. Place the vinegar, apple cider, 2½ tablespoons sorghum, shallots, bourbon, Dijon, garlic, salt, and pepper in a medium bowl and whisk together. Slowly pour in the olive oil and whisk to emulsify. Taste and adjust the seasoning as necessary.

2. Place the frisée, apples, and onions in a mixing bowl, add ¼ cup of the dressing, and toss to coat. Add additional dressing as necessary. Add the chives and toss to combine. Taste and adjust the seasoning as necessary.

3. Evenly divide the pork belly among six plates and drizzle evenly with the 6 tablespoons sorghum. Sprinkle the crushed peanuts over the pork belly and garnish each plate with an equal portion of the frisée and apple salad. Serve immediately.

THOUGHTFUL TIP

The art of the cure is an important step in building flavor. Just like in our recipe for braised duck legs, we use a salt and sugar cure to help tenderize the pork belly by drawing moisture out of the meat. This not only helps to build flavor but also helps prepare the meat for further preservation, like smoking over wood fire.

Pan-Roasted Wild Grouper

WITH BROWN BUTTER SHRIMP AND ANCHOVY CAPER SAUCE

SERVES 4

With briny capers, anchovies, confit garlic, and herbs, the sauce is the star of the show in this simple winter fish dish. It gives a punchy and vibrant tang to the gently cooked grouper and rich, buttery shrimp. Here I use grouper, but any firm and flavorful white fish will work. And while it's not in the recipe, I like to serve this alongside rice or a whole grain such as farro.

ANCHOVY CAPER SAUCE
- 6 cloves Confit Garlic (page 272)
- 6 white anchovy fillets
- 1 tablespoon rinsed capers
- Zest from 1 large lemon
- 3 tablespoons freshly squeezed lemon juice
- ½ cup chopped chives
- ¾ cup extra virgin olive oil
- Kosher salt, to taste
- Freshly ground black pepper, to taste

GROUPER AND SHRIMP
- Four 6-ounce skin-off grouper fillets, pin bones removed
- Twelve 21/25 count, peeled and deveined shrimp
- ½ teaspoon kosher salt, plus extra to taste
- ¼ teaspoon ground white pepper, plus extra to taste
- 2 tablespoons extra virgin olive oil
- 4 tablespoons unsalted butter
- 1 tablespoon freshly squeezed lemon juice
- 4 lemon wedges

ANCHOVY CAPER SAUCE

1. Place the confit garlic, anchovies, capers, lemon zest, lemon juice, chives, and olive oil into a food processor and process until fully combined. Taste and add salt and pepper as necessary. Set aside or cover and refrigerate for up to 3 days.

GROUPER AND SHRIMP

1. Preheat the oven to 425°F.

2. Season the grouper and shrimp with salt and white pepper.

3. Place the olive oil in a large oven-proof sauté pan and set over medium-high heat. Once the oil shimmers, add the grouper to the pan. Cook until the grouper is beginning to brown, 4 to 5 minutes.

4. Place the pan into the oven and roast for another 4 to 5 minutes, until the internal temperature reaches 140°F.

5. Remove the pan from the oven and transfer the grouper to a plate. Cover with foil to keep warm.

CONTINUES →

6. Pour out the oil from the pan, return the pan to medium-high heat, and add the butter. As the butter begins to foam and turn light brown, add the shrimp, and cook for 2 to 3 minutes. Flip and cook for another 1 to 2 minutes on the other side. Add the lemon juice and toss to evenly combine.

7. Divide the grouper evenly among four plates. Top the grouper with shrimp and spoon over the anchovy sauce. Serve with lemon wedges.

THOUGHTFUL TIP

Capers are the unripened green flower bud of the caper bush, or Flinders rose, that grow wild in the Mediterranean. Once they are harvested, the buds are dried and then preserved by packing in salt or pickling brine. These little buds provide a lemony, briny tang and a salty and floral boost when added into a sauce or used as a garnish.

Pork Milanese, aka "Fried Pork Chops"

WITH PRESERVED SUMMER VEGETABLES, GRAIN MUSTARD DRESSING, AND HEIRLOOM PEPPER SAUCE

SERVES 2

Pork chops are a quintessentially American dish, but their roots run deep. Head to Germany and eat a pork schnitzel, or ride on over to Italy and try a pork Milanese, or here in the States belly up for a fried pork chop sandwich. While the pork chops many of us ate growing up made it to the table dry and tough (Did someone say, "Shake 'n Bake?"), my pork Milanese will end up crispy, juicy, and tender. In the middle of winter, when the temperature is cold and the sun is low, the fixings get thin because our farms are producing less. So, it's a great time to dip into your preserved veggie stash in your pantry to brighten up your crispy pork chops.

MUSTARD DRESSING

1½ tablespoons aged sherry vinegar

1 tablespoon whole-grain mustard

1 tablespoon freshly squeezed lemon juice

1 teaspoon honey

1 teaspoon minced garlic

½ cup extra virgin olive oil

Kosher salt, to taste

Freshly ground black pepper, to taste

PEPPER SAUCE

½ cup Preserved Jimmy Nardello Peppers (page 271)

2 cloves Confit Garlic (page 272)

3 tablespoons extra virgin olive oil

Kosher salt, to taste

PICKLED VEGETABLES

½ cup Sour Corn (page 271)

½ cup Pickled Tomatoes, cut in half (page 268)

½ cup Pickled Okra, cut into rings (page 264)

½ cup Pickled Yellow Squash, diced (page 268)

2 tablespoons chives, cut into 1-inch pieces

2 tablespoons basil leaves, torn

Freshly ground black pepper, taste

PORK CHOPS

Two 16-ounce bone-in pork chops

½ gallon Standard Brine (page 274)

1 cup all-purpose flour

3 teaspoons kosher salt, plus extra to taste

2½ teaspoons freshly ground black pepper, plus extra to taste

3 large eggs

1 cup Panko bread crumbs

2 tablespoons thyme leaves

1 cup canola oil

MUSTARD DRESSING

1. Place the vinegar, mustard, lemon juice, honey, and garlic into a small bowl and whisk to combine. Add the olive oil in a steady stream while whisking continually until emulsified. Taste and adjust the seasoning with salt and pepper as necessary. Cover and refrigerate for up to 1 week.

PEPPER SAUCE

1. Place the preserved Jimmy Nardello peppers and confit garlic in a small food processor and process on high speed until pureed. With the processor running, add the oil to emulsify the sauce. Taste and adjust the seasoning as necessary with salt. Cover and refrigerate for up to 5 days.

CONTINUES →

PICKLED VEGETABLES

1. Place the sour corn, pickled tomatoes, pickled okra, pickled yellow squash, chives, and basil in a small bowl. Add ¼ cup of the mustard dressing and toss to combine. Taste and adjust the seasoning with black pepper, as necessary.

PORK CHOPS

1. Place the pork chops into a clean container, cover with the brine, and refrigerate for 4 hours.

2. Remove the pork chops from the brine, rinse, and pat dry.

3. Lay a piece of plastic wrap or parchment onto a cutting board or clean work surface. Cover the pork chops with a piece of plastic wrap and pound the pork chops to ½ inch thickness.

4. Place the flour, 1 teaspoon of the salt, and 1 teaspoon of the black pepper into a flat-bottomed container and whisk to combine.

5. Place the eggs, 1 teaspoon of the salt, and ½ teaspoon of the black pepper in a flat-bottomed container and whisk to combine.

6. Place the bread crumbs, thyme, 1 teaspoon of salt, and 1 teaspoon of black pepper into a food processor and process until the bread crumbs are finer, about 30 seconds. Place the mixture into a flat-bottomed container.

7. Dredge the pork chops on all sides in the flour mixture and pat off the excess.

8. Dredge in the egg mixture next. Finally, dredge in the bread crumb mixture. Set aside.

9. Place a large cast-iron skillet over medium heat and add the canola oil. Once the oil shimmers, add the pork chops, in two batches if necessary, and fry until golden brown, 6 to 8 minutes. Flip the pork chops and cook until the pork chop reaches an internal temperature of 160°F and is golden brown, 6 to 8 minutes.

10. Place 3 tablespoons of the pepper sauce across the bottom of two large plates.

11. Place a pork chop on top of each plate and garnish with the vegetables. Serve immediately.

THOUGHTFUL TIP

Chef Sean Brock said, "He who dies with the biggest pantry wins." He would have gotten along well with my grandmother, who also preserved everything from her garden for moments like these when options are slim. In the middle of winter we need flavor! Dive headfirst into your pantry and pull out those preserved and pickled vegetables you've been putting up all year in preparation for the cold months.

Baked Sheepshead Fish
WITH BELUGA LENTILS, MIREPOIX, AND VADOUVAN BUTTER

The first time I put sheepshead on a menu I wondered why it wasn't selling. For me, it obviously wasn't the head of a certain type of livestock, but rather a wonderful ocean fish that offers one of the most delicious flavors from the coast. Known as the convict fish, because of its black and white stripes, its diet consists of crabs, shrimp, oysters, and mussels giving it a flavor that is sweet with a slight shellfish flavor. How can they eat through the shells? With gnarly teeth, sheepshead are able to eat and grind down the hard shells of some of the ocean's tastiest shellfish and mollusks.

VADOUVAN SPICE

2 tablespoons ground cumin

2 teaspoons (about 5) curry leaves

1¼ teaspoons garlic powder

¾ teaspoon fenugreek seed

¾ teaspoon brown mustard seed

¼ teaspoon ground turmeric

¼ teaspoon ground nutmeg

¼ teaspoon chili powder

4 whole cloves

2 green cardamom pods

VADOUVAN BUTTER

1 tablespoon extra virgin olive oil

4 tablespoons minced shallot

1 teaspoon peeled, minced ginger

1 teaspoon minced garlic

6 curry leaves, finely chopped

1 tablespoon Vadouvan Spice (recipe included)

½ cup unsalted butter, room temperature

1 tablespoon lime zest

½ teaspoon kosher salt

LENTILS

1 tablespoon extra virgin olive oil

½ cup small-dice bacon

¼ cup small-dice yellow onions

¼ cup peeled, small-dice carrots

¼ cup small-dice celery

4½ cups water

1½ cups beluga lentils

½ teaspoon dried thyme

½ teaspoon kosher salt, plus extra to taste

Freshly ground black pepper, to taste

2 tablespoons unsalted butter

2 tablespoons freshly squeezed lemon juice

SHEEPSHEAD

2 pounds sheepshead fish fillet, skinned, pin bones removed

2 tablespoons extra virgin olive oil

½ teaspoon kosher salt

½ teaspoon ground white pepper

4 slices Vadouvan Butter (recipe included)

VADOUVAN SPICE

1. Place the cumin, curry leaves, garlic powder, fenugreek, mustard seed, turmeric, nutmeg, chili powder, cloves, and cardamom pods in a small bowl and stir to combine.

2. Transfer the spices to a small sauté pan and set over medium heat. Toast the spices for 1 minute, or until aromatic. Remove the pan from the heat and transfer the spices back to the bowl to cool to room temperature.

3. Place the spices into a spice grinder and grind. Store in an airtight container at room temperature for up to 2 months.

VADOUVAN BUTTER

1. Place the olive oil in a small sauté pan, set over medium heat, and add the shallots. Cook, stirring often, until the shallots are translucent, about 3 minutes. Add the ginger, garlic, and curry leaves and cook for 3 to 4 minutes, stirring often.

2. Add the vadouvan spice and cook until aromatic, 1 to 2 minutes. Remove from the heat and scrape onto a plate to cool.

3. Place the butter into the bowl of a stand mixer fitted with the paddle attachment and add the shallot and spice mixture, lime juice, and salt and mix on medium speed until fully incorporated. Taste and season with additional salt as necessary.

4. Place the compound butter onto plastic wrap and roll into a cylinder. Refrigerate for up to 1 week or freeze until needed.

LENTILS

1. Place the olive oil and bacon into a medium saucepan, set over medium-low heat, and cook the bacon until it is brown and crispy and has rendered its fat, 6 to 7 minutes. Transfer the bacon to a paper towel–lined plate to drain.

2. Add the onions, carrots, and celery and cook until the onions are translucent, 4 to 5 minutes. Add the water, lentils, thyme, and salt and raise the heat to medium and bring to a simmer. Cook the lentils, stirring occasionally, until they are tender, 25 to 30 minutes.

3. Add the reserved bacon, butter, and lemon juice and stir to combine. Taste and adjust the seasoning with salt and pepper as necessary. Keep warm.

SHEEPSHEAD

1. Preheat the oven to 425°F.

2. Cut the sheepshead into four equal portions and dry the flesh with a paper towel. Rub a sheet tray with 1 tablespoon of the olive oil.

3. Place the fish onto the oiled sheet tray and rub the fish with the remaining olive oil and season with the salt and white pepper.

4. Place the fish into the oven and roast 10 to 12 minutes, until a meat thermometer reaches 140°F and the fish flakes.

5. Remove from the oven and top each piece of fish with a slice of the vadouvan butter.

6. Divide the lentils among four bowls and top each with a portion of sheepshead. Serve immediately.

Red Wine–Braised Beef Short Ribs
WITH BLUE CHEESE AND GREEN APPLE SLAW AND CUMIN CHILI SAUCE

SERVES 4

Beef short ribs braised in red wine is one of my all-time favorites. In this classic dish, the meat becomes tender and rich in flavor from slow braising in red wine. To help balance the richness of the short ribs, in place of a more traditional preparation I like to provide a tangy coleslaw made with green apples and buttermilk blue cheese, and serve it with a thick spoonful of cumin chili sauce.

CUMIN CHILI SAUCE

8 dried ancho chile peppers

½ cup white wine vinegar

½ cup granulated sugar

One 2-inch piece ginger, peeled and sliced

8 whole garlic cloves, smashed

2 teaspoons paprika

2 teaspoons ground cumin

1 teaspoon ground turmeric

1 tablespoon lime juice

2 tablespoons lime zest

2 tablespoons olive oil

1 tablespoon kosher salt

½ teaspoon ground black pepper

RED WINE–BRAISED SHORT RIBS

6 pounds bone-in beef chuck short ribs

4 tablespoons canola oil

1 tablespoon kosher salt, plus extra to taste

1 teaspoon freshly ground black pepper

2 bottles dry red wine

1 medium yellow onion, large dice

6 stalks celery, large dice

5 carrots, peeled and cut into large dice

4 whole garlic cloves, smashed

2 bay leaves

12 thyme sprigs

1 teaspoon black peppercorns

2 tablespoons unsalted butter

GREEN APPLE SLAW

¼ cup mayonnaise

¼ cup sour cream

¼ cup apple cider vinegar

2 tablespoons freshly squeezed lemon juice

2 tablespoons granulated sugar

1 teaspoon Dijon mustard

1 teaspoon minced garlic

4 cups thinly sliced green cabbage

1 green apple, cored and julienned

½ cup crumbled buttermilk blue cheese

¼ cup thinly sliced red onion

2 carrots, peeled and julienned

2 tablespoons thinly sliced scallions

Frank's RedHot, to taste

Kosher salt, to taste

Freshly ground black pepper, to taste

CUMIN CHILI SAUCE

1. Place the dried chile peppers in a small bowl and cover with boiling water. Set aside for 15 minutes. Remove the peppers from the hot water and set aside until cool enough to handle. Remove the stems and discard. Roughly chop the peppers.

2. Place the peppers, vinegar, sugar, ginger, garlic, paprika, cumin, and turmeric into a small saucepan, set over medium-high heat, and bring to a boil. Reduce the heat and simmer for 5 minutes. Remove from the heat and cool to room temperature. Transfer to a blender, add the lime zest, lime juice, and olive oil and puree until smooth. Taste and adjust the seasoning with salt and pepper. Refrigerate for up to 5 days.

RED WINE–BRAISED SHORT RIBS

1. Preheat a grill or grill pan to high heat.

CONTINUES →

2. Rub the beef with 2 tablespoons of the canola oil and season with the salt and pepper. Sear the short ribs until browned and caramelized, 6 to 8 minutes. Flip and sear on the back side for another 3 to 4 minutes. Set aside to cool. Transfer to a deep-sided container and refrigerate.

3. Place the red wine into a large saucepan, set over medium-high heat, and bring to a simmer. Using a stick lighter, flambé the wine. Turn off the heat and allow the flame to burn out. Add the onions, celery, carrots, garlic, bay leaves, thyme, and peppercorns to the red wine. Place the wine mixture into the refrigerator to cool completely.

4. Place a double fold of cheesecloth over the beef short ribs so it hangs over the side of the container. Pour the wine mixture over the beef and cover. Refrigerate overnight.

5. Preheat the oven to 300°F. Remove the cheesecloth from the container by bringing the sides together and squeezing excess wine back over the beef.

6. Heat a large, heavy-bottom saucepan or Dutch oven over medium-high heat and add the remaining 2 tablespoons of canola oil. Add the vegetable mixture from the marinade to the pan and sauté until caramelized, 6 to 8 minutes. Add the wine to the pan and bring to a simmer, 8 to 10 minutes. Remove the pan from the heat.

7. Gently add the short ribs to the pan and cover with a parchment paper round. Cover the pan with a tight-fighting lid and place into the oven. Braise for 3 to 3½ hours, or until the beef is fork-tender and coming away from the bone.

8. Remove the short ribs from the pan and place onto a cutting board; remove the bones from the meat. Keep warm.

9. Place the pan back on the stovetop, set over medium heat, and bring to a simmer. Reduce the braising liquid by three-fourths. Add the butter and whisk to combine. When ready to serve, spoon the sauce over the beef and serve with chili cumin sauce and green apple slaw.

GREEN APPLE SLAW

1. Place the mayonnaise, sour cream, vinegar, lemon juice, sugar, Dijon, and garlic in a large mixing bowl and whisk to combine.

2. Add the cabbage, apple, blue cheese, onions, carrots, and scallions and toss to combine. Taste and adjust the Frank's RedHot, salt, and pepper as necessary.

THOUGHTFUL TIP

While beef short ribs can be braised in all sorts of different liquids, I prefer red wine. You can use red wine as a marinade, because the acidity in the wine helps break down the tough meat before cooking. That marinade can then be used to braise the meat. After you've finished cooking the meat, remove it from the pan and reduce the red wine braising liquid to make the perfect red wine sauce to put the exclamation point on this dish!

Lemon Pound Cake

WITH BRIE ICE CREAM

SERVES 8

This might be my favorite dessert. Sweet, lemony, rich pound cake served warm with a scoop of brie ice cream. Yes—brie ice cream! The combination of the lemon-tinged cake glazed in a sweet lemony topping makes for a dessert you'll want to make all the time. Adding in buttery, creamy brie cheese in the form of ice cream takes this to the next level of explosive winter desserts. This recipe was born by combining the best of a cheese course into a dessert.

LEMON POUND CAKE

1 cup plus 1 tablespoon unsalted butter, room temperature

3 cups all-purpose flour, plus extra for pan

1 tablespoon baking powder

¾ teaspoon kosher salt

3 cups sugar

½ cup coconut oil

5 large eggs

1 cup whole milk

1 tablespoon lemon zest

6 tablespoons plus 2 teaspoons freshly squeezed lemon juice

2 tablespoons water

2 tablespoons sugar

Brie Ice Cream (see page 277)

1. Preheat the oven to 350°F. Grease a Bundt pan with 1 tablespoon of the butter. Dust the pan with flour, shake off the excess, and set aside.

2. Place the flour, baking powder, and salt into a medium bowl and whisk to combine.

3. Place the 1 cup of butter, sugar, and coconut oil into the bowl of a stand mixer fitted with the paddle attachment and mix on low speed until well combined. Add the eggs one at a time, beating until well blended, stopping to scrape down the sides of the bowl at least once.

4. Add the dry ingredients in three additions, alternating with the milk. Beat on low speed just until blended after each addition. Add the lemon zest and 6 tablespoons of the juice, and beat just until combined.

5. Pour the batter into the prepared Bundt pan, place in the oven, and bake 50 to 55 minutes, until a cake tester inserted into the cake comes out clean.

6. Remove the cake from the oven and place the cake pan onto a rack to cool for 15 minutes. Turn the cake out onto the rack to cool completely.

7. Place the water and sugar into a small saucepan, set over high heat, and bring to a boil, 3 to 4 minutes. Remove the pan from the heat and stir in the 2 teaspoons lemon juice.

8. When the cake is cool, transfer to a platter and brush with the glaze. Serve with Brie Ice Cream.

Blood Orange Rum Smash

A smash cocktail, also known as a smasher, or smash up, is a cocktail closely related to a julep cocktail. It's a combination of a base spirit, seasonal fruit, ice, and mint. Sounds a little vague? Well it is, because it's widely accepted as a family of cocktails rather than a specific recipe. First made in the 1800s, the difference between a julep and a smash is that the mint is stirred into a julep, and in a smash it's muddled in with the fresh fruit. Many smashes are made with whiskey, but you'll find them using everything from herbal gin to tequila these days. The combination of a high-quality white rum and blood oranges make a refreshing Sunday sipper to brighten up those snowy winter weekends.

1 blood orange, sliced
2 tablespoons mint plus 4 leaves for garnish
4 ounces white rum
1½ ounces blood orange juice
1 ounce Grand Marnier
1 ounce simple syrup
4 dashes orange bitters

1. Place all but two of the blood orange slices into a cocktail shaker. Add the mint and rum, and muddle until the oranges are fully mashed.

2. Add the blood orange juice, Grand Marnier, simple syrup, and orange bitters.

3. Fill the shaker with ice, cover, and shake vigorously for 30 seconds.

4. Double strain the cocktail into rocks glasses filled with ice. Garnish with the remaining two blood orange wheels and fresh mint leaves.

THOUGHTFUL TIP

Try making my smash with aged rum, or pineapple rum, to add a deeper, richer flavor to this classic drink. Make sure to use pellet or crushed ice to step your cocktail up a notch, and thank me later.

Citrus Limoncello

In an effort to make sure no one gets scurvy this winter, I have decided to share my limoncello digestif recipe. One drink and you'll be certain to get your daily dose of vitamin C, and you may even forget that it's winter for a few hours! Winter is the heart of citrus season in America. From blood oranges to Meyer lemons to grapefruit and kumquats, it's time to get your daily dose and add some tang to your life.

10 lemons
One 750-milliliter bottle 100 proof vodka
2 cups simple syrup
Lemon peel twists, for serving

1. Bring water to a boil in a large pot set over high heat. Place the lemons in the pot for 30 seconds to melt the wax coating.

2. Remove the lemons from the pot and rinse under cold water to cool. Pat dry.

3. Remove the rinds from the lemons using a sharp vegetable peeler, making sure not to remove any of the white pith. Reserve the flesh for another use.

4. Place lemon rinds in a large glass or other nonreactive container and cover with the vodka. Place a tight-fitting lid on the container and leave at room temperature for 2 weeks to 1 month to infuse.

5. Strain the alcohol into another container and add the simple syrup.

6. Funnel the limoncello into sterilized bottles and cover. Store, refrigerated, until ready to serve. Keep under refrigeration, until needed.

7. Serve 2 ounces of cold limoncello in a digestif glass and garnish with a twist of lemon peel.

THOUGHTFUL TIP

If you want to experiment with my limoncello recipe, substitute the lemon peel for any seasonal citrus. One of my favorites is grapefruit cello. These citrus cellos are also fun to use when cooking. I like to reduce the limoncello and use it in desserts for sorbets or for vinaigrettes when making salads.

BEING A THOUGHTFUL EATER

Our choices, without a doubt, have a cause and effect on the world around us. We are preprogrammed to nourish ourselves and chase after the most delicious food. Now that you're on this journey to become a thoughtful eater, it's important that you continue to think before you act. By making choices that are not only good for our planet but also good for our health and our bodies, we can help to keep our planet sustained: for ourselves, our children, and beyond. "One of the very nicest things about life is the way we must regularly stop whatever it is we are doing and devote our attention to eating," said Luciano Pavarotti. As human beings we are all connected to food, and to the earth that grows our food and provides for us. Slow down and enjoy where our food comes from, how it's grown, and how we can sustain our farms and oceans for generations to come.

Access to food is a privilege that we are lucky to have. It's our responsibility to understand this privilege and learn to take advantage of our own diets. While cooking takes time to learn, we can all start small: ask questions about the food we are eating, question the path of our food system takes, and learn how we get our food on the table. Many hands are needed to provide the food we eat. Let's put value on this privilege, and on the people, the farms, and the process it takes to get there.

And let's learn to cook! Beyond this book, find recipes that work for you and your family. This takes time and experimentation to discover what everyone in your house will eat, but you can make it fun and get them involved. Bring your children and family into the kitchen and teach them skills they can use for a lifetime. Plant a garden with them and watch their minds grow as the plants grow in the soil. Taking time to grow your own food, even if it's just fresh herbs on a kitchen counter, connects you to our ecosystem in a way that's much deeper than going on a grocery run or ordering takeout. Stop by your local farmers' market and support your local economy. Ask the farmers about what they are growing and try something new. Who knows? You might even find a new vegetable that you never knew you'd love. Spend a Sunday afternoon learning to can, pickle, and preserve extra vegetables: These things help to save you money and also helps to save food from going to waste. You'll help to brighten up your winter days, and your taste buds will thank you when you pop open a can of vegetables you put up yourself in the summertime. Take a walk in the woods and see what's growing on the forest floor around you. Be adventurous! Get involved and be thoughtful about what you're eating, because you vote with your fork. Eating is activism. You can be the change you've always wanted to see in yourself and the world around you.

Do you remember that song that goes, "When the moon hits your eye, like a big pizza pie?" Well, that is certainly love indeed. Cooking brings people together, and no matter who you are or where you're from I am certain that some of your best memories have occurred sitting across the table sharing a meal with your friends and family. Cooking with love helps touch the people you're feeding, and they can feel the goodness in the food you're creating. Give second helpings of love and positivity. Take the time to cook someone a meal from the heart and watch their expression change. Now *that's* amore!

Onward, Thoughtful Eaters! The future is bright, and we've got one planet to live on, so let's cook from the heart, live seasonally, and be thoughtful about how we eat and how we work to make our planet a more delicious place to live!

Santé!

Appendix:
FOUNDATIONAL RECIPES

263

Pickles and Preserves

Not all pickles are created equal, and when you learn to put some sour power in your pantry, you'll soon be adding the right amount of tang to your next dish, appetizer, or cheese and charcuterie platter. Pickling is a great way to extend the shelf life of a vegetable, add flavor to a dish, and keep food from wasting in your fridge.

If you want to take the preservation a step further, instead of pickling vegetables in the refrigerator you can process them for longer-term storage. To do so, place the vegetables into a clean quart-size canning jar and pour hot brine over the vegetables. Then seal each jar with a clean seal and ring, and place the jars into a boiling water bath (making sure each jar is covered by at least an inch of water), and process in the water bath for 10 minutes, or more depending on the recipe. Remove the jars with canning tongs and allow them to cool to room temperature. Listen for each lid to pop, indicating it has sealed. Your vegetables are now good to keep in a cool, dark place at room temperature for 6 months to 1 year. During the cooler winter months, you can open a jar of sunshine anytime you want.

B and B Pickles

MAKES ABOUT 2 QUARTS

1½ pounds cucumbers, sliced into 3/16-inch-thick rounds
1 medium onion, julienned
¼ cup kosher salt
3 quarts ice cubes
2 cups apple cider vinegar
2 cups water
½ cup granulated sugar
4 teaspoons yellow mustard seeds
1 teaspoon red pepper flakes
1 teaspoon ground turmeric

1. Place the cucumbers, onions, and kosher salt in a large bowl and toss to combine. Top the cucumbers with the ice cubes. Set aside at room temperature to allow to crisp, for 3 to 3½ hours.

2. Drain the cucumbers and evenly divide between two 1-quart glass containers with lids.

3. Place the vinegar, water, sugar, mustard seeds, red pepper flakes, and turmeric in a medium saucepan, set over high heat, and bring to a boil. Stir to dissolve the sugar and salt.

4. Pour the pickling liquid over the cucumbers and onions. Set aside to cool to room temperature. Cover and refrigerate for up to 2 months.

Pickled Okra

MAKES 1 QUART

1 pound small, young okra, washed, dried, and stems cleaned
1½ cups distilled vinegar
¼ cup sugar
2 tablespoons kosher salt
5 garlic cloves, peeled
4 thyme sprigs
2 bay leaves
1 teaspoon whole black peppercorns
1 teaspoon yellow mustard seeds
1 teaspoon red pepper flakes
½ teaspoon fennel seeds
¼ teaspoon cayenne pepper

1. Place the okra in a clean, 1-quart glass jar, packing down as needed to fit.

2. Place the vinegar, sugar, salt, garlic, thyme, bay leaves, peppercorns, mustard seeds, red pepper flakes, fennel seeds, and cayenne pepper into a small saucepan. Set over high heat and bring to a boil. Stir until the sugar dissolves.

3. Carefully pour the boiling liquid over the okra to completely cover. Use a small dish or weight to ensure that all okra is submerged in the liquid. Set aside at room temperature until cooled.

4. Cover and refrigerate for at least 4 hours before serving. Store refrigerated for up to 2 months.

Dilly Beans

MAKES ABOUT 1 QUART

1 pound young, tender, thin string beans
3 dill sprigs
1 cup apple cider vinegar
1 cup water
3 garlic cloves
1 tablespoon kosher salt
½ teaspoon red pepper flakes
½ teaspoon yellow mustard seeds

1. Rinse the beans and trim the stem end. Place the beans and the dill in a 1-quart glass jar with a lid.

2. Place the vinegar, water, garlic, salt, red pepper flakes, and mustard seeds in a small saucepan, set over high heat, and bring to a boil. Stir to combine.

3. Pour the liquid over the beans. Set aside to cool to room temperature. Cover and refrigerate for at least 4 hours before using.

4. The beans can be stored in the refrigerator for up to 2 months.

Pickled Ramps

MAKES 1 QUART

1 tablespoon kosher salt, plus extra for blanching
2 pounds ramps, cleaned and green leaves cut to 1 inch above red stem
1 tablespoon whole black peppercorns
1 teaspoon mustard seeds
½ teaspoon caraway seeds

½ teaspoon fennel seeds
½ teaspoon cumin seeds
2 bay leaves
1 cup white wine vinegar
1 cup sugar

1. Place a medium pot of water over high heat. Add enough salt to taste like the ocean and bring to a boil. Add the ramps and blanch for 30 seconds. The ramps should be tender crisp. Transfer the ramps to a bowl of ice water to stop the cooking.

2. Drain the ramps, pat dry, and place them into a sterilized 1-quart jar.

3. Place the peppercorns, mustard seeds, caraway seeds, fennel seeds, and cumin seeds into a small sauté pan, set over medium-high heat and toast until aromatic, 2 to 3 minutes.

4. Transfer the spice mixture to the jar with the ramps.

5. Place the 1 tablespoon kosher salt, bay leaves, white wine vinegar, and sugar in a small saucepan. Set over medium-high heat and stir until the salt and sugar dissolves, about 2 minutes. Pour over the ramps. Seal the jar and set aside to cool to room temperature. Refrigerate for up to 1 month.

Pickled Rhubarb

MAKES ABOUT 1 QUART

1 pound rhubarb stalks, trimmed
2 teaspoons mustard seeds
2 whole star anise
1 bay leaf
½ teaspoon whole black peppercorns
½ teaspoon whole cloves
1 cup apple cider vinegar
1 cup water
1 cup sugar
½ teaspoon kosher salt

Pickled Ramps

1. Cut the rhubarb stalks in half and place them in a 1-quart glass jar or other lidded, nonreactive container. Add the mustard seeds, star anise, bay leaf, peppercorns, and cloves.

2. Place the vinegar, water, sugar, and salt in a small saucepan, set over medium-high heat, and bring to a boil. Stir until the sugar dissolves, about 1 minute. Remove from the heat and cool to room temperature.

3. Pour the cooled liquid over the rhubarb, cover, and refrigerate overnight before using. Store, refrigerated, for up to 3 months.

Pickled Fresno Peppers

MAKES 2 QUARTS

2 cups sherry vinegar

2 cups water

5 tablespoons granulated sugar

5 tablespoons kosher salt

1 pound Fresno peppers, sliced into ⅛-inch rings

1. Place the vinegar, water, sugar, and salt into a medium, nonreactive saucepan, set over high heat, and bring to a boil. Decrease the heat to low and simmer for 5 minutes.

2. Place the peppers in a 2-quart heatproof, glass container and add the hot liquid. Set aside to cool to room temperature. Cover and refrigerate for up to 6 months.

Pickled Red Onions

MAKES ABOUT 1 CUP

1 medium red onion, julienned

1 cup sugar

1 cup white vinegar

1 cup water

2 tablespoons kosher salt

1 teaspoon Pickling Spice (recipe follows)

1. Place the red onions into a 2-cup glass jar or other heatproof container.

2. Combine the sugar, vinegar, water, salt, and pickling spice in a small saucepan, set over medium-high heat, and bring to a boil. Stir until the sugar and salt dissolves.

3. Pour the boiling pickling liquid over the onions and set aside and cool to room temperature. Once cool, cover and refrigerate for up to 2 weeks.

Pickling Spice

MAKES ABOUT ¾ CUP

2 tablespoons black peppercorns

2 tablespoons yellow mustard seeds

2 tablespoons coriander seeds

2 tablespoons dill seeds

1 tablespoon allspice berries

1 teaspoon red pepper flakes

10 bay leaves, crumbled

1. Combine all the ingredients together and store in an airtight container.

Pickled Green Strawberries

MAKES 4 PINTS

2 pounds green strawberries, washed and hulled, about 2 quarts

½ yellow onion, julienned

2 cups apple cider vinegar

2 cups water

½ cup sugar

¼ cup kosher salt

4 teaspoons yellow mustard seeds

1 teaspoon red pepper flakes

1 bay leaf

1. Cut the strawberries in half if they are large. Otherwise, leave them whole.

2. Evenly divide the strawberries and onions into four sterilized pint canning jars.

3. Place the vinegar, water, sugar, salt, mustard seeds, red pepper flakes, and bay leaf into a medium saucepan, set over high heat, and bring to a boil. Stir until the sugar and salt dissolves. Remove from the heat and carefully pour over the strawberries and onions, dividing the liquid evenly among the jars. Depending on the size of the strawberries, there may be some liquid left over.

4. Process the cans in a pressure cooker or boiling water bath to seal, or allow the pickles to cool to room temperature and refrigerate for up to 1 month.

Pickled Tomatoes

MAKES ABOUT 1 QUART

1 quart cherry tomatoes
2 garlic cloves, smashed
1 teaspoon whole black peppercorns
2 bay leaves
1 cup apple cider vinegar
1 cup water
1 tablespoon kosher salt
1 tablespoon granulated sugar

1. Place a large pot of water over high heat and bring to a boil. Place ice and water in a large bowl and set aside.

2. Using a paring knife, cut an X on the stem side of the tomatoes and place them into the boiling water for 20 seconds. Use a slotted spoon to transfer the tomatoes immediately to the ice bath.

3. Peel and discard the skins.

4. Place the garlic, peppercorns, and bay leaves into a 1-quart glass canning jar and top with the tomatoes.

5. Place the vinegar, water, salt, and sugar into a small saucepan, set over high heat, and bring to a boil. Stir to dissolve the sugar and salt.

6. Pour the liquid over the tomatoes, leaving a ½-inch headspace.

7. Gently tap the jar on the counter to remove any air bubbles and add a seal with the lid.

8. Process in a hot water bath for 40 minutes. Remove the jar and allow to cool to room temperature. Check the seal and store in a cool dark place for up to 1 year. Refrigerate once opened.

Pickled Yellow Squash

MAKES ABOUT 1 QUART

2 garlic cloves, smashed
1½ teaspoons whole black peppercorns
1 teaspoon coriander seeds
1 teaspoon red pepper flakes
2 bay leaves
12 ounces (about 2) yellow squash, large dice
½ cup julienned yellow onion
1 cup water
¾ cup apple cider vinegar
1 tablespoon honey
1½ teaspoons kosher salt

1. Place the garlic, peppercorns, coriander, red pepper flakes, and bay leaves into a 1-quart canning jar. Add the squash and onions and set aside.

2. Place the water, vinegar, honey, and salt into a small saucepan, set over medium heat, and bring just to a boil. Stir to dissolve the salt and honey.

3. Pour the liquid over the squash and leave ½ inch of headspace at the top of the jar.

4. Place a seal and lid on the jar.

5. Process in a hot water bath for 15 minutes. Remove the jar from the water bath and set aside to cool to room temperature. Check the seal and store in a cool dark place for up to 6 months. Refrigerate once opened.

Preserved Lemons

8 small to medium lemons, washed
3 tablespoons coriander seeds
3 tablespoons fennel seeds
2 cups kosher salt
1 dried guajillo pepper
6 thyme sprigs
½ cinnamon stick, crushed
2 bay leaves, crumbled

1. Starting at the top of each lemon, cut an X into it, stopping about ¼-inch from the bottom. You want to have a quartered lemon that is held together at the base. Set aside.

2. Place the coriander and fennel in a small sauté pan set over medium heat and toast until fragrant and beginning to brown, about 3 minutes.

3. Transfer the toasted spices to a medium bowl and add the salt, guajillo pepper, thyme, cinnamon stick, and bay leaves. Stir to combine.

4. Working over a large bowl, stuff a lemon with a handful of the salt mixture, using your thumb to gently break into the flesh, allowing the juices to run out. Drop the lemon into the bowl. Repeat with all the lemons and then toss everything to combine.

5. Pack the lemons into a 1-quart glass jar with a lid, pressing down so they are completely covered in their own juices. Add any remaining juice and seasoning from the bowl. Seal the jar and set aside at room temperature for 3 to 4 weeks or until the rinds have softened.

6. Store tightly sealed at room temperature for up to 6 months or refrigerated for up to 1 year.

7. To use the preserved lemons, remove the white pith, rinse, and pat dry.

Strawberry Preserves

MAKES ABOUT 1½ QUARTS

4 pounds fresh ripe strawberries, hulled and quartered
¼ cup freshly squeezed lemon juice
2½ cups sugar

1. Place the strawberries and lemon juice into a large, nonreactive saucepan, set over medium-high heat, and bring to a boil.

2. Once the mixture comes to a boil, reduce the heat to low and simmer, stirring occasionally, until the strawberries release their juices and begin to break down, 30 to 35 minutes.

3. Add the sugar, stir to combine, and increase the heat to medium. Bring back to a simmer and cook until the preserves have thickened and coat the back of a spoon, about 45 minutes.

4. Remove the preserves from the heat and skim off any foam from the top.

5. Ladle the hot preserves into sanitized glass jars, leaving about ½ inch of headspace between the preserves and lid.

6. Wipe the jars clean and seal the jars with the lid. Allow to cool completely and refrigerate until ready to eat. Refrigerate for up to 1 month.

Blackberry or Raspberry Preserves

MAKES 1 PINT

12 ounces blackberries or raspberries
⅔ cup sugar
1½ teaspoons freshly squeezed lemon juice

1. Place the fruit and the sugar in a small bowl and stir to combine. Set aside for 30 minutes to macerate.

2. Place a small plate in the freezer.

3. Transfer the berry mixture to a small heavy-bottom pot, add the lemon juice, and stir to combine. Set over medium-low heat and bring to a simmer. Cook at a low simmer for 20 minutes.

4. Check the consistency of the preserves by placing a small spoonful of the preserves across the frozen plate. Drag the spoon across the center of the small mound. If the preserves hold their shape without running, it is done. If it is still runny, cook for another 5 minutes and test again.

5. Remove from the heat and place into a sterilized canning jar or lidded container. Cool to room temperature and refrigerate for up to 1 month. If preferred, can in a water bath.

Preserved Plum Sauce

MAKES 2 PINTS

2 pounds plums, rinsed, pitted, and cut into large dice
1 cup light brown sugar
½ cup granulated sugar
½ cup finely diced yellow onion
½ cup apple cider vinegar
½ cup plum wine
1 tablespoon yellow mustard seeds
1 clove garlic, chopped
½ teaspoon ground ginger
¼ teaspoon kosher salt

1. Sterilize two pint canning jars, lids, and seals by washing in hot soapy water, rinsing, and drying well before using.

2. Place the plums, brown sugar, granulated sugar, onion, vinegar, wine, mustard seeds, garlic, ginger, and salt into a medium heavy-bottom saucepan or Dutch oven. Place over medium-high heat and bring to a simmer, about 15 minutes. Decrease the heat to low and cook, stirring frequently, until the plums

are tender and falling apart and the mixture has slightly thickened, 25 to 30 minutes.

3. Remove from the heat. Pass the mixture through a food mill set over a second, heavy saucepan. Set the pan over medium-low heat and cook stirring frequently to prevent scorching, until the mixture has reduced to 4 cups, about 30 minutes. Remove the pot from the heat.

4. Prepare another pot of boiling water to process the plum sauce in the jars.

5. Immediately spoon the hot plum sauce into the prepared jars, leaving a ½-inch head space in each jar. Wipe the rims of the jars clean with a clean towel or paper towel.

6. Seal the jars. Carefully place the sealed jars in the boiling pot and process for 10 minutes. Turn off the heat and leave the jars submerged in the water for 5 minutes.

7. Carefully remove the jars from the water and turn upside down on the counter to seal and cool to room temperature, 2 to 3 hours.

8. Store in a dark place for up to 1 year. Refrigerate the jars upon opening and use within 1 month.

Espelette Pepper Jelly

MAKES ABOUT FIVE 8-OUNCE JARS

3 red bell peppers, seeded and coarsely chopped
3 cups sugar
1 cup apple cider vinegar
2 tablespoons piment d'Espelette
1 tablespoon ground sweet paprika
Two 3-ounce pouches liquid pectin

1. Place the red bell peppers into a food processor, and pulse to a coarse puree.

2. Transfer the puree to a heavy bottom, non-reactive saucepan. Add the sugar, vinegar,

piment d'Espelette, and paprika and set over medium heat. Bring to a simmer and cook, stirring occasionally, until the mixture begins to thicken, 6 to 8 minutes.

3. Remove the pot from the heat and stir in the pectin.

4. Return the pot to the heat and cook for 1 minute, stirring constantly. Remove the pot from the heat.

5. Ladle the pepper jelly into sterilized 8-ounce canning jars, leaving ½ inch of head space. Wipe the jar with a damp towel and cover and seal with sterilized lids.

6. Gently place the jars into a wide, deep-sided pot and cover with water by 2 inches, set over high heat and bring to a boil. Once the water is boiling, process the jars for 10 minutes. Turn off the heat and allow the jars to sit in the water for 5 minutes.

7. Remove the jars from the water with canning tongs. Invert and place on the counter until they reach room temperature.

8. Store in a cool, dark place for up to 1 year. Refrigerate once opened.

Preserved Jimmy Nardello Peppers

MAKES 1 QUART

1½ pounds (8 to 10) Jimmy Nardello Peppers
¾ cup sugar
¾ cup aged sherry vinegar
¾ cup water
4 thyme sprigs
2 garlic cloves, smashed
1 teaspoon kosher salt

1. Roast the peppers over an open flame on the stovetop until they are charred on all sides. Place the peppers in a bowl, cover with plastic, and allow to steam for 10 minutes. Remove

from the bowl and peel away the skin. Make a slit down the side of the pepper and remove the seeds. Set aside

2. Place the sugar, vinegar, and water into a medium saucepan, set over high heat and bring to a simmer, and stir to dissolve the sugar. Add the peppers, bring to a simmer, and then remove from the heat.

3. Place the thyme, garlic, and salt into a sterilized 1-quart canning jar. Place the peppers in the jar and cover with the pickling liquid, leaving ½ inch headspace in the jar.

4. Run a knife around the inside of the jar to remove any bubbles. Wipe the lid clean and close with the seal and ring.

5. Process in a hot water bath for 5 minutes. Remove from the water bath and cool to room temperature. Refrigerate or store in a cool dark place for up to 1 year. Refrigerate after opening.

Sour Corn

MAKES 1 QUART

6 ears (about 4 cups kernels) yellow corn
2 cups spring water
1½ tablespoons kosher salt

1. Cut the kernels from the cobs and reserve the cobs for another use. Place the corn in a clean quart-size canning jar and set aside.

2. Place the water and salt in a large measuring cup or small bowl and whisk to dissolve. Use spring water, as tap water often contains chemicals that can prevent lacto fermentation.

3. Pour the brine over the corn. Keep the corn below the brine by using a canning weight. Cover the jar with a double layer of cheesecloth and secure with a rubber band or

butcher's twine. Set aside at room temperature for 7 days to ferment.

4. Check daily and if a white film forms on top of the brine, remove it and discard. Taste after 7 days to see if the corn is sour. If so, remove the cheesecloth and cover with a seal and canning ring. Refrigerate for up to 6 months, keeping the kernels submerged in the brine.

Condiments, Stocks, and Sauces

The foundation of all great recipes start with stocks and sauces. They are the special touch that help to elevate a dish to the next level. There are five mother sauces—béchamel, velouté, espagnole, hollandaise, and tomato—that the French created to derive a multitude of deliciousness. Taking the time to build on the foundation of a great stock, sauce, or condiment will help your dishes stand out to your guests. Use these recipes to aid in working from this cookbook or keep them in your back pocket as the base for creativity in your future cooking endeavors.

Confit Garlic

MAKES 2 CUPS

40 garlic cloves (about 3 heads), peeled
2 cups extra virgin olive oil

1. Place the garlic and the olive oil into a small saucepan, making sure all the garlic cloves are completely submerged in the oil.

2. Set over medium heat and bring to a light simmer, 7 to 8 minutes. Cook until the garlic is tender and light gold in color, 20 to 25 minutes.

3. Remove from the heat and set aside to completely cool.

4. Transfer to an airtight container and refrigerate for up to 3 weeks.

Jalapeño Lime Butter

MAKES 1 CUP

1 jalapeño pepper, stemmed and seeded
1 garlic clove, minced
2 teaspoons lime zest
1 tablespoon freshly squeezed lime juice
1 teaspoon kosher salt
¼ teaspoon freshly ground black pepper
3 sprigs cilantro, finely chopped
½ cup unsalted butter, room temperature

1. Place the jalapeño, garlic, lime zest, lime juice, salt, pepper, and cilantro into a food processor and puree until smooth.

2. Add the butter to the food processor and process until fully incorporated. Use a rubber spatula to scrape down the sides of the bowl and process until thoroughly combined. Taste and adjust seasoning if needed.

3. Lay out a sheet of plastic wrap on a counter and place the butter on top. Wrap the butter and roll into a 1-inch-wide log. Refrigerate until firm before using. Refrigerate for up to 1 week.

Cured Egg Yolks

MAKES 6 EGGS

2 quarts kosher salt
6 egg yolks

1. Pour half of the salt in a ½-inch layer across the bottom of a nonreactive container.

2. Create small divots in the salt, using the back of a spoon, for each of the egg yolks, making sure that they are at least ½ inch apart.

3. Place the egg yolks in the divots and cover the eggs with the remaining salt so that you can no longer see any of the yellow from the yolk.

4. Refrigerate to cure for 7 days.

5. Place a rack in a small sheet tray or pan. Carefully remove the cured yolks from the salt and place on the prepared pan. Return to the refrigerator to dry for another 7 days.

6. Once the yolks are dry and firm, store them in the refrigerator tightly covered for up to 1 month. Grate and use as a topping.

Gremolata

MAKES ABOUT 1 CUP

1½ cups packed, roughly chopped parsley
Zest from 1 lemon
3 tablespoons freshly squeezed lemon juice
2 tablespoons rinsed capers
2 tablespoons minced shallot
2 garlic cloves, minced
¼ cup extra virgin olive oil
¼ teaspoon kosher salt, plus extra to taste
Freshly ground black pepper, to taste

1. Place the parsley, lemon zest, lemon juice, capers, shallots, and garlic into a food processor and pulse to roughly chop.

2. With the motor running, slowly add the olive oil. Season to taste with salt and pepper.

3. Use immediately or refrigerate for up to 1 day.

White Wine and Herb Vinaigrette

MAKES ABOUT 2 CUPS

¼ cup white wine vinegar
1 tablespoon Dijon mustard
1 tablespoon honey
1½ teaspoons minced shallots
1½ teaspoons minced garlic
½ teaspoon kosher salt, plus extra to taste
Pinch freshly ground black pepper, plus extra to taste
¾ cup blended oil
1½ teaspoons finely chopped basil
1½ teaspoons finely chopped parsley
1½ teaspoons finely chopped thyme

1. Place the vinegar, mustard, honey, shallots, garlic, salt, and pepper into a blender and puree until smooth. With the blender running, slowly add the oil until emulsified.

2. Transfer to a small bowl and stir in the basil, parsley, and thyme and taste. Adjust the seasoning as necessary. Refrigerate for up 1 week.

Green Goddess Dressing

MAKES ABOUT 1 CUP

¾ cup Duke's mayonnaise
3 cloves Confit Garlic (page 272)
3 white anchovies
3 tablespoons chopped basil
3 tablespoons chopped chives
3 tablespoons chopped parsley
1 tablespoon extra virgin olive oil
2 tablespoons water
¾ teaspoon white vinegar
¼ teaspoon Aleppo pepper
Kosher salt, to taste

1. Place the mayonnaise, confit garlic, anchovies, basil, chives, parsley, olive oil, water, vinegar, and Aleppo pepper in the bowl of a food processor and process until pureed, 3 to 4 minutes.

2. Taste and season with salt as needed. Transfer to an airtight container and refrigerate for up to 5 days.

Vegetable Stock

MAKES 1 GALLON

3 yellow onions, peeled and rough chopped
4 large carrots, peeled and rough chopped
4 celery stalks, rough chopped
1 leek, rinsed and rough chopped
5 garlic cloves, peeled
1 bunch thyme
¼ bunch parsley stems
2 bay leaves
1 tablespoon whole black peppercorn
1 gallon water

1. Place the onions, carrots, celery, leek, garlic, thyme, parsley, bay leaves, and peppercorns in a large saucepan. Add the water and make sure it covers the ingredients by 2 inches. Add more water if necessary.

2. Set over high heat and bring just to a boil. Reduce the heat to low and simmer for 1 hour. If necessary, skim any foam that forms on the surface.

3. Remove from the heat and set aside to cool to room temperature. Strain through a fine mesh strainer and discard the solids. Refrigerate for up to 1 week or freeze until ready to use.

Chicken Stock

MAKES 2 QUARTS

2 whole chicken carcasses or bones from 2 chickens
2 tablespoons canola oil
1 yellow onion, peeled and large diced
2 stalks celery, large diced
1 large carrot, peeled and large diced
1 cup parsley stems
3 garlic cloves, peeled
10 thyme sprigs
1 bay leaf
1 teaspoon whole black peppercorns
Water

1. Preheat the oven to 400°F.

2. Rub the chicken carcasses with the canola oil and place on a sheet tray.

3. Place in the oven and roast for 30 minutes or until golden brown.

4. Place the chicken in a large saucepan or stockpot and add the onions, celery, carrots, parsley, garlic, thyme, bay leaf, and peppercorns. Cover with water by 3 inches. Set over high heat and bring just to a boil. Reduce the heat to low and simmer for 4 hours. If necessary, skim any foam that forms on the surface.

5. Remove from the heat and strain through a fine mesh strainer and discard the solids. Set aside to cool to room temperature. Refrigerate for up to 1 week or freeze until ready to use.

Shrimp Stock

MAKES 2 QUARTS

Shrimp shells from 2 pounds of shrimp
1 cup large-dice onion
½ cup large-dice celery
2 garlic cloves
6 thyme sprigs
1 bay leaf
1 teaspoons whole black peppercorns
½ gallon water

1. Place the shrimp shells, onion, celery, garlic, thyme, bay leaf, peppercorns, and water in a large saucepan or stockpot.

2. Set over high heat and bring just to a boil. Decrease the heat to low and simmer for 30 minutes. If necessary, skim any foam that forms on the surface.

3. Remove from the heat and strain through a fine mesh strainer and discard the solids. Set aside to cool to room temperature. Refrigerate for up to 1 week or freeze until ready to use.

Standard Brine

MAKES 1½ GALLONS

1½ gallons water
2 cups kosher salt
½ cup light brown sugar
½ cup granulated sugar
2 bay leaves
1 bunch thyme
6 garlic cloves
2 teaspoons whole black peppercorns

1. Place the water in a large pot, set over high heat, and bring to a boil. Remove from the heat and add the salt, brown sugar, granulated sugar, bay leaves, thyme, garlic, and black peppercorn. Stir until the salt and sugar have dissolved.

2. Cool to room temperature before refrigerating. Bring to 41°F before using. Refrigerate until ready to use.

Rosemary Applesauce

MAKES 1 QUART

2 tablespoons unsalted butter
¼ cup diced shallots
2 pounds Granny Smith apples, peeled, cored, and cut into large dice
1 cup dry white wine
2 cups water
1 tablespoon chopped rosemary
1 teaspoon kosher salt, plus extra to taste
Freshly ground black pepper, to taste

1. Place the butter in a medium heavy-bottom saucepan, set over medium heat, and add the shallots. Cook, stirring occasionally, until translucent, 3 to 4 minutes.

2. Add the apples, stir to combine, and cook until just beginning to soften, 2 to 3 minutes.

3. Add the wine and reduce to ¼ cup, 5 to 6 minutes.

4. Add the water and bring to a simmer, stirring occasionally.

5. Reduce the heat to medium-low and cook until the apples have broken down and cooked into a thick applesauce, 15 to 20 minutes.

6. Remove the applesauce from the heat and add the rosemary and salt. Taste and adjust the seasoning with salt and black pepper to taste. Serve immediately or cool completely and refrigerate in an airtight container for up to 2 weeks.

Ice Cream and Dairy

Making your own fresh cheeses and ice cream may sound intimidating, but nothing beats the fresh flavor of homemade dairy products in your kitchen. Use these recipes as a base for your own creativity in the kitchen and you'll never go back to store-bought again. Brie Ice Cream is going to be your new favorite ice cream to serve alongside your baked goods and pies.

Crème Fraîche

MAKES 2 CUPS

2 tablespoons cultured whole buttermilk
2 cups heavy cream
½ teaspoon lemon zest

1. Combine the buttermilk and heavy cream in a nonreactive container. Cover and set aside at room temperature until it has thickened to the consistency of sour cream, 16 to 20 hours.

2. Add the lemon zest and fold to combine. Store in the refrigerator for up to 2 weeks.

Ricotta or Farmer's Cheese

MAKES ABOUT 1 QUART

½ gallon whole milk
2 cups buttermilk
1½ tablespoons kosher salt
1 tablespoon freshly ground black pepper (optional)

1. Place a layer of cheesecloth in a large fine mesh strainer and set in a deep bowl.

2. Place the whole milk and buttermilk into a large saucepan and set over medium heat. Stir frequently for 5 minutes to prevent the milk from burning. Decrease the heat to maintain a simmer and do not allow to boil.

3. Cook until the mixture reaches 100°F, then stop stirring. Leave, undisturbed until the

temperature reaches 175°F. Turn off the heat and leave for another 5 minutes without stirring.

4. Use a slotted spoon to scoop the curd (solids) into the cheesecloth-lined strainer. Leave to drain for 10 minutes. Stir in the salt.

5. Gather the cheesecloth around the curds and tie at the top with a rubber band. Hang the bundle from your faucet or set a ladle handle across the top of a pot and hang the bundle from the ladle handle. Drain for 30 minutes. Transfer the ricotta to an airtight container and refrigerate for up to 1 week. Add 1 tablespoon freshly ground black pepper for Black Pepper Ricotta.

6. Reserve the whey (leftover liquid) for cooking grains or grits.

Stracciatella

MAKES ABOUT 1 CUP

2 quarts water
½ cup kosher salt
1 cup large-diced mozzarella curd
½ cup heavy cream
¼ teaspoon freshly ground black pepper, plus extra to taste

1. Place the water and salt into a medium pot and bring to a bare simmer.

2. Place the diced mozzarella curd into the pot. Using a long metal slotted spoon, stir the curd until it just begins to melt on the sides.

3. Using the slotted spoon, quickly transfer the curd to a medium bowl, draining away as much water as possible. Set aside until cool enough to handle, 3 to 4 minutes.

4. Working with your hands, shred the mozzarella into fine threads. Add the heavy cream and black pepper and stir to combine until it is the consistency of ricotta cheese. Taste,

and adjust seasoning as necessary. Cover and refrigerate up to 1 week.

Peach Ice Cream

MAKES ABOUT 1-QUART

2 medium peaches, peeled, pitted, and cut into large dice
1¼ cups sugar
½ teaspoon freshly squeezed lemon juice
1½ cups heavy cream
1½ cups whole milk
1 tablespoon bourbon, flambéed
1 teaspoon vanilla bean paste
¼ teaspoon kosher salt
5 egg yolks

1. Place the peaches, a third of the sugar, and the lemon juice into a medium bowl and stir to combine. Set aside at room temperature to macerate for 30 minutes. Transfer the mixture to a blender and puree until smooth.

2. Transfer the puree to a medium saucepan, add another third of the sugar, the heavy cream, milk, bourbon, vanilla, and salt, and whisk to combine. Set over medium-low heat and cook, whisking often, until the mixture reaches 159°F.

3. Place the egg yolks and the final third of the sugar into a medium bowl and whisk to combine. Slowly pour the cream mixture into the egg mixture, while whisking continually, until combined. Return the entire mixture to the saucepan, return to medium heat, and continue to cook, stirring frequently, until the mixture coats the back of a spoon, 6 to 8 minutes. Strain the mixture through a fine mesh strainer into another container. Refrigerate until completely chilled.

4. Process in an ice cream maker according to the manufacturer's instructions.

Cinnamon Brown Butter Ice Cream

MAKES ABOUT 2 QUARTS

1 quart half-and-half
1 cup heavy cream
1 cup sugar
1 teaspoon vanilla extract
1 teaspoon ground cinnamon
4 tablespoons unsalted butter
10 large egg yolks

1. Place the half-and-half, heavy cream, ½ cup of the sugar, vanilla, and cinnamon in a medium saucepan, set over medium-high heat, and heat until the mixture begins to simmer, 7 to 8 minutes.

2. Place the butter in a separate small saucepan, set over medium-high heat, and cook until it turns a golden brown and has a nutty aroma, 5 to 6 minutes. Slowly whisk the brown butter into the ice cream base.

3. Place the remaining ½ cup of sugar and egg yolks into a separate bowl and whisk until well-combined and lightened in color, 2 to 3 minutes.

4. Temper the egg yolk mixture into the hot cream by adding small amounts at a time while whisking continually. Once you have added half of the egg and sugar mixture to the hot cream, pour the entire cream mixture back into the pot with the remaining cream. Decrease the heat to low and cook, stirring continually, until the mixture thickens and coats the back of a spoon. Strain through a fine mesh strainer and cool to room temperature.

5. Refrigerate until cold and then process in an ice cream maker according to the manufacturer's instructions. Freeze for up to 1 month.

Brie Ice Cream

MAKES ABOUT 1½ QUARTS

2 cups heavy cream
2 cups whole milk
¼ vanilla bean, split and scraped
6 egg yolks
¾ cup sugar
4 ounces Brie, trimmed of white bloomy rind and large dice
4 drops almond extract

1. Place the heavy cream, milk, and vanilla bean seeds and pod in a medium saucepan, set over medium heat, and stir occasionally until the mixture begins to steam, 6 to 7 minutes.

2. Place the egg yolks and sugar in a medium mixing bowl and whisk to combine.

3. Once the cream mixture is hot, ladle small amounts into the eggs while whisking continuously.

4. After adding about ½ cup of hot cream to the eggs to temper, pour the mixture back into the pot and stir continuously until the mixture begins to steam again and slightly thickens, 2 to 3 minutes. Remove the vanilla bean.

5. Add the Brie and stir vigorously to melt. Add the almond extract and stir to combine.

6. Pour the mixture through a fine mesh strainer to remove any stray bits of vanilla bean or cheese rind. Cover and refrigerate until chilled.

7. Process in an ice cream maker according to the manufacturer's instructions.

Culinary Resources

Where can you find all these awesome tools and essentials for your own kitchen? I've listed some of my favorite places to go shopping for hard-to-find ingredients and tools so that you can create your own *thoughtful kitchen*. You'll find everything from my favorite plates and cookware to the stores and farms where I source the ingredients I use at home and in my professional restaurant kitchens.

MCQUEEN POTTERY: Beautiful, minimalist pottery handmade in eastern Tennessee by LeAnne McQueen. Her pottery appears in some of the best restaurants and hotels.

MMCLAY CERAMICS: San Francisco Bay Area ceramicist MaryMar Keenan produces some of the finest ceramics around with beautiful styles and glazes.

HEATH CERAMICS: This OG pottery company helped to put custom pottery on the map.

LE CREUSET: They create colorful enameled cast-iron cookware from France that will brighten up any kitchen. Their Dutch oven is one of my favorites to cook with at work and at home.

ALL-CLAD: Made in Canonsburg, Pennsylvania, this is some of the heaviest-duty stainless steel cookware around.

LODGE CAST IRON: Hailing from South Pittsburg, Tennessee, Lodge Cast Iron has been producing heirloom quality cast iron cookware since the 1800s. Take care of your cast iron and it can be handed down for generations.

JB PRINCE: This is where chefs shop for quality kitchen tools and equipment and hard-to-find specialty tools. Their pastry tool selection is one of the best for pastry chefs and bakers.

WILLIAMS SONOMA: The go-to location to invest in building out your kitchen. From cookware to kitchen tools to design pieces to set the table, this store is your one-stop shop for high-quality tools and more.

KORIN: With a robust online store, and retail location in New York, this is the source for professional quality Japanese knives, kitchen tools, and barware. Many items are imported directly from Japan. This is where I go to find razor-sharp knives to use in a restaurant kitchen.

J.Q. DICKINSON SALT-WORKS: Ancient ocean water sea salt from Appalachia. How cool is that? Hailing from my home state of West Virginia, this is where you'll find the perfect finishing salt for any dish.

SUNBURST TROUT FARMS: Enjoy farm-fresh and sustainable rainbow trout and caviar wherever you live in the United States—they ship nationwide.

ANSON MILLS: Check out this South Carolina purveyor of heirloom Carolina Gold Rice, heirloom dried pea, farro, benne seeds, and more.

FARM & SPARROW: A small batch artisan mill, grain collection, and seed project located in Mars Hill, North Carolina, that showcases the regional terroir of Appalachian landrace grains and legumes.

MARSH HEN MILL: Nestled into the low-country town of Edisto Island, South Carolina, Marsh Hen Mill provides heirloom Carolina Gold Rice, benne seeds, Sea Island red peas, and heirloom corn grits.

KEEPWELL VINEGAR: Buy small batch vinegars and misos from two former pastry chefs who are creating specialty ingredients you can't find anywhere else.

MISO MASTER: Stock up on organic and GMO-free varieties of miso made in the traditional Japanese method.

LUSTY MONK: Enjoy a spicy, coarse-ground, small-batch mustard the way it was intended to be made. This is my absolute favorite whole-grain mustard.

SPICEWALLA: Founded by Chef Meherwan Irani as a way to get his favorite spices direct from India, Spicewalla has grown into one of the preeminent spice importers with the highest quality fresh spices and spice blends.

BLIS GOURMET: The first time I tried their bourbon barrel-aged maple syrup was an epiphany. They sell a number of small-batch sauces that are worth stocking up on in your larder.

FOODS IN SEASON: You'll find high-quality specialty ingredients like wild salmon, elk, venison, truffles, and mushrooms fresh and direct from the source.

MIKUNI WILD HARVEST: They offer a range of products, from wild mushrooms to fresh seafood and hard-to-find specialty products. This is a wonderful place to order direct.

THE CHEF'S GARDEN: When you need fresh vegetables that you can't find at the farmers' market, The Chef's Garden is where to go. They provide some of the highest quality, sustainable produce in the country.

Acknowledgments

W. W. NORTON & COUNTRYMAN PRESS:
I always wanted to put my English degree to good use, not to mention my culinary degree. Since I became a chef, I always dreamed of writing my own cookbook. Thank you for believing in me and giving me the platform to tell my story. You've made me a believer in following the process and have made a dream come true.

ANN TREISTMAN: My amazing editor who helped to steer my dreams into reality. I can't thank you enough for taking a chance on me and bringing this book to life.

JOHNNY AUTRY: I told you we'd make this cookbook happen! It only took 12 years! Thank you for your keen eye to make my food look better than expected. Thank you for traipsing around the country with me to find all the right shots! You are one of the most creative people I've had the opportunity to work with, let alone call a friend. Your calmness and Dad jokes kept me afloat, and your skill set is the best in the industry.

CHARLOTTE AUTRY: I think we accomplished the *vibe* shift—no doubt due to your amazing styling skills. Thank you for making my food, the background, and the atmosphere *thoughtful* in every way even when I second guess myself. You are a center of poise and expertise. And when in doubt, don't forget to drip, or you might drown.

ELLEN SCORDATO: You took a risk to take me on as a client, and a first-time cookbook author. You coached me through my proposal and helped to find the perfect publisher. Thank you for bringing me to the table.

TAMIE COOK: Thank you for crossing the T's and dotting the I's and making sure my recipes were game tight, and for keeping me organized.

CATHERINE CAMPBELL: Your encouraging words and keen eye have helped to get me, and this book, ready for the bookstore stand. I appreciate your soft-spoken critiques as much as your votes of confidence to go and get it. Thank you.

CHEFS CLAYTON ROLLISON, VIRGINIA WILLIS, SAIF RAHMAN, AND PAUL SMITH: Thank you for your friendship and for taking my phone calls so I could wax and wane about this book. I appreciate you being there for me, and for your guidance and advice.

MY INSTRUCTORS AT THE CULINARY INSTITUTE OF AMERICA, CHEF JAMIE WEST, CHEF PETER TIMMINS, CHEF RICHARD ROSENDALE, CHEF DONALD BARICKMAN, CHEF CRAIG DEIHL, AND SO MANY OTHERS: Thank you for taking in this young punk and molding him into a man. I'm not sure what path I would have gone down if you had not taken the time to teach me a craft and talk to me about leadership and life.

OUR TEAMS AT THE MARKET PLACE, HAYMAKER, BILLY D'S FRIED CHICKEN, AND LITTLE GEM: Your leadership, skill set, and demeanor set you apart from your peers. Your help in this book is extraordinary, and I can't thank you all enough for working your behind-the-scenes magic. You are truly stewards of our community, and your work helps make our world a better place through your commitment not only to excellence, but to making people happy through food and hospitality. You all make me a better person each and every day. Thank you for believing in me and believing in creating a better food system.

TRACY MOORE: Thank you for keeping our businesses afloat with your business acumen, your professionalism, and your positivity. We've definitely been on a roller-coaster ride over the years! Thank you for keeping me organized and listening when I have some new scheme and dream.

OUR FARMERS AND FISHERMEN AND FORAGERS: Gaining Ground Farm, Fair Share Farm, Full Sun Farm, Boy and Girl Farm, Brasstown Farm, Sunburst Trout Farms, Hickory Nut Gap, Craig Hastings Mushrooms, "The Mushroom Man" Alan Muskat, Brad Spivey at Zero Acres Farm, Cloister Honey, Joyce Farms, Moonsprouts, and many, many more! Your commitment and integrity to farm sustainably has pushed me to be a better chef and steward of the land.

APPALACHIAN SUSTAINABLE AGRICULTURE PROJECT: If it weren't for the founding work of Charlie and Emily Jackson, I wouldn't have found the Local Food Guide that changed my mind to move to Asheville and dive headfirst into the local food movement. Your work resonates and defines an entire region's ethos toward sustainable food systems.

JENNY: You are my best friend and the love of my life. You have supported my "art project" since day one, and even when we don't agree, I know you have always believed in me. You've pushed me to be a better man and gave me the world when you made me a husband and a father. You have influenced my cooking in ways I cannot describe, and as we grow old, I will always see you in my mind, walking down the streets of Hanoi, radiant and glowing, and telling me to come and chase you. I will always chase you, and promise to take you on more adventures.

KIRA AND COLE: When I met your mother I fell in love for the first time. When I held each of you in my arms when you were born, I truly learned what love is. You bring me more joy than anything life could offer. Because of you I am more evolved as a person. Kira, your spirit knows no bounds. You have a creative mind and heart of gold. Cole, your radiant energy shines bright, and your fearlessness makes me a stronger person. I will always be here for you both along your own *thoughtful journeys*.

JAYPRAKASH AND NIRAJANA PARMAR: When I showed up unannounced at your home to ask for permission to marry your daughter, you made me pani puri. I knew right then and there that I would love being a part of your family. You shared your family, your culture, and your love of flavorful and healthy food with me that led me down a new path of spice exploration. Thank you for always being there to help when I'm out chasing my dreams.

ANNA AND ELIZABETH: It's tough being the middle child, and you both showed me how to take charge and also how to be caring. Thank you for helping with "my newspaper route," and damn if I didn't make life hard when we were kids. I know my ADD personality and stubbornness as your brother was not easy some days, but thank you for being there for me, constantly providing

encouragement, and always being my intrepid taste testers. And yes, one day I'll put a dipping trio on the menu.

MOM AND DAD: I don't know where to even begin. You should win an award for dealing with my BS. We had a bumpy start as I began this culinary journey, and while you were unsure of my career path you still stood behind me. You listened when I was scared and gave advice when I had questions and helped to pick me up when I was down—no matter what. While my journey seemed different and stranger than the norm, you continued to stay beside me, and you encouraged me to make the right choices even when you didn't have the answer. Thank you for believing in me and helping to make this delicious dream come true.

THOUGHTFUL READERS AND OUR AMAZING RESTAURANT GUESTS: You've offered me the opportunity to hone my culinary artistry, to find faith in myself, and to push limits that I didn't know I had in me. Thank you for trusting me with your taste buds and coming along for this adventurous ride.

Index